Advance Praise for *Conversion Optimization*

"The Web is unique in its ability to deliver this almost improbable win-win: You can increase revenue AND make your customers happy. Yet most websites stink. Worry not, Khalid and Ayat to the rescue! Buy this book to follow their practical advice on how to create high-converting websites that your visitors love."

—Avinash Kaushik
Author of *Web Analytics 2.0* and *Web Analytics: An Hour A Day*

"Khalid Saleh and Ayat Shukairy are two of the world's leading practitioners of conversion optimization, and they distilled their years of experience into this terrific book that guides you on the journey from clicks to sales. This is a must-read for online marketers and web operations managers alike."

—Scott Brinker
President & CTO, ion interactive

"I am always surprised by the value of picking up a good compilation of insights, examples and recommendations and getting refreshed. Is it time for a new bottleneck review or a Life Time Value recalculation? When did you last spend time on your bounce rate? Have you updated your personas? Khalid Saleh and Ayat Shukairy have been there and done that and share lessons learned in a very readable and informative way. Refer to this book and get instruction on the things you know you should be doing. It will pay off in sales."

—Jim Sterne
Founder, eMetrics Marketing Optimization Summit,
Chairman, Web Analytics Association

Conversion Optimization

Khalid Saleh and Ayat Shukairy

O'REILLY®

Beijing · Cambridge · Farnham · Köln · Sebastopol · Tokyo

Conversion Optimization

by Khalid Saleh and Ayat Shukairy

Published by O'Reilly Media, Inc., 1005 Gravenstein Highway North, Sebastopol, CA 95472.

O'Reilly books may be purchased for educational, business, or sales promotional use. Online editions are also available for most titles (*http://my.safaribooksonline.com*). For more information, contact our corporate/institutional sales department: (800) 998-9938 or *corporate@oreilly.com*.

Editor: Simon St.Laurent
Production Editor: Holly Bauer
Copyeditor: Audrey Doyle
Proofreader: Marlowe Shaeffer
Production Services:
  Newgen North America

Indexer: Ellen Troutman Zaig
Cover Designer: Karen Montgomery
Interior Designer: Ron Bilodeau
Illustrator: Robert Romano

Printing History:

  November 2010: First Edition.

ISBN: 978-1-449-37756-4
[LSI]   [2012-03-16]

It's difficult to live up to the standards that many great thinkers and innovators have set before us. But they are our inspiration. This book is hopefully a stepping stone to many great things that we will do in our lives with the grace and blessings of God.

This book is dedicated to those who do good but are never recognized. For those who have dedicated their lives to the betterment of others.

This is book is dedicated to our parents, who spent their lives guiding us to achieve success through the fulfillment of our dreams.

And finally, this book is also dedicated to our children. We encourage you to always think big and strive for greatness, but continue to have humility and gratitude to He who blessed you.

CONTENTS

Preface . . . . **x**

1   **The Journey from Clicks to Sales**. **1**
    Converting Visitors to Buyers   2
    Landing Pages   4
    Fifteen Years of Change   7
    Conversion Rates   10
    What You Can Accomplish   16

2   **The Numbers Behind Your Website** **21**
    Macro Conversions   22
    Key Performance Indicators   24
    Micro Conversions   27
    Building Budgets for Ecommerce Sites with Conversion Rates   28
    Lifetime Value (LTV) of a Customer   32
    Budgeting for Lead Generation Sites   34
    Monetization Models and Conversion Rates   36
    Bounce Rate   38
    Exit Rate   41
    Quality of Traffic (Visitors)   47
    Resources   58

3   **Getting to Know Your Customers: Developing Personas**. **59**
    What Are Personas?   61
    Benefits of Personas   63
    Market Segmentation Versus Persona Development   65
    A Case Against Personas   68
    Back to the Basics: Creating Customer Profiles   70
    Brief History of the Four Temperaments   73
    The Four Temperaments and Personas   75
    Putting It All Together   78

	Your Website from a Different Perspective	79
	Personas and Copy	81
	Adjusting Your Selling Process Through Personas	83
4	**From Confidence to Trust**	**85**
	Value Proposition	87
	Continuity	96
	Congruency	105
	Social Proof	109
	Membership/Professional Organizations or Affiliations	111
	External Reputation	112
	Design Aspects	114
5	**Understanding the Buying Stages**	**119**
	Deciphering the Buying Stages Online	120
	Complexity of the Product and the Buying Funnel	140
6	**FUDs**	**143**
	The Buying Decision and FUDs	145
	Getting "Personal" with FUDs	146
7	**Appealing with Incentives**	**159**
	What Are Incentives?	161
	Incentives Versus Value Proposition	163
	Positioning Incentives	164
	Behavioral Incentives	171
	How to Apply Incentives	172
	Additional Tips for Using Incentives	173
8	**Engagement**	**175**
	Measuring the Effectiveness of Engagement	176
	Social Media	178
	Customer Reviews	182
	Cross-Sells and Upsells	184
	Customer Feedback Tools	189
	Informational Videos	189
	Virtual Closets	190
	Virtual Help	190

9 Testing: The Voice of Visitors **193**
The Basics of Testing   194
Creating a Successful Test   199
Forty-Nine Things You Can Test on Your Website   203

10 Be Iterative **229**
When Conversion Optimization Succeeds   230
When Conversion Optimization Fails   231
The Upward Spiral   233

Index. **235**

Preface

PAINFUL LESSONS LED TO THE CREATION OF THIS BOOK.

In late 2005, I (Khalid) had the opportunity to lead the design and implementation of one of the largest ecommerce websites in North America, with a huge budget: $15 million. My team of 20 senior ecommerce developers and I built a "feature-rich" website that integrated with several external systems in a miraculous three months. While I pushed my team to work harder and spend more nights at the office, the marketing team assembled first-year revenue projections: $500 million!

Excitement built as the go-live deadline was approaching. However, I still had concerns: will visitors come to the site? On the go-live day, I sat with the other two architects to monitor the server's performance. I was wrong. The website received tens of thousands of visitors during the first hour. Everyone was ecstatic. Yes, visitors were coming.

As the hours passed, though, my earlier tension built up again. Despite the site receiving tens of thousands of visitors, *customers placed fewer than 10 orders in those first critical hours*. Ten orders was all we had to show our client for their $15 million investment. It was a disaster.

Why weren't these visitors converting into customers? Looking back, the low number of orders wasn't at all surprising.

We worked with an ad agency to create the design for the website. During the three months of implementation, we never discussed conversions, or even orders. In most cases, a few technical people, with little usability experience, decided how to design different pages, where to place elements, and how visitors would flow through the website. Both the technical and design companies promised the client a lot and delivered a great-looking website. It just did not convert.

That painful experience was not unusual. As more companies moved to the Web, most of them focused on driving visitors to their websites—the more eyeballs a website gets, the greater the chance that orders will be placed. However, the percentage of visitors placing orders was small compared to the total number of visitors. Marketers noticed this, and the practice of conversion optimization was born. While other areas of online marketing have developed tremendously in the past 15 years, conversion optimization is still in its infancy.

We started our practice in 2006 with a simple goal: create usable websites that visitors love, and generate more orders from these sites for clients. Consulting on conversion optimization projects suffers from the same problems as consulting in other fields. The quality of work a client receives is dependent on the skill set of the consultant working for them. Some clients we talked to felt that conversion optimization, while promising, involves random guessing and a lot of finger crossing. Since the early days of our company, we knew we had to establish a process and follow a methodology to generate consistent results for clients.

This book describes the Conversion Framework™, a process we developed in 2007 and have evolved since. The framework is built around eight principles: the first six principles cover how visitors interact with different websites and whether they are persuaded to stay or decide to leave. These principles are:

- Understanding your website visitors through persona creation

- Creating confidence and trust

- Understanding the impact of the buying stages

- Dealing with FUDs (fears, uncertainties, and doubts)

- Using incentives

- Engaging users

As you apply these principles to your website or campaign, you will begin to see what changes need to be made.

The seventh principle of the Conversion Framework asks you to test any change you make against your original design. By applying the science of online testing, you will measure the impact of any change you make on your bottom line. The eighth and final element of the Conversion Framework asks you to make a long-term commitment to conversion optimization—a willingness to iterate. Conversion optimization is not something you do only once. It is a long-term effort when done correctly. It should pay for itself for a very long time.

We have deployed this framework on hundreds of websites in different vertical markets to help increase conversion rates. The framework removes the guesswork from the conversion optimization process. It will provide anyone interested in optimization with a specific methodology to produce consistent results. The framework puts buyers at the heart of your optimization effort. It forces you to think of buyers' needs, wants, motivations, and fears. By focusing on buyers, you will ultimately persuade more of them to become your customers. We continue to test the Conversion Framework and refine it every day.

How Should You Read This Book?

This book is divided into two sections. The first two chapters introduce online marketing concepts you'll need to understand as you read the rest of the book. Chapter 1 covers some of the basic concepts in conversion optimization, and Chapter 2 explains some of the analytics concepts and mathematical formulas behind conversion optimization. These two chapters will provide you with enough information to understand the general concepts and numbers behind conversion optimization. A novice reader should start here.

If you are familiar with online marketing and have been doing it for a while, you can skip to the second section of the book, which starts with Chapter 3. This section is focused on the eight principles of the Conversion Framework.

Who Should Read This Book?

You may be a marketing and ecommerce professional who is interested in discovering new ways to maximize the ROI for the campaigns under your purview. You might be a sales professional looking for a way to optimize your sales funnels and increase output. You could be a web designer who is looking for ways to translate your beautiful designs into money for your clients. You may be a web developer or a software engineer creating great websites or ecommerce portals, but you have never focused on creating applications with revenues or users in mind—this is where one of the authors of this book started. Or you might be a small-business owner who is looking for quick tactics to implement on your website.

Who Should Not Read This Book?

We cast a wide net when we wrote this book, but there are a few people who might not enjoy it. Developers whose work stays far from the actual user of their application (i.e., developers of backend applications) aren't likely to enjoy this book. Those who believe that conversion optimization is only about testing may not like our approach to optimization. Finally, those who are looking for pure tactics and are not concerned with the theory behind conversion optimization might find some of the chapters in the book boring.

About the Examples in This Book

Most of the examples in this book come from our practice and our clients. This is only natural since we are discussing a process and a methodology that was initially developed to serve our clients. In addition, most of the screen captures from analytics programs come from our own websites; for those that don't, we made sure the websites and their data remained confidential.

If You Like (or Don't Like) This Book

If you like—or don't like—this book, by all means, please let people know. Amazon reviews are one popular way to share your happiness (or lack thereof). Or you can leave reviews on the book's website:

http://www.oreilly.com/catalog/9781449377564

The book's website also provides a link to errata. Errata give readers a way to let us know about typos, errors, and other problems with the book. The errata will be visible on the page immediately, and we'll confirm it after checking it out. O'Reilly can also fix errata in future printings of the book and on Safari, making for a better reader experience pretty quickly.

We hope to update this book's content in future editions, including implementing readers' suggestions and other input.

How to Contact Us

Conversion optimization continues to grow every day. As such, we continue to fine-tune some of the elements we've outlined in the book. Please let us know about any errors you find, as well as your suggestions for future editions, by writing to:

O'Reilly Media, Inc.
1005 Gravenstein Highway North
Sebastopol, CA 95472
800-998-9938 (in the U.S. or Canada)
707-829-0515 (international/local)
707-829-0104 (fax)

We have a web page for this book, where we list errata, examples, and any additional information. You can access this page at:

http://www.oreilly.com/catalog/9781449377564

To comment or ask technical questions about this book, send email to:

bookquestions@oreilly.com

For more information about our books, conferences, Resource Centers, and the O'Reilly Network, see our website at:

http://www.oreilly.com

Safari® Books Online

 Safari Books Online is an on-demand digital library that lets you easily search over 7,500 technology and creative reference books and videos to find the answers you need quickly.

With a subscription, you can read any page and watch any video from our library online. Read books on your cell phone and mobile devices. Access new titles before they are available for print, and get exclusive access to manuscripts in development and post feedback for the authors. Copy and paste code samples, organize your favorites, download chapters, bookmark key sections, create notes, print out pages, and benefit from tons of other time-saving features.

O'Reilly Media has uploaded this book to the Safari Books Online service. To have full digital access to this book and others on similar topics from O'Reilly and other publishers, sign up for free at *http://my.safaribooksonline.com*.

Acknowledgments

We have been blessed by God with wonderful opportunities like this book. We have also been blessed with a wonderful, supportive family throughout the writing process, and we wouldn't have been able to complete this book without them. Special thanks go to Reem for being there whenever we called. Thanks also to Yaman Shukairy, Chris Goward, and Feras Alhlou for taking time from their busy schedules to review and provide insight on the book. We also want to thank John Hossack from VKI Studios and Trevor Claiborne from Google for allowing us to use the YouTube case study in the book. We are also thankful to Shereen Mir who was responsible for helping us secure the book deal. Special thanks to Simon St.Laurent for providing support and guidance on our first book!

CHAPTER ONE

The Journey from Clicks to Sales

SELLING ONLINE IS HARD.

Although customers are just one click away on the Internet, merely reaching them is not enough. Potential customers are bombarded with more than 3,000 advertising messages every day.* The competition for their attention is fierce. They are also savvier than they were 20 or 30 years ago. If you want to increase sales, you must connect with your customers in new ways, capture their interest, give them control over their relationship with you, and gently guide them toward a conversion.

Every sales transaction is made up of a buying process and a selling process. In the buying process, the customer realizes his need or desire for a particular product or service, identifies and evaluates the different options available to him, and finally makes a purchase. The selling process is the flip side of this. In this process, the sales executive must establish a rapport with the buyer, qualify the buyer's needs, demonstrate how her product meets those needs, deal with the buyer's objections, and ultimately close the sale.

Although the Internet revolutionized how buyers and sellers communicate, the buying and selling processes have not changed much. The Internet gives buyers increased information and makes different products and retailers more accessible. Sellers, of course, have new ways to reach potential buyers.

* *http://www.ucsusa.org/publications/guide.ch1.html*

The different stages of the selling process represent a funnel that many *potential* buyers or prospects enter on one side, and few *actual* buyers exit on the other. As potential buyers go through this sales funnel, many will exit at different stages for different reasons. The exit points represent holes in the sales funnel. Optimizing the sales funnel focuses on plugging these holes.

This process of sales optimization is complex. However, we can learn a lot about it from retail chains. No other retailer has perfected the art of maximizing revenue per visit as much as Wal-Mart has. Initially, they relied heavily on keeping prices lower than the competition and achieving profitability through higher sales volumes. Although this strategy remains at the heart of Wal-Mart's marketing approach, its marketing mix has evolved tremendously over the past 20 years. The retail giant pays very close attention to every little detail of its sales process. Before a single visitor sets foot into a Wal-Mart store, plans are laid out and executed carefully to select the right location for the store, as well as its layout, merchandising displays, atmosphere, consistency in branding, and store traffic flow.

As a result, Wal-Mart continues to be one of the world's largest and most successful retail companies. Regardless of whether you like Wal-Mart, the company's planning, attention to detail, and successful execution provide critical lessons. As Wal-Mart has proven, choreographing every step and element of the sales process translates into more revenue. You must get into the minds of your customers. You must optimize your selling process to meet the needs of your customers. Ultimately, you must guide your customers through the sales funnel toward a conversion.

Converting Visitors to Buyers

The Web's interactivity makes conversion fast. You can convert a prospective customer into a paying customer more quickly on the Web than in other media. People receive various messages through advertising and promotional media attempting to persuade them to take action. Although traditional offline media can broadcast those messages, it's hard for people to act on them immediately. On the Web, a prospect could receive a message and, in mere minutes click on a link and buy a product.

Although this is wonderful, converting a prospect online is not that easy. The speed at which the conversion can occur is matched only by the speed at which the conversion will unravel, creating new kinds of challenges. Online prospects can become distracted and within seconds decide to navigate to another website, never to return to yours. So, how can you minimize the chance of your prospect leaving your site, and maximize the results of your online promotion?

Conversion optimization analyzes the behavior of consumers, focuses on what motivates a particular market segment to react in a certain way to marketing elements, and advises companies on how to adjust their marketing and sales mix in response. As the name suggests, conversion optimization is focused on increasing the percentage of visitors that "convert" into buyers for a marketing campaign. Conversion optimization is a departure from traditional marketing, where it is sometimes difficult to measure and quantify the impact of a particular campaign. Quantitative measurements provide a foundation. Although you should define a conversion based on your own specifics, you must be able to track the number of conversions during a certain period.

The process of conversion optimization starts with quantifying the numbers for each campaign you run. Different campaigns will track different kinds of conversions. For a retailer, these numbers might be the number of orders the retailer receives in one month or the average order value during the same period. For a law office, it might be the number of website inquiries or the number of new cases signed up. An online news website or magazine might track the number of subscriptions or how often stories are viewed. A nonprofit organization might track the donations collected in one week or one month.

After establishing an initial baseline, the next stage is to understand the story behind the numbers. Why did your target market react a certain way to a specific campaign? What did they love or hate about it? What could you have done better? Again, the customer is at the heart of this analysis. We will dig deeper into consumer behavior throughout the book and give you more specific examples to help you understand your customers' behavior.

Armed with the knowledge from the analysis stage, you are finally ready to move to the optimization process. Because conversion optimization is focused on results, we rarely recommend making drastic changes where you lose track of which elements are impacting your audience. This can be one of the biggest challenges in conversion optimization. Many website operators and marketers are deeply frustrated by their low conversion numbers and are eager to find new ways to maximize revenue. As a result, they change hundreds of elements in a single campaign, hoping that these changes will have a positive impact on their bottom line.

We have done conversion optimization long enough to know that although some of the changes will have a positive impact, a few of them will have a negative impact. Many are likely to have little to no impact at all. Making too many changes at once dilutes the impact of such changes, making it difficult to track which elements actually helped—or hurt—your campaign.

Conversion optimization is an iterative process. You start by understanding your market and making assumptions about how your market interacts with your website. You then adjust your marketing and sales processes to test these assumptions and to measure how your market actually responds. Exactly measuring a customer's response on the Web is far superior to measuring a customer's response in any other medium—learn all you can from the response. Changes to a marketing campaign that increase revenue are rewarding. But instances where adjustments cause a decrease in revenue present valuable information about your market. Changes to a website or campaign that do not move the needle in any direction should be cause for concern.

Conversion optimization starts when a visitor views a particular ad and clicks to visit your website. A properly designed campaign, site, collection of web pages, and check-out process will give your prospects the information they are looking for and will increase your chances of converting them. However, a poorly developed website can undermine an otherwise successful promotional campaign.

Landing Pages

We are used to entering terms into a search engine and receiving results that are relevant to our query. If your website or campaign is displayed on the search engine results pages (SERPs), you have a chance of a consumer clicking on that listing and landing on your website.

Figure 1-1 shows how a SERP is divided into two main sections: organic results and paid results. The organic search results are your first chance to get visitors to your website. Organic search results appear in the order that search engines determine is most relevant to a particular query after crawling millions of pages on the Web. The competition for the coveted first place in organic search results is fierce. The discipline of search engine optimization (SEO) focuses on achieving a higher ranking in the SERPs. Paid results on a search results page are your second chance to get a customer to click through to your website. Although paid advertising is competitive, it is far less complex to appear first as a paid listing compared to the organic listings. In the paid listing section, advertisers pay only when a customer actually clicks on an ad.

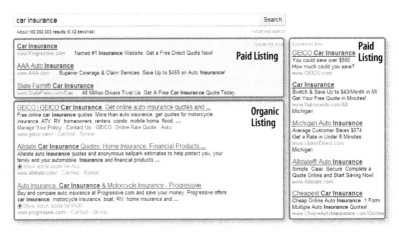

Figure 1-1. *Search results page*

Search is only one way to drive customers to your website. Many companies send regular promotions and advertisements to their email lists. Figure 1-2 shows an example of a promotional email we received from Amazon.com offering large discounts on textbooks. The goal of this particular email is to get us to take action: visit the site and place an order.

Figure 1-2. *Email marketing*

Banner advertising is another technique you can employ to drive visitors to your website. Although most paid search results rely on a model in which advertisers pay when a user actually clicks on the ad and lands on your website, most banner advertising is sold based on the number of times a banner is displayed. Figure 1-3 shows how metroPCS uses a banner ad to drive visitors to its website.

Figure 1-3. *Banner advertising*

The techniques for driving traffic to a website are similar to the techniques for driving customers to a retail outlet. Think of the advertising that media retailers use to convince customers to visit their store: yellow page listings, TV commercials, print advertising, radio ads, telemarketing campaigns, snail mail ads, and many other forms. Table 1-1 compares some of the online and offline advertising media. Ultimately, the goal is to convince a potential customer to come to the store and make contact with the retailer.

Table 1-1. *Online versus offline advertising media*

Offline	Online
Yellow pages	Directories
Billboards	Banner ads
Direct mail	Email campaigns
TV/radio advertising	Online ads
Print advertising	Content ads
Conferences	Webinars and virtual conferences
Telemarketing	NA

Regardless of the medium, the goal of most advertising is to drive customer demand. When you click on any of the different types of online advertisements or organic search results, you will be directed to a *landing page*. A landing page is the first page a visitor sees after clicking on or entering a specific link or web address. Figure 1-4 shows a banner ad for American Express. When you click on the banner ad, you will arrive at the landing page displayed in Figure 1-5.

In the offline world, as customers see your different ads, they might at some point get in their car and drive to your store. The entrance point and the first thing customers see when they walk into a physical store mirror the online landing page. That physical "landing page" is the first chance for a brick-and-mortar retailer to make a positive impression on a customer.

In the overall process of marketing, most of a company's time and resources are spent on creative, production, media placement, and similar tasks. Often, without the proper attention, a landing page is marginalized, giving the impression that the strength of the overall campaign is all that is needed to attract customers. However, getting a prospect to the landing page does not mean success; it is just the start of the road to success.

Although you *might* get away with paying little attention to a customer's entrance point (landing page) in the physical world, data shows that consumers are not very tolerant of poorly designed online landing pages. There is a large difference between how customers react to an online landing page and how they react to a physical store's equivalent. Our analysis of hundreds of online advertising campaigns shows that more than 50% of online visitors leave landing pages in fewer than five seconds without continuing to the rest of the website.

When was the last time you drove to a retail outlet, stayed in the store for five seconds, and then just walked out? This does not happen often. Yes, the time investment required for a physical store visit might have a lot to do with this. But other factors, which we will discuss later in the book, also prompt customers to leave an online landing page right away.

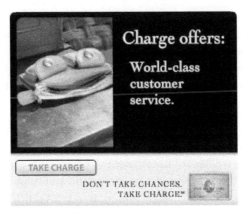

Figure 1-4. *Banner ad for American Express*

Figure 1-5. *American Express landing page*

Fifteen Years of Change

In 1995, when the first ecommerce stores began to appear online, marketers spent a lot of time convincing both large and small companies that they needed an online presence. Many companies thought the rush to the Web was similar to the gold rush: it was unjustified, and it would eventually die down. By the end of 1996, fewer than 50,000 websites were online and fewer than 2.6 million transactions were conducted on ecommerce websites.*

---

* http://www.acjournal.org/holdings/vol2/Iss3/articles/Online_Shopping.htm; http://www.docstoc.com/docs/7069364/ANALYZING-E-COMMERCE-GROWTH-FROM-THE-PERSPECTIVES-OF-INNOVATION-DIFFUSION

In the three years that followed, more companies embraced the Web, though often without focus. Many companies established an online presence because doing so was supposed to increase brand reach and open new revenue streams. As ecommerce was still in its infancy, very few companies could figure out how to actually generate online revenue or create sustainable business models. Having a website became a business goal in and of itself.

During these first few years, companies struggled to determine the technical and marketing complexities of selling online. At the same time, consumers were hesitant to hand over their credit card information to an online business. Security and privacy concerns for a brand-new medium were valid and stopped many customers from considering ecommerce as a viable option. In a 1998 article published in the *New York Times*, "Security Fears Still Plague Cybershopping," the reporter points out the following:

> While not many of the 19.7 million Americans who visited commercial Web sites from their homes in 1997 have reported problems with Internet credit-card use, some surfers—and security experts—say they are concerned enough about Internet crime that they would rather auction off their firstborn child than use a credit card to buy something on the Web.*

We've come a long way, haven't we?

You Must Market Your Site

Back in 1999, at the height of the dot-com era, we worked with a software client who wanted to capture the online customer relationship management (CRM) space. The company was funded by a group of technologists who believed that their $40 million startup would take the Web by storm. They projected that the site could generate more than $100 million in its first year of operation. The company's entire marketing plan seemed to center on a one-minute flashy spot during the Super Bowl.

Sound familiar? The first day the site was live, it had fewer than 1,000 visitors. Things did not improve. With no real online marketing plan to promote the website, the numbers continued to dwindle. Management learned a very hard lesson: it is not enough to build a website; you must spend the money to bring visitor "traffic" to it. Of course, our client was very similar to numerous other startups during the dot-com bubble. Too many companies assumed a website was a great marketing tool in and of itself. The reality is that for this marketing tool to be successful, you first must market the marketing tool!

Companies were quick to learn from their mistakes. By the late 1990s, companies started spending millions of dollars to advertise and bring traffic to their websites. By 2005, online advertising reached $12 billion. The online channel has been growing

* *http://www.nytimes.com/1998/07/30/technology/security-fears-still-plague-cybershopping.html*

steadily since 2003 and is on track to surpass the $61 billion annual level of ad spending for the first time in history by 2010.* Online advertising budgets, as displayed in Figure 1-6, are expected to continue to grow by close to 10% annually† worldwide to surpass $110 billion by 2015.‡

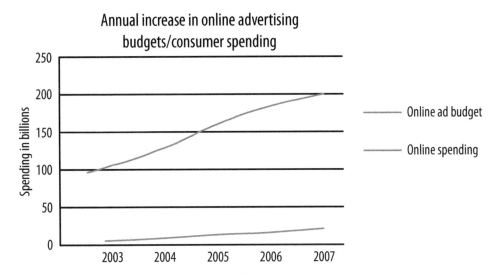

Figure 1-6. *Online advertising budgets versus spending*

For the most part, the purpose of these large investments is to drive as many consumers to a website or a landing page as possible. By the end of 2007, data from our ecommerce customers showed that 50% of online marketing budgets was spent on SEO. In 2008, spending on SEO increased to close to 60%.

Once Visitors Arrive, Convert

Many companies are making huge investments in their effort to drive as many consumers as they can to their websites. Yet, companies are discovering that it is not enough to drive visitors to their websites; it is just as critical, if not more so, to convert these visitors into actual consumers or leads. The concept of conversion is by no means a new idea. Print advertisers have discussed response rate and conversion ratios for years. Most direct mail campaigns convert at 1% or less.§ Online conversion rates did not do a whole lot better. Data reported by Shop.org reflects a continuous decline

---

* *http://www.bizreport.com/2010/06/forecast-by-2015-online-ads-to-surpass-110-billion.html#*

† *http://www.comscore.com/Press_Events/Press_Releases/2010/8/comScore_Reports_Q2_2010_U.S._Retail_E-Commerce_Spending_Up_9_Percent_vs._Year_Ago*

‡ *http://www.bizreport.com/2010/06/forecast-by-2015-online-ads-to-surpass-110-billion.html#*

§ *http://www.gaebler.com/Direct-Mail-Response-Rates.htm*

in online conversion rates. In June 2007, the Fireclick Index reported an average ecommerce conversion rate of just 2.2%. Fireclick Index data shows an average conversion rate of 1.7% in August 2010.[*]

As a result, most firms are increasing their investment in conversion optimization. From our experience, the majority of Fortune 500 companies are allocating close to 5% of their online marketing budgets to conversion optimization efforts. Based on the current trends, we expect that by 2015 most companies will spend close to 15% of their online marketing budgets on conversion optimization, and the remaining 85% will be spent on other forms of online marketing (SEO, paid advertising, email, banner ads, etc.).

—— **DON'T FORGET!** ——
- A lot of traffic does not necessarily translate into a lot of customers.
- Conversion optimization is crucial because it is not enough to just drive traffic to your website.

Conversion Rates

Whether you are trying to measure the health of your website, the success of your paid advertising, or the ROI in an online marketing campaign, you'll often discuss conversion rates. The term *conversion rate* has many definitions. For the purposes of this book, we define conversion rate as the percentage of visitors exposed to a campaign who take the desired action of that campaign. Since there are different goals and ways to measure conversion, this definition should be general enough to use with different media.

There are hundreds of millions of business websites, most of which fall into one of these categories:

Ecommerce websites
> Mirror their physical store counterparts by offering products to their visitors. A conversion on an ecommerce store happens when a visitor places an order with the site.

Lead generation websites
> Are not designed for consumers to place orders on them, but rather are designed to capture leads. The actual conversion process takes place offline. Many professional services firms such as consulting companies and law firms rely on their website to drive leads for their business. A conversion on a lead generation website takes place when a visitor successfully fills out a contact form and submits it online.

* *http://index.fireclick.com/*

Content-based websites

Rely on publishing content to drive visitors to the site. Content sites usually sell advertising to generate revenue. A conversion on a content-based website is more difficult to quantify compared to a conversion on an ecommerce or lead generation website. These sites charge their advertisers based on the number of monthly views and visitors to the site. So, having more visitors or more page views will lead to higher advertising revenue. Thus, a conversion might take place when a visitor views more articles, spends more time on the site, visits the site regularly, or even subscribes to a newsletter.

Brand websites

Are designed to increase brand reach and awareness within a certain market. Although other types of websites can define measurable conversion goals, brand websites have vague notions of what a conversion is.

Social media websites

Are designed to help different audiences connect and communicate with each other. Examples of these websites include blogs, Facebook, and LinkedIn. Social websites introduce a new challenge in redefining what a conversion is within a social network.

Of course, a website does not always fit into a single mold. Although ecommerce companies sell products to customers, which is their main conversion goal, they still have other website conversion goals, such as increasing brand awareness or getting visitors to subscribe to a mailing list. A content website that relies on online advertising—such as an online magazine—might also sell paid subscriptions to access premium content on the site.

The discussion in the book will focus primarily on ecommerce and lead generation websites, although you can easily apply the same concepts to other kinds of websites.

Calculating Conversion Rates

The primary goal of an ecommerce website is to sell products to consumers. The conversion rate for an ecommerce website in a particular period is the total number of orders the site receives divided by the number of visitors to the site. If a website gets 10,000 visitors in one month, and of those only 120 visitors place an order, the conversion rate for that site is 1.2%:

Conversion rate = 120 / 10,000 = 1.2%

Of course, a conversion on an ecommerce website does not happen in one step; it is a multistep process. Let's say you want to buy a copy of *The Tipping Point,* so you go online and search for the book in Google. Figure 1-7 shows the many search results for "The Tipping Point." Data tells us that the first listing among organic results gets the highest number of clicks on a search results page, which is usually around 45%. Figure 1-8 shows "The Tipping Point" product page at Amazon.com, which you would land on if you click on the first search result.

Although product pages on an ecommerce website can have different goals, the main goal is to get visitors to click on the "add to cart" button. Of course, clicking on this button does not translate into a sale. Website visitors have many options after clicking on it. For example, they might get a phone call and forget about purchasing *The Tipping Point*. They might become distracted and navigate to other products. Or they might want the book enough to actually click on the "checkout" button to start the order. Of course, they still have to go through the different steps of the checkout process, with each step getting them closer to the final goal of placing an order. Only when a visitor clicks on the "Place your order" button in Figure 1-9, the final step in the Amazon.com checkout process, has Amazon.com secured an order and a conversion.

Figure 1-7. Google search results for "The Tipping Point"

Figure 1-8. "The Tipping Point" product page at Amazon.com

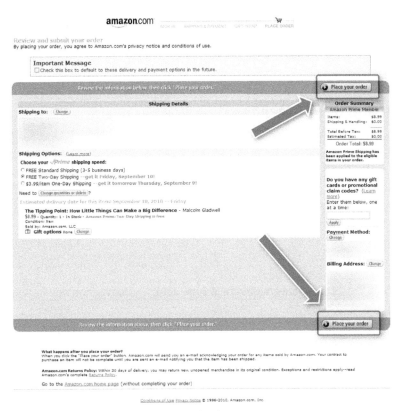

Figure 1-9. *The final step in the Amazon.com checkout process*

Figures 1-7 through 1-9 show a typical "order funnel" for many ecommerce websites. This funnel might start with visitors arriving at different pages (landing pages) in the website. Although an ecommerce website may or may not have full control over where a visitor lands initially on the site, it does have control over the design of the order funnel, such as the checkout process. Each step toward the final order page is a *micro conversion*. Small victories build toward the final, ultimate victory: a visitor placing an order, or a *macro conversion*. A macro conversion will only take place if the ecommerce store is able to convert the visitor at each micro conversion.

An online order funnel is very similar to a physical sales funnel. Think of a company that is looking to purchase an expensive piece of software. Evaluating the different software packages is similar to looking at a category page with different products listed in it. Narrowing the options to a particular software package mirrors looking at the product pages in an ecommerce store. Then there is the physical-world "checkout," finally executing the agreement. The only time you reach a deal is when each step in the process successfully leads to the next step.

Conversion Rate Averages

Online conversion rates have been on the decline since companies started tracking them. Although we used to talk to our clients about average site conversion rates of around 5%, these figures no longer hold true. Most websites struggle to convert visitors into clients, and the numbers aren't improving. Table 1-2 shows the Fireclick Index average conversion rate based on the industry in June 2007 and June 2008. Most (though not all) categories report a decline in conversion rates.

Table 1-2. *Fireclick Index average conversion rate by industry in June 2007 and June 2008*

Type of site	Conversion rate in June 2007	Conversion rate in June 2008
Catalog	5.80%	4.60%
Software	3.90%	3.30%
Fashion and Apparel	2.30%	2.20%
Specialty	1.70%	2.30%
Electronics	0.50%	0.70%
Outdoor and Sports	0.40%	2.40%

On the other end of the spectrum, some ecommerce sites report double-digit conversion rates. Table 1-3 shows the top converting ecommerce websites according to Nielsen's MegaView Online Retail report in June 2007.* Next to each top converting website we included the industry averages as reported by the Fireclick Index.† Table 1-4 shows the top converting ecommerce websites according to Nielsen's MegaView Online Retail report in March 2010,‡ as well as the industry averages.§

---

* *http://www.internetretailer.com/2007/06/26/lane-bryant-catalog-site-tops-online-retailers-in-conversion-rat*
† *http://index.fireclick.com/*
‡ *http://www.marketingcharts.com/direct/top-10-online-retailers-by-conversion-rate-march-2010-12774/*
§ *http://index.fireclick.com/*

Table 1-3. *Top converting websites in June 2007 compared to industry averages*

Type of site	Conversion rate	Industry average
Lane Bryant Catalog	24.7%	2.3%
QVC	16.7%	5.8%
Oriental Trading Company	15.2%	5.8%
Blair.com	14.5%	2.3%
Jessicalondon.com	13.7%	2.3%
Symantec	13.5%	3.9%
Roamans	13.5%	2.3%
The Sportsman's Guide	12.2%	0.4%
Christianbook.com	11.9%	5.8%
Lillian Vernon	11.8%	1.7%

Table 1-4. *Top converting websites in March 2010 compared to industry averages*

Type of site	Conversion rate	Industry average
Schwan's	40.6%	2.1%
Woman Within	25.3%	1.7%
Blair.com	20.4%	1.7%
1800petmeds.com	17.7%	2.1%
Vitacost.com	16.4%	2.1%
QVC	16.0%	5.2%
ProFlowers	15.8%	2.1%
Office Depot	15.4%	5.2%
Oriental Trading Company	14.9%	2.1%
Roamans	14.4%	1.7%

Although most online retailers are able to convert 2.3% of their visitors into customers, retailers such as Lane Bryant convert 24% of their visitors into customers. Yes, some online retailers are able to capture 10 times as much business compared to their competitors. Some even sustain that rate over years.

—— **DON'T FORGET!** ———————————————————————

Conversion optimization is ultimately about lost sales, helping you to get back some of the money you are leaving on the table.

What You Can Accomplish

Conversion optimization can bring a company a staggering increase in revenue. For many companies, conversion rate optimization translates into hundreds of thousands of dollars of additional revenue. For example, a client of ours that runs an ecommerce furniture store had annual sales of around $20 million. The initial three months of conversion optimization generated a 30% increase in online sales, which translated to around $600,000 in additional sales per month. With large numbers such as these, you may be wondering: why wouldn't every company jump on the conversion optimization bandwagon?

Before we answer that question, let's compare ecommerce conversion rates to those of the physical world. Although there is no published data on the average physical-store conversion rate, informal surveys show that most offline stores convert around 25% of their in-store traffic into actual purchases. When a store runs a large discount, those conversion rates shoot up even more significantly. Think back to Black Friday 2009. Even in a bad economy, thousands of customers waited in lines for hours in front of retail stores looking for good deals.

So, why are website operators content with low conversion rates? We've encountered three common reasons:

Conversion data is difficult to track

In the case of a standalone ecommerce website where the company does not operate a traditional physical store, calculating conversion is clear. The line is not so clear in the case of a mixed operation, where the company sells both offline and online. Many websites that have a physical-store presence report that offline retail sales increase as a result of their online advertising.

Research by Yahoo! and comScore shows that consumers who were exposed to online advertising are more likely to research products online and then to make their purchases offline.* And although more and more people are purchasing online, data shows there is a segment of visitors who are more comfortable completing a purchase offline. In that case, consumers complete the research online, but the actual purchase (conversion) takes place in the physical store.

---

* *http://www.comscore.com/Press_Events/Press_Releases/2007/07/Yahoo!_and_comScore_Online_Consumer_Study*

So, although the reported online conversion rate is low, the overall conversion rate for the company is actually higher. The question of attributing offline sales to online visits presents a challenge that many companies continue to struggle with.

Acquiring visitors costs money

Acquiring website visitors, whether via organic search results or through paid advertising, used to be cheap. As a result, most ecommerce stores did not worry about their low conversion rates. This is no longer the case. Search engine optimization whereby a website ranks at the top of the natural search results requires more time, effort, and money today. Paid results requiring bids of between $3 and $5 per keyword are typical in most industries. It is not unheard of to pay more than $10 in certain competitive markets. As traffic gets more expensive, more website operators will look for ways to maximize ROI on the current traffic they are getting.

The world of conversion optimization is mystical

This is perhaps the biggest reason we have *not* seen a real push toward improving conversion rates in the past few years. Conversion optimization is a blend of science and art. It is the intersection of creative, marketing, and analytical disciplines. It would be easier to state that there is a simple formula you can apply to increase your conversion rate. And yes, there might be a few tweaks you can make here and there to quickly increase your conversion rate a bit. But it takes time and patience to move from a 2% to a 10% conversion rate.

Can You Really Achieve a Double-Digit Conversion Rate?

CEOs and VPs of marketing ask this question every day. Many of them have accepted low conversion rates as a fact of doing business online. They believe that achieving a double-digit conversion rate is farfetched, or even impossible. Some executives have not only accepted low conversion rates, but will argue that there is no way to increase sales conversion rates. Having helped hundreds of companies increase their sales, we know the possibilities are endless. The question is not whether you can achieve a double-digit conversion rate; the question is whether you are willing to do what it takes to achieve a double-digit conversion rate.

Expectations for conversion optimization results should be combined with realistic expectations regarding the amount of work required to achieve these results. Because many clients do not understand the investment and commitment required from their team, they give up too soon. Conversion rates won't increase overnight. You must start by understanding the visitors you are trying to convert. You then have to create hypotheses about these visitors and why they interact the way they do with your website. Then you have to validate these hypotheses by making changes to your website and tracking the customer response. All of these steps require time, resources, and a financial commitment, which is why they must be done accurately and with great focus.

The Numbers Game

In the physical world, many executives believe sales is a numbers game. The more calls or appointments you book, the more sales you will generate. Let's assume your sales force is able to convert 10% of their appointments into actual contracts. What would it take to generate more transactions? You shouldn't discount the fact that making more calls and appointments, if the same averages hold, will translate into more transactions. But most experienced organizations understand the value of trying to convert more of their current pipeline into transactions. Developing new leads and making initial contacts with them is a lot more expensive than focusing on the current pipeline and increasing its output.

The same rules apply to the online world. Sales is both a numbers game and a quality game. You should figure out ways to increase the number of qualified companies or individuals entering your sales pipeline. It is even more important to increase the conversion rate of the current funnel. But which of the two is a better option? In the long run, much as in the physical world, the cost of acquiring new visitors to a website or a campaign is expensive. Converting more of your current funnel into actual paying clients typically costs less.

Conversion optimization puts your customers at the heart of the sales process and yields better results by following three main approaches:

- Determine current strong techniques that are working for your organization and enhance them.

- Discover weak points in your selling approach and replace them with better tactics that have worked for your particular market.

- Continue evaluating the sales funnel and test new elements to increase its conversion rate.

Over the long run, conversion optimization will generate more customers with the same investment in time and money.

Where Are Your Real Conversion Bottlenecks?

One of our clients is a large provider of desktop sharing software, and spends tens of thousands of dollars on pay-per-click (PPC) and banner ads to drive traffic to the landing page of its most popular software product.

This wasn't enough, though. According to its vice president of marketing, the company's landing page was "simply not converting."

He was correct. For every 1,000 visitors who landed on the page, the company generated five orders. That page had a measly 0.5% conversion rate. The VP of marketing gave the optimization team one month to increase the conversion rate; otherwise, they'd have to stop spending money on advertising altogether. Our team was brought on board as a last-ditch effort to rectify the situation.

As the optimization team dug deeper into the page and different campaigns, they discovered that there were many issues with the way our client understood conversion. The first landing page we evaluated was very typical and did not allow visitors to place an order directly on the page. The page explained the software features and benefits, and presented the visitor with an option to place an order with a clearly marked "Start Your Service" button. Clicking on the button took the visitor through a three-step checkout process.

Focusing on a single landing page does not usually produce results. The Conversion Framework asks you to examine the full path, from the point a visitor lands on the site until the point the visitor successfully places an order. Since the client used the same checkout funnel for many other products, they did not want us to evaluate the funnel, and instead wanted our team to focus on the landing page.

When we examined the data more carefully, we discovered that the landing page visitors were actually clicking on the "Start Your Service" button more than we were told. Four percent of the landing page visitors clicked on the button to place an order for the service. As a micro conversion point, all the landing page could do was persuade visitors to move forward in the conversion funnel and start the checkout process. And although 4% was not great, it was doing a lot better than the 0.5% conversion rate the client's team thought it did.

Of the visitors who clicked on the order button and started the checkout process, only 12.5% completed the checkout and placed an order with the client. The remaining 87.5% were leaving the checkout process. As a result, the overall conversion rate for the campaign was 0.5% (12.5% * 4% = 0.5%).

Our team suggested examining the checkout process to determine why most visitors were not converting. The client, however, insisted that we focus our effort on optimizing the landing page itself. After one month of optimization, we were able to increase the landing page conversion (click-through) to the checkout process from 4% to 14.88%.

Although that was a significant increase in the click-through rate, final orders were still not coming through. Most visitors continued to exit the checkout process. At that point, the client refocused on the checkout process. Completing checkout process optimization increased the overall conversion rate from 0.5% to 6.1%.

CHAPTER TWO

The Numbers Behind Your Website

UNDERSTANDING THE NUMBERS BEHIND YOUR WEBSITE is an important step toward conquering the conversion problem.

However, too many companies jump into conversion optimization without a real plan or a methodology to identify promising areas for optimization. A simplistic process won't help you to understand why customers abandon the sales funnel.

A client recently came to us after working with another landing page optimization company. That company looked at conversion from a very linear perspective: pick a single landing page, test 32,000 different designs of that page, and one of these designs will be bound to convert better than the original. Predictably, that costly and time-consuming approach did not produce any results for the client. Who would have thought that none of the 32,000 combinations would beat the original design?

Conversion rate optimization takes a more sophisticated approach, requiring the following two elements:

- Identifying areas of the sales funnel that should be optimized

- Following a repeatable process to optimize these areas

Without these two elements, your optimization efforts are destined to fail. Regardless of the approach you follow, you will ultimately pick an area to optimize. The question becomes: what should you modify in that particular area or step? If your prospecting during the sales process is weak, what changes should you make to it to ensure that you are able to convert better? If you are looking for consistent results, your answers must move beyond the random guessing game of changing too many elements and hoping that one of the changes will increase conversions.

Macro Conversions

Most websites have more than one conversion goal. The primary goal of an ecommerce website is to capture orders. Forgetting other conversion possibilities, though, will hurt the ecommerce website in the long run. If you do not persuade a visitor to place an order during her first visit, getting her email address and sending her regular email promotions will increase the chances that she will come back to your website and eventually convert. *Macro conversions* refer to overall or ultimate conversions on a website. In contrast, *micro conversions* refer to the smaller steps or conversions a visitor must take to achieve a macro conversion.

Conversion optimization starts by pinpointing the conversion goals for your website. Typical conversion goals for an ecommerce website include:

- Capture visitors' orders.
- Capture visitors' email addresses.
- Allow visitors to download product manuals.
- Allow visitors to locate nearby stores.
- Allow visitors to create a registry or add to wish list.

A lead generation website might have some of the following conversion goals:

- Capture visitors' information as sales leads.
- Allow visitors to call into a business.
- Allow visitors to download a white paper.

The next step is to identify a value for each of these conversions. It is easy to place a numerical value on a customer placing an order with an ecommerce website. But what is the value for getting an email address? If an ecommerce site allows visitors to use a store locator to find the store nearest to them, it is important to track the number of offline conversions that take place at the specific store compared to the number of leads sent to it. If within a 30-day period, 2,000 website visitors use the store locator functionality to find a store within a specific zip code, you should answer the following questions:

- How many of these visitors actually made it to the store?
- How many of those who visited the offline store actually ended up buying an item?
- What was the average order value these customers placed?

Some of these questions are more complicated to track than others, and they will all require some form of integrated online and offline system to find concrete numbers. Ultimately, your goal is to assign values to the different *macro* conversion goals on the site. Since these goals generally compete with each other, assigning values will help you find the right balance among them. Let's take an example of a website that has two conversion goals. Conversion goal A has a $30 value. Conversion goal B has a $5 value. Consider two different designs that lead to different conversion rates for these two goals:

Conversion goal	Conversion rate for first design	Conversion rate for second design
Goal A	0.18%	0.25%
Goal B	0.80%	0.33%

Which design should we choose?

Assuming that each design receives 1,000 visitors, let's calculate the financial value for each. For the first design:

Conversion goal	Conversion rate for first design	Number of conversions	Value per conversion	Value of design
Goal A	0.18%	1.8	$30	$54
Goal B	0.80%	12	$5	$60

This calculation shows that the first design generates a total of $114.

For the second design:

Conversion goal	Conversion rate for second design	Number of conversions	Value per conversion	Value of design
Goal A	0.25%	2.5	$30	$75
Goal B	0.50%	5	$5	$25

This calculation shows that the second design generates a total of $100. Based on the assumptions we stated, the first design will generate more value.

With a standalone landing page, such as a page designed to capture leads only, we recommend that you have one macro conversion goal for the page. Many clients struggle with this recommendation. Since visitors are landing on the page, these clients would like to take the opportunity to allow visitors to navigate to different services. This approach causes a lower overall conversion rate.

Key Performance Indicators

Key performance indicators (KPIs) are specific metrics that help organizations measure and track their business performance. Each conversion goal for a website could have one or several KPIs attached to it. For example, a conversion on an ecommerce website will have any of the following KPIs:

- Number of conversions within a time period

- Average order value

- Number of items ordered

At the start of your conversion optimization process, invest time in identifying KPIs to measure, track, and ultimately improve.

These KPIs should have a meaningful business value attached to them. Sometimes marketing or technology departments focus on a metric and ignore the fact that it might *not* have a real business value. For example, the number of page views per month for an ecommerce website holds little business value by itself. The conversion rate or the average order value, on the other hand, has a direct impact on the company's bottom line. Although general KPIs are shared across industries and within the same vertical markets, it is common for different organizations to have unique KPIs. It is also natural for departments within a single organization to have different KPIs that they are interested in tracking and improving.

KPIs should be trackable. You should be able to express them numerically. To measure an organization's progress toward its goals, you have to be able to measure current performance and future progress.

Finally, the question you should ask to determine whether a KPI should be tracked is, *"What is the business value?"* For example, if a person wants to track the number of monthly visitors to a website, we ask, "What is the business value?" There may be no business value in simply increasing the number of visitors.

Common KPIs for Ecommerce Websites

The following are some of the common KPIs tracked by many ecommerce websites:

Conversions
    The number of orders a website captures remains the most critical factor for an ecommerce website.

Average order value
    This KPI calculates the average amount a customer spends when placing an order with an ecommerce website. In some instances, a conversion optimization project or particular optimization software will focus on increasing the average order value

as opposed to increasing the number of orders. Most companies consider that increasing the average order value is more challenging than increasing conversion rates. The total monthly revenue generated by a website is equal to the average order value multiplied by the number of orders in the same month.

Number of items per order

In few instances does the number of items per order have a direct impact and business value associated with it. It's typical of upsell and cross-sell software to focus on this metric since it shows the capability of the software to increase the number of items customers are ordering. We rarely see real value in tracking this metric on our projects, but again, this will vary based on the business and the client.

Checkout process abandonment rate

This represents the number of visitors who start the checkout process but never place an order with the site. It is typical for an unoptimized checkout process to have abandonment rates anywhere from 45% to 80%. We have seen few ecommerce websites with checkout abandonment rates close to 92%. To put this in perspective, an 80% abandonment rate means that for 100 website visitors who start the checkout process, only 20 of them successfully complete it. The remaining 80 visitors leave the website without placing an order. From our experience, the best optimized checkout process has an abandonment rate of 20%.

Common KPIs for Lead Generation Websites

The following two metrics are the most common KPIs tracked for lead generation websites:

Conversions

The number of leads a website generates compared to the number of monthly visitors. This is the most important KPI for lead generation websites.

Offline close ratio

This ratio represents the number of leads that are generated online and from which the sales team is then able to capture business. Some companies consider this ratio to be the real conversion rate ratio for a website. And although this ratio measures to some extent the quality of leads a website is generating, there are external factors that the website has no way of controlling, such as the ability of the sales team.

Common KPIs for Content Websites

Content websites generate their revenue either by selling online advertising or by selling monthly subscriptions to premium content. Based on the revenue model, the following are some of the common KPIs tracked:

Monthly visitors
> Advertisers are willing to pay more for websites that have a higher number of visitors. This metric can have a direct impact on the amount of money a company can charge for displaying banner advertising on a specific section of its website.

Monthly page views
> Similar to the number of monthly visitors, this metric measures the website's ability to engage its visitors. The more a website is able to engage visitors, the more pages these visitors will view. Some content websites will intentionally break down articles into four or five sections to force readers to navigate to more pages, thus inflating this KPI. This metric should be monitored closely to ensure that users are actually spending time "reading" the content and not bouncing from page to page (which indicates that they have not found what they are looking for).

Common KPIs for Subscription Websites

For websites that rely on selling premium content to registered users, the registration process abandonment metric tracks the percentage of visitors who start the registration process compared to those who complete it. This metric is similar to the checkout process abandonment rate for an ecommerce website, and it tracks the following KPIs:

Free-to-paid account conversion ratio
> In many instances, these websites will offer free access to their content for a limited time. The goal is to allow website visitors to experience the content and determine whether a paid membership will bring them additional value. Ultimately, the goal is to convert these free accounts into paid ones. This ratio tracks the percentage of visitors who start with a free account and then convert into a paid account. This ratio will vary tremendously based on the type of website, the cost of membership, and the perceived value of the content.

Active paid membership base
> At the surface, this metric may seem to have little business value, as it doesn't affect revenue directly. However, it can be useful for predicting the possibility of subscribers canceling their membership and thus reducing the website's revenue. Some subscription websites measure the average activity for their membership and how frequently they log in to the website. For example, if a customer logs in to the site once every two weeks initially, but then does not log in for four weeks, the chances of that user canceling the subscription increase.

Subscription cancellation ratio

This ratio tracks the number of cancellations within a time period. Tracking this ratio allows subscription-based websites to react to spikes in cancellation by understanding why this happens and coming up with a plan to address the causes.

Average subscription length

This number tracks the average period a person remains subscribed to the website. This will help the website operators understand their revenue model. Analyzing the different subscriber behavior between long-time subscribers and short-term subscribers can help reduce the number of short-term subscriptions.

Micro Conversions

Macro conversion goals and KPIs set the overall vision. For any of these macro conversions to take place, visitors must go through a series of *micro* conversions on the site. Each micro conversion moves visitors farther down the conversion path until a final macro conversion takes place. When a visitor places an order with an ecommerce website, a macro conversion occurs. Compare that to the micro conversion on a product page. Product pages on most ecommerce websites serve to persuade customers to add an item to their cart. When the customer clicks on the "add to cart" button, a micro conversion happens. This micro conversion moves the visitor down the conversion funnel. If our ultimate goal on a website is to increase *macro* conversions, increasing our *micro* conversions is the best way to achieve that.

A single page on the site can have several micro conversion goals. For example, customers can use a product page to perform any of the following tasks:

- Add an item to the cart

- Read product reviews

- Check product availability in a physical store

- Compare products

Each of these represents a micro conversion. With several conversion goals on a single page, you should start by prioritizing the different goals and determining the *primary conversion objective* of the page. As you work through this prioritization, you will find that many of the micro goals support the site's macro conversions. Reading product reviews persuades customers to buy an item. Clicking on the "add to cart" button is necessary for them to make a purchase.

The primary conversion goal on a page drives all of its elements, including copy, design, and layout. Goals that distract visitors from the primary conversion goal should be reworked or removed. Never lose focus of your main objective on the site (conversion). When you lose focus, your conversion rates will drop. It's that simple.

When you begin to optimize a particular page, ask the following:

- What are the different micro conversions that can take place on this page?
- How do we prioritize the different micro conversion goals?
- How do we focus the page to support the most important micro conversion goal?
- What would stop visitors from taking the micro conversion path?

Figure 2-1 shows the relationships among micro conversions, macro conversions, and website KPIs.

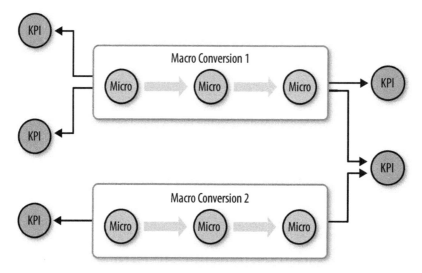

Figure 2-1. *The relationships among macro conversions, micro conversions, and website KPIs*

----- **DON'T FORGET!** -----

- Make sure your landing page is clear, easy to read, and focused on your conversion objectives or goals.
- Even though your site may have multiple goals, your pages should have one primary conversion objective.

Building Budgets for Ecommerce Sites with Conversion Rates

How much revenue a conversion generates is important when determining a budget for a campaign. In the simple case of a sale on an ecommerce website, that number usually is the *average order value* (aka AOV) you receive from a conversion:

Average order value = Total revenue from orders / Total number of orders

If a website generates $10,000 of revenue from 25 orders, the average order value is $400:

Average order value = $10,000 / 25 = $400

That revenue only comes from customers who actually convert, of course. The basic conversion rate equation is:

Conversion rate = Total number of visitors who take an action / Total number of visitors

Two elements control the success of paid online advertising campaigns:

- The cost associated with running the campaign. There are usually two costs you must account for: the cost to drive traffic to the landing page, and the cost of designing and optimizing the landing page.

- The revenue generated by the campaign as determined by its conversion rate, and the revenue generated by a conversion.

When creating a campaign, you will need to plan and budget for both of these elements. Several scenarios could affect the campaign's profitability, so you have to consider the following questions:

- What budget should you set for an advertising campaign?

- What is the average cost per click you should spend while remaining profitable?

- How will the campaign conversion rate impact profitability?

- What is the absolute minimum conversion rate for the campaign to generate a profit?

An example may help show how these questions connect. Let's say a company has been selling widgets in the traditional market for more than 10 years. Based on historical data, the company nets $75 of profit for each unit sold. The company decides to experiment with selling widgets online. The marketing team will run a pay-per-click (PPC) campaign that directs prospects to a landing page where they can place orders for the widgets.

In planning the campaign, the marketing team makes the following assumptions:

- The widgets landing page should receive 100,000 visitors during the campaign.

- The company never ran any paid advertising before, so it is estimating the campaign to start with a 1% conversion rate.

The profit a campaign is expected to generate is important when determining its marketing budget. In this example, the campaign is expected to generate $75,000 in profit:

Number of orders = Number of visitors * Conversion rate

Number of orders = 100,000 * 1% = 1,000 orders

Gross profit = 1,000 * $75 = $75,000

However, this calculation does not take into account the additional cost associated with the new medium (online marketing). The marketing team has to plan for additional costs, which include:

1. The cost of designing the landing pages for the campaign

2. The cost of landing page optimization software and consulting fees

3. The cost of acquiring 100,000 visitors

Let's assume this project will have a fixed cost of $15,000 to handle items 1 and 2 (design, software, and optimization costs):

Number of orders = Number of visitors * Conversion rate

Number of orders = 100,000 * 1% = 1,000 orders

Gross profit = 1,000 * $75 = $75,000

Cost of design and software = ($15,000)

Gross profit = $60,000

So, the company is left with $60,000 to cover the cost of acquiring visitors. How much should the company spend to acquire these visitors?

The company can spend all of its profit, $60,000, and not lose any money. Based on the competitiveness of the vertical, the cost per click to acquire a single visitor to the landing page varies. We have seen clients spend as much as $15 per click. Since this is a new market the company is planning to penetrate, it is willing to spend up to 40% of possible revenue to acquire visitors:

Possible investment to acquire visitors = 40% * $60,000 = $24,000

How Much Should the Company Spend per Click?

We use the following formula to determine the average cost per click in a campaign:

Cost per click = Campaign budget / Number of visitors

Cost per click = $24,000 / 100,000 = 24 cents per click

So, if the marketing manager is bidding on a PPC campaign, his average bid should not exceed 24 cents per click to remain within the $24,000 budget. Table 2-1 shows how changing the average bid per click will have an impact on the bottom line for the campaign. With an average bid of 24 cents per click, the campaign will generate $36,000 in profit. However, if the keywords are more competitive and the team has to increase the average bid per click to 48 cents, the campaign profit will go down to $12,000.

Table 2-1. *Breakdown of campaign profitability*

Campaign parameters	First campaign, with 24 cents per click cost	Second campaign, with 48 cents per click cost
Total number of visitors	100,000	100,000
Pay per click	$0.24	$0.48
PPC spending	$24,000	$48,000
Number of orders	1,000	1,000
Profit per order	$75	$75
Total profit from orders	$75,000	$75,000
Campaign budget	($24,000)	($48,000)
Additional costs	($15,000)	($15,000)
Total profit	$36,000	$12,000

Table 2-2 shows that the company can pay up to 60 cents per click without losing any money. Paying more than 60 cents per click will put the campaign in the red. Of course, in some instances companies decide to spend money on a losing campaign because their business strategy is to try to capture or enter a new market. It is also normal for companies to increase their average bid per click when a campaign starts, and then slowly reduce it over time.

Table 2-2. *Calculating the maximum average pay per click for a campaign*

Campaign parameters	Campaign with 60 cents per click cost
Total number of orders	1,000
Profit per order	$75
Total profit from orders	$75,000
One-time costs	($15,000)
Possible profit	$60,000
Total number of visitors required	100,000
Average bid per click	$0.60

How Does the Campaign Conversion Rate Impact Profitability?

The calculations we presented assumed an average conversion rate of 1%. Table 2-3 shows the bottom-line impact of both increasing the conversion rate to 2% and reducing it to 0.5%. With a conversion rate of 2%, the company is able to generate twice as many sales, and the campaign generates a total of $110,000 in profit. A 0.5% conversion rate results in the campaign losing $1,500.

Table 2-3. *Impact of conversion rate on campaign profitability*

Campaign parameters	1% conversion rate	2% conversion rate	0.5% conversion rate
Total number of visitors	100,000	100,000	100,000
Pay per click	$0.24	$0.24	$0.24
PPC spending	$24,000	$24,000	$24,000
Average conversion rate	1%	2%	.5%
Number of orders	1,000	2,000	500
Profit per order	$75	$75	$75
Total profit from orders	$75,000	$150,000	$37,500
Campaign budget	($24,000)	($24,000)	($24,000)
Additional costs	($15,000)	($15,000)	($15,000)
Profit or loss	$36,000	$111,000	($1,500)

What Is the Minimum Conversion Rate for a Campaign to Not Lose Any Money?

While setting paid campaigns, conversion rate is usually the unknown element. We refer to the minimum conversion rate for a campaign as the *breakeven conversion rate*. As the name implies, at the breakeven conversion rate the campaign will not generate any profit or loss.

The formula to calculate the breakeven conversion rate is:

Breakeven conversion rate = Total costs / (Profit per conversion * Number of visitors)

Let's assume this company knows it will have to spend 55 cents per click. Let's walk through how to calculate the lowest possible conversion rate:

Pay-per-click budget: 100,000 * 0.55 = $55,000

Design, optimization, and software costs = $15,000

Total campaign costs = $55,000 + $15,000 = $70,000

Total number of widgets sold to cover cost = $70,000 / $75 = 934 widgets

Minimum conversion rate = 934 / 100,000 = 0.934%

Or minimum conversion rate = $70,000 / ($75 * 100,000) = 0.934%

Lifetime Value (LTV) of a Customer

Most companies see their first sale with a new customer as the initial step in a long-term relationship. If things go well, these companies will receive multiple orders from that customer, building loyalty to their brand. Our calculations in the previous sections used the profit from a single order to determine the campaign budget and its profitability. We did not take into account the fact that returning customers will likely not click on paid advertising.

Taking *lifetime value (LTV)* into account can drastically change the budget for the campaign. How to calculate LTV is beyond the scope of this book and is the subject of many debates. But for the purposes of our discussion, let's assume you are able to calculate LTV for your customers. How does LTV impact the calculation for a campaign? In our example, the company determines that the LTV of a customer is $187.50. Table 2-4 shows how using the LTV calculation versus a single sale calculation will have an impact on the campaign's bottom line.

Table 2-4. *Adding LTV to budget calculations*

Campaign parameters	24 cents per click and LTV calculation	24 cents per click and single order calculation	48 cents per click and LTV calculation	48 cents per click and single order calculation
Number of orders	1,000	1,000	1,000	1,000
LTV	$187.50	$187.50	$187.50	$187.50
Profit per order	$75	$75	$75	$75
Income	$187,500	$75,000	$187,500	$75,000
Total number of visitors	100,000	100,000	100,000	100,000
Pay per click	$0.24	$0.24	$0.48	$0.48
PPC spending	($24,000)	($24,000)	($48,000)	($48,000)
Additional costs	($15,000)	($15,000)	($15,000)	($15,000)
Net income	$148,500	$36,000	$124,500	$12,000

With an average bid of 24 cents per click, the company is able to generate $148,500 when using LTV calculations versus $36,000 when using a single sale calculation. At an average bid of 48 cents per click, the company generates $124,500 in profit versus $12,000 when using a single sale calculation.

The campaign's breakeven conversion rate also improves. The updated formula for the breakeven conversion rate is:

Breakeven conversion rate = Total costs / (Lifetime value * Number of visitors)

Let's use the same numbers from the previous example:

Pay-per-click budget: 100,000 * 0.55 = $55,000

Design, optimization, and software costs = $15,000

Total campaign costs = $55,000 + $15,000 = $70,000

Total number of widgets sold to cover cost = $70,000 / $187.5 = 374

Minimum conversion rate = 374 / 100,000 = 0.374%

Or minimum conversion rate = $70,000 / ($187.5 * 100,000) = 0.374%

When using a single sale for budgeting, the breakeven conversion rate for the campaign is 0.934%. When using the LTV, the breakeven conversion rate is lower: 0.374%. The company may experience a much lower conversion rate (lower number of orders), yet still generate profit—*although not immediately*.

You should apply LTV calculations cautiously. On the positive side, when using the customer LTV calculation, companies are willing to spend a lot more to run PPC campaigns. However, on the negative side, they are basing the LTV calculation on longer-term assumptions and predictions, which can be risky.

Some of our clients complain that the numbers for LTV keep changing. They're right. The biggest challenge is lack of concrete data. This could be the case particularly for many new businesses, but it could also happen with well-established businesses if they are not aware of this. If there is no system in place to track customer retention rates, LTV calculations are based on guesses at best.

There is also debate regarding how much data is needed to accurately assess the LTV of a customer. Is it enough to have six months' worth of data, or do you need multiple years' worth? Also, how do you determine how long a customer will remain with the company? Some LTV models calculate a customer's value to be five to seven years. That might work for some businesses, but definitely not for all.

NOTE

You may find that your competitors are willing to spend a lot more per click. Likely reasons for this include the following:

- Your competitors did not do the math, and eventually they will get to it.
- Your competitors are converting more of their traffic into customers.
- Your competitors are using the LTV model, perhaps a very optimistic LTV model, in their calculations.
- Your competitors have been advertising for a long time, and they are able to lower their PPC spend.

Budgeting for Lead Generation Sites

Calculating conversion rates gets a little more complicated for lead generation websites. With these sites, the campaign goal is to convince visitors to give out their contact information, such as an email address or telephone number, so that the sales team can follow up with these leads. The actual conversion takes place offline. The offline conversion rate is impacted by any of the following:

- The nature of the product or service

- The target market demographics

- The quality of the lead

- The ability and skill of the sales team to close the sale

The more money a customer is expected to spend, the lower the conversion rate will be. It is typical for companies selling software or consulting services that cost thousands of dollars to have an offline conversion rate of around 5%. On the other hand, lead generation businesses that require customers to make smaller investments can have an offline conversion rate anywhere from 15% to 20%.

Two elements control the success of online lead generation campaigns:

- The costs associated with running the campaign, including the cost to drive traffic to the landing page and the cost of designing and optimizing the landing page.

- The revenue generated by the campaign as determined by its offline conversion rate.

Let's take an example of a roof repair company that runs a lead generation campaign. The average profit per customer is $500. The company does not expect any repeat business from its customers. In planning the campaign, the marketing team makes the following assumptions:

- The lead generation landing page should receive 10,000 visitors during the campaign.

- The company estimates the campaign to start with a 10% online conversion rate, which is typical for lead generation campaigns.

- Based on its history, the company assumes to close 15% of the online leads.

The following shows how to calculate the campaign budget assuming an average cost of $2.50 per click:

Pay-per-click budget = 10,000 * $2.50 = $25,000

Total number of leads generated online = 10,000 * 10% = 1,000 leads

Total number of sales generated offline = 1,000 * 15% = 150 sales

Total revenue = 150 * $500 = $75,000

Net profit = $75,000 − $25,000 = $50,000

Table 2-5 shows campaign profitability based on paying an average of $2.50 and $5 per click.

Table 2-5. *Lead generation campaign profitability*

Campaign parameters	Campaign with $2.50 per click cost	Campaign with $5 per click cost
Total number of visitors	10,000	10,000
Pay per click	$2.50	$5
PPC budget	$25,000	$50,000
Online conversion rate	10%	10%
Number of leads	1,000	1,000
Offline conversion rate	15%	15%
Number of deals	150	150
Profit per deal	$500	$500
Margin	$75,000	$75,000
PPC cost	($25,000)	($50,000)
Additional cost	($15,000)	($15,000)
Total profit	$30,000	$5,000

Monetization Models and Conversion Rates

Maximizing the ROI of an online marketing campaign requires companies to invest time and money in conversion efforts to generate more orders or leads from their current traffic. Companies have two options for increasing the profitability of a landing page or a website:

- Pay more money to increase traffic to a campaign and hope the laws of statistics will hold true and your conversion rates will remain constant.

- Pay for optimization services to increase the number of orders or leads from the current campaign.

The choice is not always easy. The challenge with conversion optimization is the difficulty in estimating the improvement a company can expect as a result of the project. We recommend creating a simple financial model that outlines different possible outcomes based on target conversion improvements. This model can help determine the viability of conversion optimization and set profitability targets for the project. The following case study demonstrates how to create this model.

Showing Delay As Dollars

One of our clients is a software company that sells IT training software through a variety of channels, including:

- The company's website
- The company's call center
- Other ecommerce partners
- Direct mail catalog

Individual licenses of the software are sold to consumers who are looking to advance their careers in IT. Multiple licenses are sold to companies looking for effective ways to save on IT training costs. The client considered its website to be its most effective channel since it had the highest profit margins.

On the business-to-consumer (B2C) side, the client made $165 for each license sold through its site. Naturally, management wanted to move most of the software sales activity online. However, with 20,000 visitors per month, the site was converting at a low 2.2%.

Our team conducted a survey of the client's industry to understand what factors influenced the decision to purchase IT training software. As we investigated consumer behavior, different purchasing trends emerged among individuals buying the software and companies buying a multilicense deal. Ultimately, the product pages played a major role in deciding whether to buy the software package. Our solution focused on creating separate product pages based on each market segment.

During the initial phase of the project, the team created a financial model that showed how incremental changes in the conversion rate will have a significant impact on the company's bottom line. Even with increasing conversion from 2.2% to 2.5%, our client would see an additional annual profit of $118,800. The model demonstrated that increasing conversion rates to 4% would translate into an annual increase of $712,800 in profit. Table 2-6 shows a sample of the monetization model for the project.

Table 2-6. *Monetization model for conversion rate optimization*

Conversion rate	Monthly traffic	Total orders	Monthly increase in orders	Monthly profit impact	Annual profit impact	Cost of three months of delay
2.20%	20,000	440	–	–	–	–
2.50%	20,000	500	60	$9,900	$118,800	$29,700
2.75%	20,000	550	110	$18,150	$217,800	$54,450
3.00%	20,000	600	160	$26,400	$316,800	$79,200
3.25%	20,000	650	210	$34,650	$415,800	$103,950
3.50%	20,000	700	260	$42,900	$514,800	$128,700
3.75%	20,000	750	310	$51,150	$613,800	$153,450
4.00%	20,000	800	360	$59,400	$712,800	$178,200

—continued—

Each term in the table is defined as follows:

Conversion rate
    Current and future percentage of site visitors who place an order through the website.

Monthly traffic
    Current number of visitors to the site. We used a constant number in this table to simplify the calculations.

Total number of orders
    Total number of orders the client should expect to see as a result of the increase in conversion rates.

Monthly profit impact
    How much additional monthly profit the client should expect as a result of the increase in orders collected via the website. This number is equal to the total number of orders multiplied by $165.

Annual profit impact
    How much additional monthly profit the client should expect as a result of the increase in orders collected via the website.

Cost of three months of delay
    Based on the target conversion rates, the lost profit if the client decides to delay the project by three months.

—— **DON'T FORGET!** ——

Conversion optimization is a new area for many companies. By developing a financial model for cost/benefit analysis, you can determine how seriously to consider optimization initiatives.

Bounce Rate

Bounce rate is a popular metric used to describe the quality of a particular page on a site. There are competing definitions for bounce rate. We define bounce rate as the percentage of visitors who arrive at a landing page but leave it without ever navigating to a second page on the site. Google Analytics defines bounce rate as follows:

> [T]he percentage of single-page visits or visits in which the person left your site from the entrance (landing) page. Use this metric to measure visit quality—a high bounce rate generally indicates that site entrance pages aren't relevant to your visitors. The more compelling your landing pages, the more visitors will stay on your site and convert. You can minimize bounce rates by tailoring landing pages to each keyword and ad that you run. Landing pages should provide the information and services that were promised in the ad copy.*

* *http://google.com/support/analytics/bin/answer.py?hl=en&answer=81986*

Based on this definition, you can calculate bounce rate like this:

Bounce rate = Number of single page visits / Total number of entrances to that page

A less popular definition of bounce rate is the percentage of visitors who arrive at a landing page but leave in less than x seconds. The numerical value for x varies from one landing page to the next. It reflects a reasonable amount of time it would take for someone who clicked on a landing page to determine whether the page has what she is looking for. On most landing pages and websites, five to 10 seconds is the number we use. For our purposes, we will use our first definition throughout the discussion.

Most analytics packages report the bounce rate for the different pages on a website. These packages usually report a website average bounce rate as well. The website bounce rate is usually calculated by averaging the bounce rate for all pages on the site. Figure 2-2 shows some of the metrics reported by Google Analytics at a page level.

Page	None ≿		Pageviews ↓	Unique Pageviews	Avg. Time on Page	Bounce Rate	% Exit
1.			25,602	18,315	00:02:19	78.21%	64.20%
2.			18,980	15,531	00:01:21	56.58%	45.35%
3.			15,907	9,920	00:00:32	28.49%	15.20%
4.			12,835	10,133	00:03:00	65.70%	61.85%

Figure 2-2. *Different metrics reported by Google Analytics at a page level*

Bounce rate is a great way to get a quick read of how well a particular page is performing on your website. The traditional approach is to compare the bounce rate of a page to the site's average bounce rate. For example, if a website has an average bounce rate of 52%, pages with a bounce rate higher than that should be optimized first.

However, this approach is too simplistic. Website bounce rate can be misleading most of the time. Taking an average bounce rate of thousands of pages is too generic to measure the health of your website. A better approach is to evaluate pages with a bounce rate above a certain mark. We evaluate pages with bounce rates above 20% to 25%. This is because you can assume that around 20% of your visitors land on your website by mistake. They typed in the wrong keyword or clicked on the wrong advertising. These are the visitors who leave right away. And these are the ones who should be responsible for a 20% bounce rate. Bounce rates above 25% indicate that visitors who are interested in your product and service are not finding what they are looking for.

Finally, optimizing pages with high bounce rates will only make sense if these pages receive large numbers of visitors. Optimizing a landing page that has a bounce rate of 95% would *only* make sense if that page gets thousands of visitors in a month. The minimum number of entrances a page should receive before evaluating its bounce rate will vary based on the size of the site and its average order value. We generally recommend the following guidelines:

- For smaller websites, focus on pages with a high bounce rate if they receive a minimum of 1,000 entrances per month to that particular page.

- For mid-size to large websites, focus on pages with a high bounce rate if they receive a minimum of 5,000 entrances per month to that particular page.

These guidelines change from one client to the next, so you should develop your own minimums based on your data.

What Is Your Real Bounce Rate?

Most marketers rely on website average bounce rate as a general metric against which to measure the bounce rate of different pages of the website. If you decide to follow this approach, we recommend that you rethink how you should calculate your website bounce rate.

Website bounce rate is usually calculated by averaging the bounce rate of the different pages of the website. The theory is that with many pages on the site, data abnormalities will disappear. This theory, however, fails the real-life test. Figure 2-3 shows how bounce rate is calculated for a website that has 20 pages.

Page	Page Bounce Rate
page 1	55.00%
page 2	27.00%
page 3	32.00%
page 4	15.68%
page 5	44.35%
page 6	43.08%
page 7	7.38%
page 8	51.50%
page 9	44.48%
page 10	32.90%
page 11	24.95%
page 12	26.35%
page 13	46.73%
page 14	22.46%
page 15	23.30%
page 16	32.20%
page 17	8.85%
page 18	2.92%
page 19	18.20%
page 20	48.62%
Site average bounce rate	30.40%

Figure 2-3. *Calculating website bounce rate*

We recommend evaluating the top 10 or 20 entry pages to the site. These pages are usually also responsible for the most bounces. To determine whether your website average bounce rate might have some abnormality in it, you should calculate:

- The percentage of entrances these pages are generating to your website

- The percentage of bounces these pages are responsible for

These two percentages should be close to each another (+/− 5% deviation). If they are not, the top landing page might be skewing the overall website bounce rate. As a result, you should calculate the site bounce rate after excluding these pages.

For example, one of our client's top 10 entry pages was responsible for 32% of their website entrances. At the same time, these top 10 entry pages were generating 38% of the bounces. The website average bounce rate was 47%:

The difference between the two percentages = (38% − 32%) / 32% = 18.7%

Since the two percentages were more than 10% apart, we recalculated the website bounce rate, excluding the top landing pages. We did this by taking the average bounce rate for all the pages on the site, except for the top landing pages; the real bounce rate for the site dropped from 47% to 41%.

Exit Rate

Exit rate is the percentage of visitors who leave a website from a particular page after visiting at least one other page in the site. The theoretical definition of exit rate is not always mapped to how analytics packages calculate and display exit rate. Google Analytics, for example, uses the following formula to calculate the exit rate on a page:

Single page exit rate = Number of page exits / Number of page views

The number of page views used in the formula includes single page visits. As a result, exit rate as displayed in Google *includes* bounce rate.

Calculating Bounce and Exit Rates

Standard reporting for most analytics packages includes bounce and exit rates for different pages on a site. The following example illustrates how bounce and exit rates are calculated.

A page receives 10,000 page views within a single day, and of those views, there are 1,800 entrances. Of the 1,800 entrances to the page, 1,000 visitors leave immediately. A total of 2,500 exit the site after arriving at the page.

Bounce rate = Number of single page visits / Total number of entrances to that page

Bounce rate = 1,000 / 1,800 = 55.55%

Exit rate = Number of page exits / Number of page views

Exit rate = 2,500 / 10,000 = 25%

Notice that the 2,500 exits from the page include the 1,000 exits that resulted from a single page view.

Using Exit Rate to Determine Where to Start the Optimization Process

You might be tempted to use the single page exit rate formula to calculate the website exit rate. But since all visitors will exit your website, that rate will be 100%, which does not tell you a lot. Instead, here's an updated website exit rate:

Website exit rate = Average (Single page exit rates)

How can exit rate help you determine where to start optimization?

Figure 2-4 shows the top exit pages report from Google Analytics. You might be tempted to pick pages with exit rates higher than the site average to start optimization. A better approach is to establish a *standard acceptable exit rate* for different pages on the site based on their function. For a page to be considered for optimization, it needs to meet the following criteria:

- The page's exit rate is higher than the established acceptable exit rate based on the page function.

- The number of unique page views is higher than x, where x is dependent on the size of the site and how much revenue you can generate by reducing the exit rate for a page. For some of our clients, x is 500 page views; for others, x is 5,000 page views.

Exit Pages			
Exits **791,120** % of Site Total: 53.45%	Pageviews **8,377,256** % of Site Total: 52.91%		% Exit **9.44%** Site Avg: 9.35% (1.02%)

Page	None	Exits ↓	Pageviews	% Exit
1.		103,244	681,478	15.15%
2.		12,315	88,475	13.92%
3.		9,335	53,105	17.58%
4.		9,004	37,400	24.07%

Figure 2-4. *Top exit pages report from Google Analytics*

What Is an Acceptable Exit Rate for a Page?

Exit rate will vary from one page to the next on your website. Order confirmation pages or thank you pages for lead generation websites will naturally have higher exit rates than other pages. As a general rule of thumb, pages from which visitors are expected to leave the site can have 90% or higher exit rates. Visitors who arrive on these pages have completed the conversion action and will obviously leave the site. Pages from which visitors are expected to continue navigating through the website, such as the main home page, should have a target exit rate of less than 10% to 20%. Anything higher than that might reveal some hidden problems that need to be addressed.

Bounce and Exit Rates in Offline Sales

The world of offline sales lacks terms that mirror exit rate and bounce rate. However, adapting bounce and exit rate definitions to offline sales can be insightful.

A lead must go through different steps in the offline sales funnel before converting. The complexity of this funnel and how quickly leads move through it depend on the nature of the product or service you are selling. A typical sales funnel includes the following stages:

- Awareness

- Interest

- Evaluation

- Action

Leads enter at the awareness stage and exit as customers in the action stage. Bounce rate in the offline world is the percentage of leads that have a single touch point with your business and decide to not pursue the relationship further. It represents the percentage of leads that start at the awareness level but never move to the interest stage. High offline bounce rates indicate either a problem with the quality of the leads entering the funnel or sales issues you must address during the initial contact with leads.

Exit rate in offline sales is the percentage of leads that have multiple touch points with your business but ultimately decide not to continue within the sales funnel. It is the percentage of visitors who move from one stage to the next, starting at the awareness stage and moving farther down the process but *never* getting to the action stage. High exit rates might indicate a breakdown of your selling process or a poor qualification process.

Time Spent on a Page/Site

The time a visitor spends on a particular page or the total time he spends on your website is a good indicator of how sticky your site is and how engaged visitors are by your content. The more time a visitor spends, the more engaged he is. Both metrics, time spent on a page and time spent on the site, can reveal many details about visitors' interaction with the site. And although they both seem straightforward, their accuracy is challenged by how they are calculated based on real data.

Figure 2-5 represents the process of a visitor navigating through a website and includes timestamps for when he enters different pages. He visits three pages before exiting the website. The time spent on page 1 is calculated by subtracting the entry timestamp of 6:00 on that page from the entry timestamp of 6:03 on page 2. As such, analytics packages will report that this visitor spent three minutes on the first page. The timestamp is essential in calculating the time spent on a page.

Given the information in Figure 2-5, can you calculate the time the visitor spent on page 3? Most analytics packages will calculate the time a visitor spends on a page only if the visitor navigates to another page on the site. Without the timestamp for a fourth page in Figure 2-5, there is no easy way to determine how much time the visitor spent on page 3. The visitor could have spent one minute or 15 minutes, but since it is not tracked, the time spent on page 3 is reported as zero.

Figure 2-5. *Time-on-page calculation*

This calculation shows the *actual* time spent on a page by a single visitor. The following formula shows how to calculate the average time all users spend on a particular page:

Average time on a page = Total time spent by all visitors on the page / Number of nonexit page views

The time spent on a page for visits that exit the site from this page is reported as *zero*. Thus, these visits are *not* included in calculating the average time on the page. Since we are excluding these visits, the accuracy of reporting is questioned. The higher the exit rate for a particular page, the less accurate the reporting of its average time. Consider two different pages on a website:

- Page 1 has an exit rate of 45%, which means 45% of its visitors leave the site from that page and never navigate to another page. Since visits that result in an exit are not included in calculating the average time spent on the page, we have to exclude 45% of the visits.

- Page 2 has an exit rate of 15%, which means 15% of its visitors leave the site. Again, visits that result in an exit from the website are not included in calculating the time spent on the page. In this case, we only exclude 15% of the visits from calculating the average time on that page.

It is clear that the average time spent on page 2 is more accurate, so we only excluded 15% of the visitors from our calculations as opposed to excluding 45% in the case of page 1.

How can we calculate time spent on the site? Figure 2-5 shows that the visitor entered the website at 6:00. The last interaction the visitor had with the site was at 6:10. We do not know exactly when the visitor exited the site, but we have to work with the data available to us. So, analytics will report the time this visitor spent on the site as 10 minutes. As you can see, there again is some inaccuracy in this reporting. The following formula shows how to calculate the average time all users spend on the site:

> Average time on the site = Total time spent by all visitors on the site / Total number of visitors

Table 2-7 shows how much time three visitors spent on a website. As you can see, the third visitor shows a time spent of 0. Should we include that visitor when calculating the average time spent on the site for all visitors?

> Average time on the site = Total time spent by all visitors on the site / Total number of visitors

Including the third visitor:

Average time on the site = 15 / 3 = 5 minutes

Excluding the third visitor:

Average time on the site = 15 / 2 = 7.5 minutes

Table 2-7. *Variations in time spent on site*

Visitor	Time spent on site
First visitor	10 minutes
Second visitor	5 minutes
Third visitor	0 (bounce off first page)

So, should we count single page visitors as part of the "total number of visitors" in the preceding formula? The example demonstrates that we are artificially introducing inaccuracy to our reporting. In 2007, Google Analytics decided to remove these bounced visitors from total-time-on-site calculations. By doing so, you no longer could compare time on a site before and after the change in method calculation. For the sake of consistency over accuracy, the Google Analytics team decided to go back to including bounce visitors in their calculation of average time spent on a site.* Our discussion of the accuracy of time spent on a page should not impact the importance of this metric, but rather should prompt you to consider and apply the metric with caution.

* *http://analytics.blogspot.com/2007/09/reverting-back-to-original-average-time.html*

A high average time spent on a page indicates that visitors are either engaged by the content or struggling to understand it. There is a huge difference between the two. How do you determine which scenario is the case? Bounce rates, exit rates, and average time spent on a page help to answer this question. Pages with high bounce and exit rates indicate that visitors are not able to find what they are looking for, and thus they are leaving the site. We usually expect these pages to have a lower time-spent-on-page rate since visitors are leaving the site. High exit rates and high time-spent-on-page rates indicate that visitors are struggling with the page content. Although a high percentage of visitors are leaving, those who are staying are spending a long time trying to understand the content. This usually indicates that the page's design, copy, and presentation need to be reevaluated.

Right about now you are probably wondering: what is considered a good amount of time spent on a page?

There is no such thing as a good time-spent-on-page rate. Each page on your site will have its own ideal time for a visitor to interact with its content. Some pages, such as category pages, might have average time-spent-on-page rates of less than 15 seconds. Other pages, such as product pages, especially those full of product reviews, might require a visitor to spend two to five minutes on them. A visitor might spend 15 minutes on a well-developed and persuasive long copy landing page.

Figure 2-6 shows the average time spent on some of the top pages on our site, Invesp.com. This figure shows that a wide range of time is spent on our pages—anywhere from as much as 4:22 to as little as 35 seconds. We also have a few extensive resource pages on our site with an average time of 29 minutes.

Page	None ⌄	Pageviews ↓	Unique Pageviews	Avg. Time on Page
		25,650	18,357	00:02:19
		21,164	17,328	00:01:22
		18,665	11,769	00:00:35
		16,754	13,132	00:03:08
		15,190	9,045	00:00:41
		12,409	8,457	00:02:28
		11,606	10,494	00:04:14
		9,390	7,472	00:01:47
		7,903	4,802	00:01:53
		7,422	6,640	00:04:22

Figure 2-6. *Time spent on the top content pages of Invesp.com*

Quality of Traffic (Visitors)

The terms *quality of traffic* and *quality of visitors* are used in the online space to indicate how interested your website visitors are in the service or product you offer. These terms are mirrored in the offline world with the common sales and marketing term *quality of leads*. If you run an online advertising campaign to sell shoes, for example, you should drive visitors who are searching for shoes to your website. Although the majority of these visitors may not convert, they are well targeted for your particular product, which means your landing page is getting high-quality traffic. If, however, you drive visitors who are looking for furniture, these visitors will have no interest in what you have to offer. Your landing page in this case is receiving poor-quality traffic.

Quality has a direct impact on conversion rates, both offline and online. If your sales team has good-quality leads, they will be able to close more business. The same applies online. High-quality leads translate into more orders and higher conversions. This is an important point to keep in mind, especially when you pay for people to visit your website. So, how do you control the quality of traffic? Several factors impact visitor quality, including:

- Traffic sources

- Traffic medium

- Keywords

- Ad copy

Traffic Sources

Websites receive visitors directly, through search engines, or by referring websites. Each of these sources will drive a different quality of visitors based on the specific product or service. The breakdown of the traffic will vary from one website to the next. Figure 2-7 shows how different sources of traffic drive different percentages of visitors for different websites.

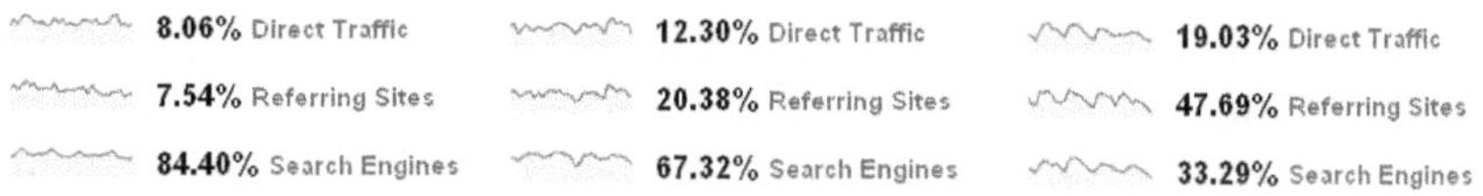

8.06% Direct Traffic	12.30% Direct Traffic	19.03% Direct Traffic
7.54% Referring Sites	20.38% Referring Sites	47.69% Referring Sites
84.40% Search Engines	67.32% Search Engines	33.29% Search Engines

Figure 2-7. *Breakdown of traffic among different websites*

Search engines provide a large amount of traffic for most established websites. With its firm grip on the U.S. market, Google usually delivers around 75% of *search* visitors. Other search engines, such as Yahoo! and Bing, drive an average of 20% of website *search* traffic.

The term *referral websites* means websites that link to your website. The amount of traffic these referrals send to your site will depend on the quality, authority, and number of visitors they have. Figure 2-7 shows how referring websites to a well-established website could be responsible for up to 50% of visitors.

The Value of Direct Traffic

As your brand becomes increasingly well known online, your website will receive a portion of its traffic from visitors coming directly to the site by typing its address in the browser address bar.

Linda Bustos of Elastic Path divided direct visitors into one of three types:[*]

- Loyal, repeat customers
- Late-stage buyers who've already visited your site through search, PPC, email, or an affiliate link, but needed time to make a purchase decision or to comparison shop
- First-time shoppers pre-sold from a newspaper article, blog post, social media reviews, or word of mouth

You should keep in mind that analytics programs report visitors as direct visitors when the software is not able to determine the referring website. So, the number of direct visitors reported by analytics software includes visitors who typed your website address directly into the browser address bar. It also includes cases in which the analytics software could not determine the referring website (search engine or a referral). That causes some analysts to question the accuracy of direct traffic reporting. Although we agree with assumptions, there are few ways to minimize the inaccuracy in reporting.[†]

[*] *http://www.getelastic.com/direct-traffic-google-analytics/*
[†] *http://blog.vkistudios.com/index.cfm/2009/7/10/Tips-Tricks-Traps-and-Tools-41-of-many-Understanding-Direct-Visits-in-Google-Analytics-UDVs*

Although we spoke here of conversion rates in general terms, we rarely do this on our projects. At a minimum, conversion rates should be tracked at the level of the different sources of traffic. General and unsegmented conversion rates do not tell us a whole lot about how well your website is performing. Table 2-8 shows a breakdown of traffic and conversion rates based on traffic sources. Let's analyze some of the metrics from this table. For this particular website, search engines drive 84% of the traffic, direct visitors drive 9.5% of the traffic, and referring websites drive 6% of the traffic. The low percentage of both referring websites and direct traffic indicates that the site is still new.

The breakdown of conversion rates based on traffic source is typical where direct traffic has a much higher conversion rate compared to the referring website or search engine traffic. This is because direct visitors recognize the brand and have some affinity to it. Thus, they are more likely to convert. In this example, direct traffic has a 75% higher conversion rate compared to other sources. Since the website receives a low percentage of its traffic from direct visitors and these visitors convert at a higher rate, this presents a possible opportunity for the site to focus on bringing more direct traffic to it.

Finally, let's look at engagement metrics for the different traffic sources. The average time on the site for the different sources is comparable. Search traffic browses more pages on the site. It is typical for direct traffic to have a lower pages-per-visit ratio. Direct visitors are more familiar with the site and know how to navigate around it. The metric that should jump out at you is the higher bounce rate for direct and referring websites. Both of these sources show about a 40% increase in bounce rate compared to search traffic. That should be alarming. It is especially unusual for direct traffic to have a higher bounce rate compared to other sources of traffic. This represents a great opportunity to optimize landing pages.

Table 2-8. *Breakdown of traffic based on source*

Source	Visits	Conversions	Conversion rate	Pages per visit	Average time on the site (in seconds)	Bounce rate
Referring website	5,712	107	1.87%	6.71	363	35.84%
Direct traffic	9,268	283	3.05%	6.82	357	35.98%
Search	82,291	1,423	1.73%	8.06	356	26.81%

Although overall search traffic converted at 1.73%, there are large differences in conversion rates based on the search engine, as shown in Table 2-9. Google, which drives 92% of the search traffic, converts at 1.69% compared to Bing, which only drives 3.60% of the search traffic yet converts at 2.30%. Does that mean Bing provides higher-quality traffic? It is difficult to conclude this with the current data. You could assume that since Bing drives a lot less traffic, the quality of these visitors will naturally be better compared to Google. This is not necessarily the case. We do notice there is a point where bringing more visitors to a site drives down the quality of conversions.

Table 2-9. *Breakdown of search traffic*

Source	Visits	Conversions	Conversion rate	Pages per visit	Average time on the site (in seconds)	Bounce rate
Google	75,128	1,270	1.69%	8.02	356	26.79%
Yahoo!	3,261	61	1.87%	7.82	329	31.34%
Bing	2,959	68	2.30%	9.24	396	21.39%

Social media sites

With today's prevalence of social media websites, many companies are starting to rely on these sites as a major source of visitors. Some of the larger social media websites, such as Digg and StumbleUpon, are known to send tens of thousands of visitors in a single day to a website. The problem is that visitors from these sites usually bounce off right away. Figure 2-8 shows the social media traffic Invesp.com received for a particular story. Traffic from StumbleUpon had a bounce rate of 83% with an average time spent of 18 seconds. The average time a visitor spends on Invesp.com is 1:53.

	Source	None	Visits	Pages/Visit	Avg. Time on Site	% New Visits	Bounce Rate
1.	twitter.com		7,664	1.86	00:01:20	73.36%	78.89%
2.	stumbleupon.com		6,972	1.22	00:00:18	95.11%	83.89%
3.	facebook.com		2,816	1.90	00:01:22	75.75%	76.42%

Figure 2-8. *Quality of social media traffic*

Focusing on bounce rate caused usability expert Jakob Nielsen to describe social media traffic as *low-value referrers* with the following characteristics:

> …People arriving through these sources are notoriously fickle and are probably not in your target audience. You should *expect* most of them to leave immediately, once they've satisfied their idle curiosity. Consider any value derived from Digg and its like as pure gravy; *don't worry* if this traffic source has a sky-high bounce rate.*

Stan Schroeder published an article on Mashable.com discussing the value of social media websites:

> Yes, Digg or Reddit or StumbleUpon users will swarm to your page, probably won't click on anything else, they'll probably stay only a couple of seconds, and there's no way in hell you can convert them to buy anything. This is true. Angry website owners have often described such users as lazy bums with a short attention span; I think it's simply because they're smart and they don't want to waste time. When I'm on Digg, I don't want to waste time either; I want to read and see the stuff that really interests me, and move on.†

* *http://www.useit.com/alertbox/bounce-rates.html*
† *http://mashable.com/2008/07/01/nielsen-digg-traffic/*

With most of our clients, social media sites never convert. Unless your website uses the number of visitors as a KPI to drive revenue, thousands of visitors are meaningless and have no real business value to you. You should evaluate these sources of traffic based on your established KPIs. For an ecommerce website, evaluate the conversion rate and average order value for visitors from these sites.

At this point, you may be wondering: is social media useless or of no value from a conversion perspective?

Not necessarily. How well a website ranks for a certain keyword depends on the number of inbound links it receives from other websites. Even if most social traffic never converts, usually visitors within that traffic are genuinely interested in your story. These interested visitors will likely link to you. These links can provide you with a higher ranking within search engines and drive traffic that actually converts. The other value in social media websites is engagement. Social media traffic allows you to converse with a community interested in what you have to offer.

Traffic Medium

With each traffic source used to drive visitors to your website, you can use different media specific to that source. For example, you can receive traffic from Google using either organic media or a paid placement. The following are the common media used to drive traffic in a campaign:

Organic traffic
> Search engine algorithms will determine which page of your website will appear when people search for a particular term. This, however, is remedied by the fact that it is in the interest of search engines to display relevant results to a particular search term. You can also use search engine optimization (SEO) techniques to influence which of your pages appears for a certain keyword.

Banner advertising
> The best way to control this traffic is by carefully selecting the websites on which to display the banners.

PPC advertising
> PPC provides greater control over which keywords will trigger advertising to display for users, offering the most control over the quality of visitors to a website. However, in some instances, companies still manage to drive poorly targeted visitors to their site due to lack of proper research.

Email advertising
> Of all the different media to drive visitors to your website, a good email list can generate conversion rates that are three to five times higher than other media.

The analysis that comes from segmenting data based on its medium can reveal a lot of information about your visitors, as well as the effectiveness of traffic coming through a particular medium. We generally like to combine the traffic source and medium in our conversion analysis. At a minimum, we recommend segmenting your website data into the following buckets:

- Google paid traffic

- Google organic traffic

- Yahoo! paid traffic

- Yahoo! organic traffic

- Bing paid traffic

- Bing organic traffic

We usually like to compare traffic from the same source but from different media (organic or paid). Table 2-10 shows an example of the breakdown of a PPC campaign on the three major search engines: Google, Yahoo!, and Bing. The last column shows that the campaign drove a total of 51,280 visitors to the landing page at a cost of $18,932.90, generating 607 conversions. The overall campaign conversion rate is 1.18% (607 / 51,280).

Table 2-10. *Breakdown of conversion rates for a PPC campaign on different search engines*

Campaign parameters	Google paid traffic	Yahoo! paid traffic	Bing paid traffic	Total/ average
Number of visitors	25,130	17,110	9,040	51,280
Average cost per click	$0.47	$0.30	$0.22	$0.33
Total cost	$11,811.10	$5,133.00	$1,988.80	$18,932.90
Conversion	310	227	70	607
Conversion rate	1.23%	1.33%	0.77%	1.18%
Cost per conversion	$38.10	$22.61	$28.41	$31.19

When you look at the segmented data, however, you will notice that traffic from different sources converted at different levels. Visitors from Bing converted at 0.77%, compared to an average conversion rate of 1.33% for visitors from Yahoo! and 1.23% for visitors from Google. At first glance, you may think you should focus on Google and Yahoo! and drop Bing from your advertising campaign. However, when you examine the cost per conversion, you can see that Bing has a much lower cost per conversion compared to Google. Although Bing traffic completed fewer transactions, it made up for it with the lower cost per click. Again, look beyond the obvious trends to gauge the most effective use of your marketing dollars.

Keywords

You can control which keywords drive visitors to your website. PPC, for example, offers the most control over visitor quality. By selecting the correct terms to bid on, you can ensure that visitors who land on your website are interested in what you have to offer. To measure the quality of the keywords driving visitors to your website, you should examine the bounce rate at the keyword level. Higher-quality keywords targeted to match the landing pages should have a bounce rate of 20% or less. If you notice a specific term has a bounce rate higher than 20%, you should ask the following questions:

Are you targeting the correct keyword?
   In some instances, certain words carry different meanings in different industries. If visitors are using the keyword in another context, you should try to eliminate that word to avoid driving lower-quality visitors to your website.

Do the page design and message match visitor intent as identified by the keyword?
   In some instances, you are targeting the correct words; however, the particular landing page design does not appeal to visitors. If that is the case, you will have to redesign the landing pages to appeal to your market.

Table 2-11 shows the top landing pages report for one of our client websites. Each top page has a high bounce rate in the 70% range. At first glance, this might indicate that the design or copy of these pages is not appealing to visitors. But it is too early to make such a judgment.

Table 2-11. *Bounce rates for some top landing pages*

Page	Entrances	Bounces	Bounce rate	Exits
Page 1	7,980	5,791	72.57%	7,258
Page 2	3,097	1,988	64.19%	2,945
Page 3	2,414	1,852	76.72%	2,202
Page 4	1,395	1,073	76.92%	1,302

Table 2-12 breaks down page 1 traffic from the top landing page report based on the keyword that drives visitors to the page. The results show that "Kw1," which drives 59.60% of that page's entrances, has the highest bounce rate of 82.40%. Let's exclude "Kw1" from the page calculations and see the impact on the bounce rate for the page:

Page entrances excluding "Kw1" entrances = 7,890 − 4,759 = 3,131 entrances

Page bounces excluding "Kw1" bounces = 5,791 − 3,921 = 1,870 bounces

Page bounce rate excluding "Kw1" = 1,870 / 3,131 = 60%

Table 2-12. *Breakdown of page 1 traffic based on keyword*

Keyword	Entrances	Bounces	Bounce rate
Kw1	4,759	3,921	82.40%
Kw2	553	182	33.00%
Kw3	478	130	27.20%
Kw4	387	74	19.20%
Kw5	323	95	29.34%

So, although the page is working well for most other terms, its content is not persuading visitors searching for that particular keyword to stay on the site. This usually happens because of one of the following reasons:

- The particular keyword has multiple meanings and the landing page targets a meaning different from the one in which visitors are interested. For example, consider a visitor searching for the word *stud*. Can you guess what she might be searching for? This word has several different meanings. A visitor searching for *stud* could be looking for animals retained for breeding. If she lands on a page discussing stud poker, she will bounce immediately. There is little you can do about this problem because it is an issue concerning the relevancy of the search engine algorithm.

- The particular keyword relates directly to the landing page; however, the visitor is looking for a specific product or service that is not presented on the page. For example, a visitor searching for information on *landing pages* will most likely land on LandingPageOptimization.org. This site matches what the visitor is looking for in the general sense. However, the domain is designed to sell optimization services, so visitors looking for free resources on landing pages will likely bounce. This is yet another example of keyword quality issues that you can do little about.

- The keyword has a specific meaning, but the landing page encompasses a general meaning for that word. This is a typical problem when category or home pages are designated as landing pages on ecommerce websites. Figure 2-9 shows the landing page on Borders.com if you search for "technical books." The page allows visitors to navigate to books of all types, DVDs, and music, but they will need to drill deeper to find the Technical Books category. As a result, it is natural for some of these visitors to leave the site instead of investigating further. Driving visitors to the Technical Books category is a better option to match what visitors are looking for. This is a problem you can fix. If you are driving visitors using PPC, you have to direct the most relevant page to the search term. If visitors are landing on this page via organic search, redesigning the page so that they can determine the fastest navigational path to their destination will reduce the bounce rate.

- The keyword is well targeted for the landing page. If this is the case, the page design and copy do not match what visitors are looking for. Optimizing the landing page for conversion will reduce the bounce rate for the page.

Figure 2-9. *Borders.com PPC landing page mismatch for the term "technical books"*

Ad Copy

There are two different ways to measure the effectiveness of the ad copy used to drive visitors to a website:

Click-through rate (CTR)
 This is the percentage of visitors who view an advertisement and click on it to land on your website. Highly optimized ad copy can have CTRs close to 10%.

Conversion rate
 This is the percentage of visitors who click on a particular ad and actually convert. Highly optimized landing pages can generate conversion rates that are 10 times better than the overall website average.

Ad copy can influence the number of click-throughs to a landing page. On most of our campaigns, we are willing to accept a lower CTR if the traffic we receive has a higher chance of converting (i.e., is more targeted). For instance, if a client has a high-priced service or product, it is likely that a small percentage of those who click through are willing to pay. Very often we ask clients to place the price on the ad so that the traffic is highly targeted and qualified. Although this results in less traffic, it saves our client money since they do not pay for unqualified clicks by visitors who will be shocked by the price. Additionally, the conversion rate skyrockets because visitors to the landing page are well aware of what is in store for them as they click through. With paid campaigns, optimizing for higher-quality traffic starts with testing different ad copy and comparing the CTRs on the ads, as well as the conversion rates they generate.

How Your Ad Copy Affects Quality of Traffic

One of the simple ways to increase clicks on PPC ads is to match the ad headline to the keywords you are bidding on. However, the wording on the rest of the ad can also impact both the clicks and the quality of traffic your landing page receives.

A recent client, a design company that sells software to create ebook covers, was bidding on the keywords "e-cover software." We tested two ads with the same copy and different headlines:

> Version 1 headline: Create Ebook covers
>
> Version 2 headline: Creates Ebook covers

The only difference between the two ads is the *s* added to *Create* in the second version of the ad. The second ad had twice as many clicks on it as the first.

This is because the first version of the ad implied that the person purchasing the software will be using it to make the ecovers. The second version of the ad, however, implied that the software will be doing the work for the user.

We then tested the second version of the ad with the following copy:

> Version 1: Creates Amazing Covers For CDs, DVDs & eBooks.
>
> Version 2: Creates Amazing Covers For CDs, DVDs & eBooks. $112

The only difference between the two ads is that the price is included in the second version.

Which ad performed better?

The first version had higher clicks on it compared to the second version. But that is not enough—even though the first ad had a high CTR, the traffic from the second version converted better. This is because the second version of the ad qualified visitors before they clicked to the landing page; they knew the software's price and were still interested in the product. Those who considered the software too expensive would not click on the ad. This explains the lower click rate as well as the higher conversion rate.

Is Your Data Statistically Significant?

Some of the examples in this chapter compared different rates (bounce, exit, conversion, etc.) across traffic sources and media. We should note that comparing different rates or percentages can be a little deceptive. The fact that one particular rate outperforms another is not enough unless we determine whether the difference is statistically significant. *Statistical significance* exists when a difference between two rates is large enough that we can attribute it to something other than an expected sampling error. Consider the following example of comparing conversions among different engines:

Source	Visits	Conversions	Conversion rate
Google	75,128	1,270	1.69%
Yahoo!	3,261	61	1.87%
Bing	2,959	77	2.60%

It looks as though traffic from Yahoo! is converting better than traffic from Google. A quick calculation tells us that Yahoo! traffic provides about 10.50% uplift in conversion. The question is whether the difference is large enough to determine whether we have a significant improvement from Yahoo!. The actual mathematical formulas used to determine statistical significance are beyond the scope of this book—but no worries, you do not have to learn these formulas. Statistical significance calculators are available online that you can use to determine the validity of your conclusion.

Figure 2-10 shows that the difference in conversion rate between Google and Yahoo!—when evaluated using a statistical significance calculator—falls within the margins of error and is not noteworthy. Figure 2-11, on the other hand, shows that the difference in conversion rates between Bing and Yahoo! is statistically significant.

Figure 2-10. *Statistical significance between Yahoo! and Google*

Figure 2-11. *Statistical significance between Yahoo! and Bing*

Resources

For more information on time spent on a page/site, we highly recommend the following reading:

"Standard Metrics Revisited: #4: Time on Page & Time on Site" by Avinash Kaushik
    http://www.kaushik.net/avinash/2008/01/standard-metrics-revisited-time-on-page-and-time-on-site.html

"Time on Page and Time on Site – How Confident Are You?" by Shawn Purtell
    http://www.roirevolution.com/blog/2008/05/time_on_page_and_time_on_site_how_confident_are_yo.html

"Digg Traffic v/s Google Traffic – A Chitika Analysis Report"
    http://chitika.com/blog/2007/04/09/digg-traffic-vs-google-traffic-a-chitika-analysis-report/

Statistical significance calculator
    http://www.prconline.com/education/tools/statsignificance/index.asp

CHAPTER THREE

Getting to Know Your Customers: Developing Personas

IN CONVERSION OPTIMIZATION, THE VISITOR IS KING.

As the past two chapters have suggested, customers are at the center of the conversion optimization story. Getting to know your customers is the first step in the Conversion Framework because, after all, you're trying to please and persuade them. Most companies are aware of the importance of knowing their customers, but few understand what "knowing their customers" entails, especially online.

Companies generally face one of two challenges when it comes to integrating their marketing data into their selling process:

- Smaller companies do not have the know-how or the means to conduct market research to identify and segment their market effectively. Some of them might not appreciate the value that market research brings to their business. As a result, they must make assumptions about their customers, which could be wrong. They might also be missing important segments that can generate a large amount of revenue for their business.

- On the other end of the spectrum, many mid-size to large businesses have tons of market information but do not know what to do with it online. They are not able to integrate that data into actionable insights that can be implemented in their online marketing campaigns or on their websites.

Regardless of the size of the company, the overwhelming question is: how do you use marketing data to ensure that the website's copy, design, navigation, and overall structure will engage most (if not all) visitors, and move a large percentage of them through the conversion funnel?

When the average ecommerce store converts only 2% of its visitors into customers, it's hard not to wonder what is stopping the remaining 98% from moving forward with the purchase process. Conversion optimization starts with gathering detailed market information. The more detailed the information, the more precise the optimization process will be. You then use that data to shape how your website interacts with its visitors.

This relentless focus on customers sounds familiar to marketing folks, but it isn't always a comfortable fit with the technical or business world on the Web. It is rare to find a company with marketing and IT teams who work collaboratively when creating the company's website. IT teams may blow your mind with innovative designs, but ultimately it is the conversions that will make a difference to your bottom line. Similarly, the focus can't be on what the CEO, VP of marketing, or business owner wants, but rather on what the visitors want. If a user isn't happy, conversion rates will drop and revenue will suffer. We've all heard the classic example of the Fortune 500 company that developed a fancy website costing more than $20 million—only to find that the site did not generate the expected revenue because it did not appeal to the company's target market, nor was it user-friendly.

So, what can you learn about your visitors that will help you encourage them to "add to cart" and eventually make a purchase? To accomplish the difficult task of converting more visitors into customers, you need to consider many aspects regarding your visitors:

- What are your visitors' general buying patterns?

- What trigger words will have the most impact on your visitors?

- Can visitors find the information they are looking for to make a purchase decision right away?

- How do visitors view your website design? Does your design instill confidence in visitors?

- Which website elements persuade visitors to remain on the site, and why?

- Which website elements cause visitors to exit, and why?

- Which of your competitors are your visitors likely to consider (maybe a brick-and-mortar store or a strong competing website), and why?

The goal of asking yourself these questions is to see your website from your visitors' vantage point. By doing so, you will start to understand what they are thinking, what objections they have, and how they will navigate and browse through your site.

However, we often find that CEOs, VPs, and even IT teams impose their own perceptions of how they *think* visitors feel about or view their website, even if the visitors' answers to these questions differ from their own.

Consider how difficult it is to buy gifts for close friends or relatives. You try to put yourself in their shoes and imagine what they would like to receive. But how many times do we make the mistake of purchasing gifts we *think* they will enjoy? And to our dismay, very often we are wrong. What about an entire website and buying experience for millions of people very far removed from you? How do you create something that will capture their interest?

This is where personas become essential. Creating personas for your website was made popular by Alan Cooper, an advocate for interactive design and author of *The Inmates Are Running the Asylum*. The process was later adopted by many large user-centered design and development companies. Cooper writes in his book:

> Marketing professionals will be instantly familiar with the process of persona development, as it is very similar to what they do in the market definition phase. The main difference between marketing personas and design personas is that the former are based on demographics and distribution channels, whereas the latter are based purely on users. The two are not the same, and don't serve the same purpose. The marketing personas shed light on the sales process, whereas the design personas shed light on the development process.[*]

If you are looking to create a highly converting website, your first step is to understand your visitors through in-depth market research, analytics assessments, usability and field studies, and online behavioral monitoring. The next stage is to develop empathy toward your visitors by translating all of the data you've collected into actual personas. The final phase is to use the personas to guide every element of your selling process.

What Are Personas?

Personas are models, examples, and archetypes that humanize and individualize a specific target market. They are hypothetical individuals who represent target consumers. They are at the helm of conversion optimization. Personas will guide every aspect of your website, including user interface and screen design, process flow, and web copy development. The purpose and objective of persona creation is to relate to customers at an individualized level.

Have you ever noticed how great it feels to explain your business to a friend, a coworker, or even a client? When you sit face to face with a person to discuss your products or services, your conversation is marked by enthusiasm, focus, and most importantly, real examples. You can anticipate what questions he will have, and you can provide more examples when you sense he did not understand what you were

---

*Cooper, Allen. *The Inmates Are Running the Asylum*. Sams Publishing (2004); p. 134.

talking about. You know when to continue and when to stop by looking at him. You know what will grab his attention, and you can read his facial expressions for signs of confusion. The goal of persona creation is to bring personalization, engagement, and enthusiasm to your website. Too many websites cater to the masses and not to a single person. As a result, the copy is dull, the design is boring, and visitors are left frustrated.

Consider a site that sells art catering to two different market segments:

- Educated females ages 50 and older, with a household income of $200,000+

- Home builders who are predominately male, ages 30 to 40, with an annual income of $75,000 to $100,000

The two markets are different in gender, income, and personality traits. Their interests and motivations behind the purchase are different. One group is purchasing for themselves, the other for customers or for home staging. Your goal is to appeal to both markets equally, but how can you guarantee you can capture both groups' interest?

This is where we would introduce Denise, a 55-year-old retired accountant. Her hobby is collecting art by new artists, or replicas of classical art pieces. She enjoys decorating her home with unique art and is always looking for new designs to add to her growing collection. Denise is not concerned about price. She just wants to ensure that her satisfaction is guaranteed. Because she knows that art doesn't always look the same online as it does in person, return policies are extremely important to her.

This is also where we would introduce Zack, a 37-year-old builder who must find great, unique pieces to stage the homes his company builds so that prospects can imagine themselves living there. He also tries to find items that are neutral and will pique prospects' interests so that he can sell the items with the homes. Zack is concerned about price because his boss always puts him on a strict budget, but also because he does not generally return the items (since he uses them). He would want a money-back guarantee in case the art piece was damaged on receipt.

Because we now understand both Denise's and Zack's concerns, we can create a site that addresses both personas. We can develop empathy toward them and regard them both as people we know, people we can relate to, and people we want to please and persuade.

Geek Squad, a boutique high-end computer-support company, is a great real-world example of a company that uncovered the needs and perceptions of its customers to guide its philosophy and branding. The company was acquired by Best Buy, but its original objective was to change customers' perceptions of IT professionals. Tech support personnel have notoriously been labeled as annoying, arrogant, and difficult to work with. Geek Squad focused on customers' emotional reactions and perceptions of its services to brilliantly rebrand an entire industry as being composed of approachable, helpful individuals who are easy to work with.

Benefits of Personas

We usually aim to create four to seven personas per website or campaign, although these numbers are not set in stone. In some instances, we have to create more secondary personas to support complex sites and to make sure all segments of the market are covered. Ultimately, you will discover that catering a site to four to seven individuals with a detailed description of their interests is more successful than catering to a large group of people with a wide range of personalities, likes and dislikes, and opinions.

By creating personas, you can visualize the customers you are targeting. Understanding your site visitors' buying patterns and behaviors can help you mold an experience that will persuade them more effectively. Personas will help you focus on usability aspects that appeal to target consumers, and they will shape the content and elements throughout the site.

Of course, the benefit of creating personas is not limited to the online space. Many retailers rely on creating personas to help their sales executives understand their target market, as well as to develop empathy toward their customers. The electronics retail giant Best Buy analyzed its customer data to determine which customers are the most and least profitable. The company discovered that one of its core markets is the typical soccer mom. In the *Washington Post* article "In Retail—Profiling for Profit,"[*] this soccer-mom target market segment is described as follows:

> The main shopper for the family but usually avoids electronics stores. She is well-educated and usually very confident, but she is intimidated by the products at Best Buy and the store clerks who spout words like gigabytes and megapixels.[†]

---

[*] *http://www.washingtonpost.com/wp-dyn/content/article/2005/08/16/AR2005081601906.html*

[†] *http://books.google.com/books?id=xTMWzXuPqgwC&pg=PA186&lpg=PA186&dq=The+main+shopper+for+the+family+but+usually+avoids+electronics+stores&source=bl&ots=GoCkDNxJpV&sig=u4fvNq17tG8A7S8PgVRQomFrFP0&hl=en&ei=QhloTO7PL8WonAfB6NjBBQ&sa=X&oi=book_result&ct=result&resnum=1&ved=0CBIQ6AEwAA#v=onepage&q=The%20main%20shopper%20for%20the%20family%20but%20usually%20avoids%20electronics%20stores&f=false*

Analyzing your customer data is the first step toward creating personas. In the next step, Best Buy created a persona, Jill, to bring the soccer mom segment to life. The company also created other personas: Buzz (the young tech enthusiast), Barry (the wealthy professional man), and Ray (the family man). Creating personas is only half the battle. Ultimately, the goal is to adjust the selling process to attract and convert more of these customers into buyers. So, Best Buy sales associates are trained to spot the different types of customers and adjust their selling behavior to match that of each customer type. The article gives us insight into how Best Buy used its Jill persona to impact the sales process:

> Best Buy Co. is trying to change that by giving her the rock-star treatment at selected stores, sending sales associates with pink umbrellas to escort the Jills to and from their cars on rainy days and hoisting giant posters in the stores that pay homage to the Jills and their children, who are shown playing with the latest high-tech gadgets.*

Personas are useful beyond the selling process. A human face and life was a lot easier for engineers and developers to work with than the traditional market information used when building applications or designs. For companies such as Microsoft,[†] IBM,[‡] and QVC,[§] personas have helped developers see websites and applications beyond their perspectives. Companies can now anticipate users' perceptions by understanding what triggered specific emotions about products or services they offer.

Large video game companies, such as Microsoft in its Xbox work,[¶] use personas when developing games. To understand and appeal to varying ages and interests, game developers put themselves in their users' shoes. The interests associated with the persona of a typical 14-year-old will be different than those of a 35-year-old, yet a game such as *World of Warcraft* does a beautiful job of appealing to both the young and the old. How can two very different personas enjoy the same game? The developers of *World of Warcraft* understood that players do not enjoy this game for all the same reasons, but rather, different aspects of the game will appeal to the different personas. Only by understanding each persona, the various situations he will likely be in, what triggers certain emotions and reactions, and what hesitations he may have, were the developers able to successfully mold an experience that is catered to each persona's needs.

To recap, personas pave the way for:

- Understanding what makes different market segments tick, what appeals to them, and what turns them off

* *http://archive.mailtribune.com/archive/2005/0822/biz/stories/02biz.htm*
† *http://research.microsoft.com/apps/pubs/default.aspx?id=68469*
‡ *http://www.ibm.com/developerworks/blogs/page/cognospersonas*
§ *http://www.forrester.com/rb/Research/use_personas_to_design_for_engagement/q/id/45717/t/2?src=44421pdf*
¶ *http://www.microsoft.com/presspass/exec/rbach/05-16-05e3.mspx*

- Relating to the different personality types that will come and addressing their needs accordingly

- Understanding that all users come at different buying stages, thereby evoking empathy within site developers, marketers, and sales teams

- Understanding competition well, which market segments are likely to identify with a competitor more than you, and why

Market Segmentation Versus Persona Development

Many clients are a little confused when we first present the concept of personas to them. They tend to think of persona development as market segmentation. It is important to distinguish between the two. Although persona creation relies heavily on market segmentation, segmentation is just one part of what a persona requires. Personas created for online selling processes focus more heavily on online behavior and usability trends. Market segmentation is the division of the market or population into subgroups with similar motivations.

Widely used bases for segmenting business-to-consumer (B2C) markets include the following factors:

- Geographic factors:

  — Region

  — Size of metropolitan area

  — Population density

  — Climate (for industries impacted by it, such as heating, cooling, and sporting goods)

- Demographic factors:

  — Age

  — Gender

  — Family size

  — Generation

  — Income level

  — Occupation

  — Education

  — Ethnicity

  — Religion

- Psychographic factors:

  — Lifestyle

  — Activities

  — Interests

  — Hobbies

  — Opinions

  — Attitudes

  — Values

  — Social responsibility

  — Forms of entertainment

- Behavioral factors:

  — Benefits sought

  — Usage rate

  — Brand loyalty

  — User status (potential, first-time, regular)

  — Readiness to buy

  — Occasions that stimulate purchases

Widely used bases for segmenting business-to-business (B2B) markets include the following:

- Location

- Company type:

  — Company size

  — Industry

  — Purchase criteria

  — Psychographics

  — Business style

  — Business stage

  — Employee relations

  — Social responsibility

  — Workforce type

- Behavioral characteristics:

    — Usage rate

    — Buying status

    — Purchase procedure

The goal of each element is to get you to understand the market you are appealing to and how you can better cater to them. You should delve into the various demographics and similarities within the market to create segmentations and narrow the target market. Although market segmentation accounts for customer buying patterns and behaviors, you are still "catering to the masses." Targeting millions within a single market segment is not the same as humanizing that segment by creating a persona with a face, life story, wants, needs, and fears.

If an accounting firm targets B2B companies within the pharmaceutical and technology sectors, it has probably identified its market segments. Within each sector there are differences such as geographic location, company annual revenue, and number of employees. An example of the segments might be:

- Technology firms located in the Midwest, with annual revenue between $5 million and $10 million and 20 to 50 employees

- Pharmaceutical firms located in the Northeast, with annual revenue between $10 million and $20 million and 100 to 200 employees

When the accounting firm creates its website or a campaign that appeals to either of these two segments, the team will use terminology that is familiar to the particular industry. Relying on marketing segments, however, creates a website that is too generic and too vague. How do you appeal to pharmaceutical firms located in the Northeast? What would trigger technology firms located in the Midwest—or their staff, for that matter—to remain or convert on your website? What individuals are you targeting exactly within each sector? What fears and uncertainties will these individuals have? What motivations will these companies and individuals have for considering your service? How can you put yourself in your target market's shoes to think and behave like them on the website? Market segmentation will start you on the road to answering these questions, but it does not answer them immediately.

Compare this approach to creating a persona for the VP of marketing in the technology sector. By identifying individuals with a name, a life, interests, and online habits, you can develop empathy toward them and place yourself in their shoes. You can begin to imagine each persona coming to you at different stages of the buying process for a different set of reasons and scenarios, and address each concern accordingly. You can individualize the site and its copy to appeal to all the personas and successfully maximize the number of visitors that contact you to learn more about your service or product.

Using Personas in Ecommerce

RHDJapan is one of the largest online sellers of OEM and Japanese domestic market (JDM) race parts in the world. The company is headquartered in Tokyo, at the heart of the extreme racing world, which gives it access to the latest JDM parts at unbeatable prices. Although the website received tens of thousands of visitors every month, its conversion rate hovered in the low single digits.

The Invesp optimization team first familiarized themselves with the JDM and auto industry at large to gain a baseline understanding of it. The team then devised a plan for optimization that relied heavily on persona development. The team understood the challenge of creating personas for an international audience. The process of persona development included the following stages:

1. Gathering general demographic information, customer buying patterns, competitor information, market segments, and overall branding objectives.

2. Conducting a detailed survey to better understand the RHDJapan customer's demographics and insights about the site, the products, and branding resonations. Additionally, the team conducted phone interviews with best customers (top spenders) to gauge their perspectives on site performance, usability, and selecting RHD over other vendors.

3. Recruiting people who shared the same characteristics as RHD's target market and using them to conduct usability and field studies to monitor visitor behaviors on the site. By asking users to complete specific tasks, the Invesp team identified conversion bottlenecks and usability issues visitors struggled with.

RHDJapan wanted to broaden its reach to the European market by making more of a general marketing push through pay-per-click (PPC) and offline advertising methods throughout Europe. However, the current customer base was composed largely of U.S. customers, which RHD did not want to alienate.

The optimization team developed four primary personas and four secondary personas to address the wide range of visitors from various nationalities, needs, and concerns. The secondary personas were needed due to the complexity of this particular market.

By evaluating their analytics and identifying the needs of each persona—their objections and fears, and the various buying stages and scenarios that would bring them to the RHDJapan website—the team was able to prioritize areas of optimization and make changes that required the least amount of effort and generated the greatest ROI.

Using personas in the final optimization process paid off well. RHDJapan reported 15% uplift in conversion rate month to month during engagement.

A Case Against Personas

Not everyone agrees that personas are effective. Some argue that you do not need that much intimate knowledge to sell to customers. Some even argue that it is an invasion of space and privacy. But isn't that what marketing is all about? Persona creation does not examine the data for a particular individual; it looks at general trends, behavior, and patterns among different market segments. Yes, the goal of persona creation is to increase a particular company's revenue, but the road toward that goal is navigable only by creating a website that is user-friendly and benefits both the end user and the company.

On the opposite end of the spectrum are those who argue that personas limit a project's scope and focus because they do not have a clear relationship to real customer data. These people feel that personas distance teams from real users and needs, and that personas' success lacks hard evidence.* This theory was debunked when experts conducted experiments in which groups of students in a controlled environment were asked to solve a design brief. One group used personas, the other did not. The group that used personas produced designs with better usability.†

Buyers' behavior patterns and characteristics tend to be the same on both ecommerce websites and their brick-and-mortar counterparts. Best Buy's Jill was the most promising customer persona; however, she wasn't always purchasing from Best Buy stores, which is why Best Buy trained specific store reps to target the Jills, help them locate the desired items, and walk them to the register lest they change their mind at any point.

There are also those who argue that personas prevent you from anticipating all the particulars of your customers. Because a persona is limiting in terms of whom it "individualizes" (i.e., personality type, traits, job, income, etc.), marketers may not anticipate all of the persona's concerns. Personas are developed so that you can anticipate the many situations that visitors present to you. They guide the process of understanding the various buying, browsing, and navigating scenarios of your customers so that you can design for them. But can you anticipate every scenario? Never. No site or offline store is able to convert 100% of its visitors into customers. Clearly, some customers are there by accident (they came with a friend to your store or just landed on your site unintentionally), some are there to compare prices, and some have needs that you just do not meet. Personas maximize your reach, but like any optimization or marketing venture, you can never guarantee absolute response.

Finally, there are many frustrated online retailers who argue that personas are only effective with smaller websites, and that ecommerce websites are complex and have too many pages to effectively use personas to increase conversion rates. This shows a lack of understanding of how personas fit into the conversion optimization process. We never aim to take thousands of pages and apply personas to them. The optimization process requires a lot more thought than that. Persona development provides you with a framework to understand your website visitors. The actual conversion optimization process starts with a SWOT (strengths, weaknesses, opportunities, and threats)

---

* Compare this to theories expressed in the article, "The Personas' New Clothes: Methodological and Practical Arguments against a Popular Method," by Christopher N. Chapman and Russell P. Milham (Microsoft, Redmond, WA: 2006; *http://cnchapman.files.wordpress.com/2007/03/chapman-milham-personas-hfes2006-0139-0330.pdf*).

† Long, F. "Real or Imaginary: The Effectiveness of Using Personas in Product Design." Proceedings of the Irish Ergonomics Society Annual Conference (Dublin), May 2009, pp. 1–10.

analysis of your website, your campaign, and your sales process. The goal of the analysis is to create a conversion optimization road map. Only then will you apply personas to specific areas of the website. You are no longer talking in terms of thousands of pages, but rather in terms of a focused set that will produce the highest impact on your conversion rate.

Although we stress the importance of persona creation, personas do not comprise the entire optimization process; they are simply the first step. If you do not use and develop personas correctly, they will be useless to your site or campaign.

Back to the Basics: Creating Customer Profiles

The purpose of this book is to help you create a strategy and provide you with tactics to sell more efficiently and effectively online. And as we've emphasized before, in order to sell more, you've got to know your customers a whole lot better. You should be ready at this point to start creating personas for the different markets you are targeting. But creating personas starts with having the right customer information. The more data you have about your customers, the stronger and more effective your personas will be.

Here are some of the techniques you can use to collect general information about your clients:

Survey your current clients

Asking your current customers to answer well-crafted surveys will provide you with a wealth of information about your current market and how your products and services are fulfilling their needs. You can also use surveys to collect and track demographic, geographic, behavioral, and psychographic information about your customers.

You can do several things to increase the likelihood of customers filling out your surveys. First, offer a reward to customers who agree to fill out the survey. A $10 coupon can do wonders. Second, keep the surveys short. We like to keep surveys at around 15 questions max. We have properly designed surveys with response rates of close to 30%. We also recommend using online survey tools to create, collect, and track the survey. Of course, the tricky part of making the survey is coming up with the right questions to ask, and there are many books on creating and analyzing surveys. Remember that you are looking for patterns in the responses. Finally, most of the questions in our surveys ask customers to choose one of several answers that best describes their situation. But we also like to give customers a chance to provide input in an open format.

Conduct a zip code analysis

An ecommerce site or physical retail store has easy access to its customers' zip codes, which is another area where you can find a lot more information about your customers. You can gain considerable insights into your buyers by analyzing specific geographical location trends in terms of race, income, and socioeconomic levels. This will also help you identify top performing areas for your products, as well as underserved areas. Software packages are also available that will provide you with data breakdowns based on customer zip codes. If you are working with a tight budget, you might consider conducting the research yourself, although the process is tedious and requires good knowledge of statistical and trend analysis.

Track customer feedback

Many customers will not hesitate to let you know what they think of the overall site experience and product or service, especially if you ask. This information is valuable to collect and analyze so that you can continue to provide them with an excellent experience. There are several opportunities to ask for feedback—for example, when a customer decides to "exit" the site without purchasing, or after the customer places an order. Several applications track customer feedback.

Conduct top-customer interviews

Customers who have been with you for years are the best source of information regarding your website, products, and services. We usually ask our clients to give us a list of their top 10 loyal customers. A loyal customer is a client who has been active for more than a year, places multiple orders with the site, generates a certain revenue amount, or prefers you over any other vendors. On the other hand, repeat customers are those who may place multiple orders but are only loyal to the "best offers" available to them. Most loyal customers are willing to take the time to talk on the phone when approached to give feedback about a company.

Use design elements to learn more about your market

You can learn more about website visitors by testing different design elements and measuring how visitors respond to them. For example, we might display an image of a female to one group of website visitors, an image of a family to another group, and no image at all to a third group. By examining how different groups react to the images (or lack thereof), you can learn a great deal about your market. Chapter 9 will provide a more detailed discussion of this topic.

Analyze the competition

Evaluating top competitors is an often overlooked tool for gaining market insight. By focusing on your competitors, their approaches to marketing, how they position themselves, and how they reach their target market, you can discover new ways to reach your market and improve your offerings.

Using a combination of the methods in the preceding list should help you create a good demographic profile of your target customers. A simple *demographic profile* will look something like this:

> White, college-educated males, ages 35 to 45, with annual household income between $80,000 and $100,000. Married with children, live in the suburbs.

Behavioral profiles can be created to segment customers on your website, however, the subject is beyond the scope of this book. For this information, we recommend that you refer to your website analytics and customer database to segment customers based on their purchasing and browsing habits. A simple *behavioral profile* will look something like this:

> Customers who place an order with the website once every 10 weeks, who visit the site once every week, and whose last order was eight weeks ago.

Notice that the demographic profile focuses on customer characteristics and the behavioral profile focuses on how a customer acts on your website. This is an important distinction. Demographic profiles are valuable in defining market segments and how your product or service helps each segment. And although we cannot discount the value of demographic profiles, they are not as effective in describing how a customer will interact with your website as behavioral profiles. Jim Novo, the leading analytics expert, sums this up by stating:

> Customer behavior is a much stronger predictor of your future relationship with a customer than demographic information ever will be. You have to look at the data, the record of their behavior, and it will tell you things. It will tell you "I'm not satisfied." It will tell you "I want to buy more, give me a push." It will tell you "I think your content is boring."*

Field and Usability Studies

Field and usability studies are great for providing insight regarding how customers and visitors interact with your website.

Field studies are widely recognized in the marketing world as opportunities to observe buyers in their natural buying states. Offline studies require experts to observe buyers at a department store or the local grocery store to gauge how various types of visitors interact with the overall store layout, promotions, products, and customer reps. In the online world, we conduct field tests in a neutral location (library, coffee shop, or often a lab) to observe users' overall browsing behavior as well as their interaction and first impression of the site in question. We generally try to conduct field studies with 10 to 15 people who fall into the general description of the market. Field studies encourage little to no intrusion. We may direct users to begin looking at a site, but then they are on their own. If they decide to navigate or remain on the site, the expert will monitor every eye and mouse movement, click, and action taken. The users in these studies must match the overall marketing data (demographic) of the site.

* *http://www.jimnovo.com/profiles.htm*

Usability studies, on the other hand, are conducted with a scripted number of tasks to complete. Users are instructed to vocalize the reason behind every mouse move, every click, and every impression they have. Their task is to imagine a scenario (putting themselves in the shoes of potential buyers of the product) and complete the task at hand. The entire experience is recorded with commentary and very often includes the users' facial expressions. The users in these studies must match the overall marketing data (demographic) of the site.

An example of a usability study looks like this:

> You are shopping for a unique Christmas gift for your eccentric daughter. She's 15 and is very difficult to please. She appreciates art, and likes items that are custom-made so that nobody has anything like it. You stumble upon a site that sells customizable bed sets and decide to take a look around.

At this point, you have set up the user to identify herself with this mother (she should already match the general demographics of the market, which probably includes a mother). The user is then given a number of tasks to complete. The less detail you give, the more room you give for the user to behave according to her intuitions. If you give her specific instructions, such as identifying exactly where to click next, you are restricting her regular online behavior and skewing the test. Be as ambiguous as possible. Give her the task, but leave much up to her perceptions.

Conducting usability studies for ecommerce websites helps identify weak areas on the site and creates scenarios around them to monitor why users were unable or hesitated to continue. We like to conduct pre-persona studies whereby participants are matched with marketing data, and post-persona development whereby we locate more exact matches to our personas. It's important to locate users who have never conducted usability studies before; otherwise, the results may not be accurate since the user would know what to anticipate, and what to say.

Brief History of the Four Temperaments

Historically, categorizing human personalities into a few main groups has been controversial because humans are so unique and diverse. However, you can draw many similarities from them in terms of personality traits and overall temperaments. In 325 BC, Aristotle wrote of hedonic, proprietary, dialectical, and ethical temperaments.* In 190 AD, Galen spoke of the following four temperaments:†

---

* *http://www.ncbi.nlm.nih.gov/pmc/articles/PMC1297495/pdf/neh106.pdf*

† *http://books.google.com/books?id=GB4o-wqeyzAC&pg=PA5&lpg=PA5&dq=In+190+AD,+Galen+Sanguin ee&source=bl&ots=eBN6QnS84J&sig=1OnsmyirX_NMwtU06bC7MQyxj54&hl=en&ei=nzhoTKz7MsH6nA eo-7zCBQ&sa=X&oi=book_result&ct=result&resnum=1&ved=0CBQQ6AEwADgK#v=onepage&q=In%20 190%20AD%2C%20Galen%20Sanguine&f=false*

Sanguine

Fun, life of the party, social, affectionate, emotional, struggles with follow-through, late, and forgetful

Choleric

A doer, ambitious, energetic, passionate, and a dominating personality

Melancholic

Thoughtful, kind, considerate, highly creative, can be preoccupied with tragedy in the world (depression), perfectionist, loner

Phlegmatic

Self-content, shy, resistant to change, relaxed, rational, curious, observant, more dependable friend

In his 1921 book *Psychological Types*, Carl Jung theorized that humans use four functions when dealing with the world.[*] These are sensing, intuiting, thinking, and feeling. All humans have these functions in different proportions. Jung also noted the distinction between introversion and extroversion in personality types:

- *Introverts* have an inward focus, with a strong sense of self and feelings.

- *Extroverts* have a focus on the outside world.

Combining Jung's four functions with the two personality types yields 16 different personalities. Of course, this does not mean a human must fall into just one of these 16 types. You can consider these personality types as realms humans function within—one may overlap another more or less. In the early 1950s, David Keirsey established a relationship between the 16 different personality types and the four temperaments by Galen and Plato. Keirsey focused on human behavior and divided the four temperaments as follows:[†]

- *Artisans* are observant and pragmatic. Keirsey describes artisans' primary objective as "Sensation Seeking."

- *Guardians* are observant and cooperative. Keirsey describes guardians' primary objective as "Security Seeking."

- *Idealists* are introspective and cooperative. Keirsey describes idealists' primary objective as "Identity Seeking."

- *Rationals* are introspective and pragmatic. Keirsey describes rationals' primary objective as "Knowledge Seeking."

---

[*] Rothgeb, C.L. (Ed.) *Abstracts of the Collected Works of C.G. Jung.* H. Karnac (Books) Ltd. (1992); p. 33.

[†] Dunning, D. *Quick Guide to the Four Temperaments and Learning: Practical Tools and Strategies for Enhancing Learning Effectiveness.* Telos Publications (2003); p. 2.

The next section will give you a general concept of the four temperaments in the process of persona creation.

The Four Temperaments and Personas

Each temperament requires careful consideration of the copy, tone, layout, and navigational structure of the website being studied. Each of your personas will have one or more of these temperaments because, as we mentioned, humans fall into two or often three of the different temperaments. For most websites, you will find that creating four to seven primary personas with a mix of temperaments will serve your needs. However, depending on the complexity of the site, you might include secondary personas to reflect a more holistic consideration of all the visitors to your site.

Let's take a closer look at the four temperaments and adapt them to the online world so that we can see what each requires.

Logical Persona (Guardian)

As the name suggests, this persona trusts logic and is meticulous, methodical, and detail-oriented in nature. This persona is skeptical, self-contained, and focused on problem-solving. Someone with a logical persona will carefully read the instruction manual before assembling an item. He will want to know the process for solving a problem. This persona comprises as much as 40% to 45% of the population.*

A logical persona wants to understand every little detail about your product or service. This type of person will read page after page of information on your site. He is also the visitor who will leave your site if you fail to present answers to his questions in a logical, systematic, and easy-to-locate fashion. You can expect a logical persona to pay close attention to your methodology pages, your product or service description, technical details of your website, and your "About Us" page. A logical persona will scroll down to the end of your page. This is the persona that will do the research to find the answers.

A logical persona takes a long time to make a purchasing decision. In the meantime, this type of person will "shop around," bookmarking your site to monitor any developments or new offers, and reading your blog or newsletter.

This persona is turned off by vague terminology. Someone with this persona is skeptical, so you should provide him with concrete evidence as to why your service or product is his best choice and how it will solve his problems. Since someone with a logical persona will read many details on your website and spend the most time on it, your page should address this persona last.

---

* Wysocki, R.K., and J.P. Lewis. *The World Class Project Manager: A Professional Development Guide.* Basic Books (2001); p. 115.

Impulsive Persona (Artisan)

An impulsive persona is focused on the here and now. This type of person is spontaneous, optimistic, and unconventional, will take on tasks others might consider risky, and will do whatever it takes to accomplish her goals. This persona comprises as much as 30% to 35% of the population.*

Someone with an impulsive persona will browse the Web with her credit card in hand. However, converting her to a customer will only happen if you lay out all the information and next steps in a clear manner. This type of person can be your best or worst customer because as quickly as the conversion can happen with her, it could unravel in the same amount of time. You generally have few seconds to convince an impulsive prospect to stay on your website or to consider your products or services.

To capitalize on this temperament, it's important to provide quick benefits of the product or service being offered. You must also test which benefits resonate best with this persona type (the benefits that resonate best with the impulsive persona may vary from those that resonate with the aggressive persona). These people are turned off by lengthy paragraphs, so consider bullet points to capture their attention. Also, they hate dealing with traditional details, so providing them with general information will satisfy their curiosity. Additionally, provide those with an impulsive persona an easy way to contact your company or to "proceed to checkout" by offering clear call-to-action buttons. If they have to look around, or if you ask too many questions on a contact form, they are likely to leave your website.

Those with an impulsive persona make their purchase decision quickly. They are undisciplined in considering different alternatives. Since they scan your website quickly, you should address them second on your page.

Caring Persona (Idealist)

A caring persona is concerned about other people; he is dependable and helpful to others. He is focused on credentials and traditions. Those with a caring persona enjoy spending time with their friends, but they are very serious about their responsibilities. This persona comprises around 15% to 20% of the population.†

The caring persona wants to know how your product and service helped other customers. This persona is influenced by the number of people who shop at your store. He wants to know more about your company, its founders, and its staff. He will read your "About Us" page trying to get a better idea about your core values. Because of this, it is important to personalize these pages and avoid generic information. Authentic

---

* Laplante, P.A., and C.J. Neill. *Antipatterns: Identification, Refactoring, and Management.* CRC Press (2006), p. 18.
† Johnson, D.P. *Sustaining Change in Schools: How to Overcome Differences and Focus on Quality.* Association for Supervision and Curriculum Development (2005), p. 23.

testimonials can do wonders for someone with a caring persona. It's important to offer these people a number of different reviews on your site, and show then that you are involved with your online and local communities.

Someone with a caring persona is slow to make a purchase decision. He is not disciplined in considering different alternatives, which makes selling to him a little difficult. This type of person will spend time on your site, and we recommend that you address this persona third.

Aggressive Persona (Rational)

These individuals are competitive, ambitious, and get things done. They trust their intuition and are looking for ways to get ahead. They are highly motivated and goal-oriented. Those with an aggressive persona are on a constant quest for self-knowledge and self-improvement. They hold themselves to a strict standard of personal integrity. The aggressive persona is rare, comprising as little as 5% to 7% of the population.*

The aggressive persona is the hardest to sell to but makes for a great customer. These people are usually determined to make a buying decision but will not settle for anything less than the best. They want to know how your product or service will help them beat their competitors. They will continue to shop around for the best offer and the best company, product, or service.

This persona will give the purchase decision the right amount of time. These people are disciplined in considering different alternatives.

Those with an aggressive persona are skeptical of companies, so you should provide them with facts to establish credibility and trust. Focus on showing how your offer will help them get ahead. You can pique the interests of someone with an aggressive persona by providing a good value proposition. You should address the aggressive persona first on the page with a strong headline and benefits list.

───── **DON'T FORGET!** ─────────────────────────────

- B2B and complex transactions will be carefully reviewed in a methodical format, whereas smaller individual customer decisions are more likely to have all four temperament types as buyers.
- The ratio of temperaments within a population is 45% logical, 35% impulsive, 15% caring, and 5% aggressive.
- Within a single page, you need to have language that addresses these four temperaments.
- Persona creation is only the beginning of the conversion optimization process. Personas will guide you and help you customize your framework based on the highest impact points with the least amount of effort (LOE).

* *The World Class Project Manager*, p. 114.

Putting It All Together

Armed with customers' demographic, psychographic, and behavioral profiles and your knowledge of the four main temperaments, you are now ready to create your personas. You must keep a few important points in mind as you work through this process:

- Creating personas is *not* the same as taking your customer demographic profiles and putting an image on them.

- Personas will not always have a one-to-one relationship with each market segment because they focus more heavily on users' online behavioral aspects.

- Most websites will have four to seven primary personas. These should satisfy your most complex visitors. You can always create secondary personas that are not as strongly addressed throughout the site.

- Personas are a generalization of the demographic, psychographic, and behavioral trends of your customers. Some of our clients try to map every little detail in their customer profiles into one of the personas we create. This is not correct.

- The persona creation process is never done. Personas are works in progress. We make assumptions about the market, create the personas to match our assumptions, and continue to evolve them.

Personas grow and mature as we move forward with a project. Persona creation is a highly collaborative exercise, so we do not assign one single analyst to work on creating them. Usually a team of three or more analysts is working on this phase.

Although we will not go into great detail regarding the meticulous process of persona creation—since a single chapter can't do it justice—we'd like you to bear in mind that a lot of mapping, assessment, testing, discussions, and research go into the process. The most difficult challenge is to map online behavioral trends to demographic trends. Our emphasis is on the online behavioral aspect, although demographic information from socioeconomic and gender perspectives applies to online behavioral trends as well, so both areas do go hand in hand.

Most of the time, you will start with 15 to 20 different customer profiles. We use these profiles to develop our initial 10 personas. We then merge some of these initial personas based on characteristics, behavior, and temperaments into our final primary personas. Let's take an example of a few initial sketches we did for a medical uniforms website:

- Candice Miller – 48, nurse, hospital – NY – Candice has been a nurse for over 15 years. She is married, 1 child, and makes around $49,343 a year. Candice loves unique prints. Candice is impulsive and caring. Candice relates well to reviews of products. Candice is concerned about security.

- Clarissa Dubb – 21, medical assistant, clinic – Clarissa is completing an internship at a local clinic affiliated with her school in order to complete her degree. Not married. Long Beach, CA. Impulsive, aggressive. Clarissa is brand-conscious. She also likes newer designs and colors. As a student/employee, she has the flexibility of wearing what she wants. Clarissa reads the descriptions on the site to ensure that the design is exactly what she needs.

- Senjay Gupta – X-ray technologist, 34, married, 2 children – hospital. Aggressive. Senjay is looking for comfort. Doesn't mind paying extra for the best. Security concerns.

As you can see, these initial sketches of personas are not fully developed.

DON'T FORGET! ─────────────────────────

- Never shut the door on the persona-creation process—it is a continuous work in progress. Every day you learn more about your market, and trends change, so a persona is never constant.
- Relying on old data can be convenient and cost-effective, but ultimately you may be missing out on important market changes that will impact your bottom line and cost your company hundreds of thousands of dollars every month.

Your Website from a Different Perspective

After creating personas, the next question you should ask is how you can use them to make changes to your website. Although personas are wonderful in theory, practical examples will drive the point home. Figure 3-1 shows the main home page for a popular medical uniforms website. Figure 3-2 shows different hypothetical personas for this website. Now, how would each persona interact with the nursing page? What changes should you make to the home page based on these personas?

At a minimum, you should evaluate the page from the perspective of each persona by answering the following questions:

- What scenarios will bring this persona to this page?

- What are the first three questions this persona will ask right way?

- Do you answer each of the first three questions on the page in an appropriate location based on the temperament of the persona?

- Does this page use the trigger words appropriate for this persona?

- What are the first three concerns this persona will have after viewing the page?

- Why would this persona decide to leave your website after viewing this page?

- If this persona decides to stay on your website, what page will this persona navigate to next? What information will this persona look for on the next page?

The answers to these questions will provide you with a list of modifications you can make to the page. But this is merely a starting point. Figure 3-3 shows how each of our hypothetical personas will view and interact with the main home page. Although we gave you seven questions to answer, it is typical for us to consider more than *350* questions as part of the Conversion Framework process for each page we optimize. As you go through the book, you should develop a list of optimization questions that are specific to your website.

Figure 3-1. *Home page of a popular medical uniforms website*

Figure 3-2. *Hypothetical personas for the medical uniforms website*

Figure 3-3. *How personas will interact with the page*

Personas and Copy

In our previous example, we saw how personas impact the way a page is designed. Let's take a second example that will focus on how personas will impact the copy you include on a page. Figure 3-4 shows a picture of one of the pages of an ecommerce website that sells a variety of golf equipment. Here is an excerpt from the copy on that website:

> So you love to golf and you're searching for some new clubs, eh? Look no further! Golf Gear Review's selection of in-depth and user submitted club reviews will help you familiarize yourself with some of the top names in golf, and what folks just like you think about their clubs. Shopping on-line for golf clubs is an easy and rewarding experience. Where else can you find the best selection and prices for clubs, all at your golf-happy fingertips?

> GGR features reviews of golf clubs from nearly every manufacturer out there. Some of the companies that we have reviews on include:

> Acer, Adams, Advanced Golf Technology, Aldila, Alien, Alpha Clubs, Ashton, Aurora, Bag Boy,...

Figure 3-4. *Generic copy on an ecommerce website for golf equipment*

Now, let's consider this from the perspective of two personas:

> Lisa Jenkins, 52, an expert golfer with more than 10 years of experience. Lisa enjoys Wilson and Spalding products. Of course, because she is a woman, she looks for the products that will cater specifically to her.

What would Lisa think of the preceding copy?

Lisa loves that this site mentions the wide selection of products because that is important to her. However, the copy does not mention any products specific for the woman golfer. She also wants to know what other products the website offers besides golf clubs. She may need a specific club, but she is also looking for new golf gloves, balls, tees, and so forth.

> Greg Scott, 39, a beginner golfer. He has been promoted in his job to an executive-level position. As a result, he now is obligated to attend more social events, including golf outings, with his coworkers, managers, and sometimes even the VP of his company. Greg wants to appear like he knows what he is doing when it comes to golf.

What would Greg think of the preceding copy?

Greg doesn't know what kinds of clubs he needs. He is overwhelmed by the large product selection the website offers. He wants the right equipment, but he is not sure how to proceed. The copy does not address the needs of the beginner golfer. This is an issue for Greg.

Let's consider how small tweaks to the copy would have satisfied both Lisa and Greg.

Here is the new, improved copy:

> Golfster offers a wide selection of golf clubs for the *novice* and *expert* golfer.
>
> You can get advice on the right equipment for your *level*, *gender*, and *age*. Visit our *expert tips* for which clubs are right for you. If you already know what you need, search among the *widest selections of golf equipment* on the Web.
>
> Need some tips on golfing and which *equipment to select*? Visit our *blog* and *articles* section for the latest information from professional instructors.

Each italicized phrase or word in the preceding copy will link to a specific page on the site to address that topic. Can you see how the improved copy will better serve our two personas?

Creating persuasive copy is key to any site, and this example demonstrates how personas can clearly guide what copy elements you should include and where you should place them.

Adjusting Your Selling Process Through Personas

By creating personas for your business, you will get to know your customers at a more intimate level. Once we reveal personas to our clients, they are very excited because of the wealth of information these personas provide. We find that the sales executives begin to discover weak points in their selling process, and the web developers and designers are ready to make hundreds of changes to their sites. CEOs and VPs might think they are ready to adjust the selling process to deal with the needs, wants, and fears of the personas. But we tell them to wait and to not address this quite yet.

Whether you are working with an ecommerce website, a lead generation website, or a physical store, trying to adjust your selling process is challenging and requires more than personas. There are hundreds of elements and points that you can evaluate throughout the selling process. We mentioned that we evaluate each web page or sales funnel from 350 different angles. You can anticipate questions, concerns, and objections users may have after persona creation, but the wealth of insight the Conversion Framework methodology will provide makes your personas more valuable.

Randomly making changes to your website without following a guide or framework will lead you to disappointment and no results. If you are looking for consistent and measurable results, you have to follow the entire Conversion Framework methodology. As you look at all the different areas of your campaign, website, or sales funnel, and think of the hundreds of possible areas of improvement, you must wonder which of these will have the highest impact on your conversion rate and which will generate the greatest increase in sales while requiring the lowest level of effort (LOE). These are the areas you should focus on first. But don't worry! Your personas will guide the process by helping you identify which areas of the Conversion Framework you should adjust immediately, and which you should address later in the process.

———— DON'T FORGET! ————————————————————————————————

Depending on what you are selling, you must adjust certain temperament trends to the process. If your product or service is expensive, all customers are likely to have a more logical approach to the buying decision. This means you can expect all customers to ask "more" questions because it is a bigger buying decision and investment for them. Of course, how an impulsive persona will ask questions differs from how a logical persona will, so you must adjust your selling process to anticipate this behavioral shift.

CHAPTER FOUR

From Confidence to Trust

VISITORS WON'T BUY THINGS FROM YOU or give you contact information if they don't trust you.

Before they buy, visitors need to feel secure and to trust sellers. Brand recognition lends credibility for larger companies, but many online stores do not have the luxury of having a recognizable name. Similar issues apply offline: you're likely to lose visitors if your storefront looks sloppy or if your business is in a bad area of town. Every visitor to your online or offline store comes to you with specific intimidations and fears. They don't want to be cheated or sold at; they want to have an enjoyable and simple shopping or browsing experience.

As you are able to successfully establish trust with your customers, you will build their confidence with your company. The more confidence a customer has in your store, the more likely she will purchase from you, often coming back for more or even recommending you to others. Although a conversion from a first-time customer is important, repeat customers are more valuable. The conversion value is multiplied if you are able to gain customer loyalty.

Gaining skeptical buyers' trust is difficult, especially when you're trying to sell something expensive. The level of skepticism generally increases as the price increases. Stores that sell jewelry online report a less than 0.5% average conversion rate. Does that number reflect only the lack of trust a visitor may have? Not necessarily, but trust plays an important role when guiding the user's decision.

Consider buying a piece of expensive jewelry from an online store. You cannot see the ring up close, touch it, examine it, or try it on. You may wonder if the site is trustworthy and whether the company is honest and will deliver the item in a timely manner. How confident would you feel about the jewelry? Certainty about what you are buying would be much easier at an offline store. Of course, it is not impossible, and many online stores selling high-priced items are able to establish enough confidence with their visitors to convert.

Establishing trust with your visitors takes four steps. As you read about these steps, though, remember that this all unfolds in a matter of seconds online.

Awareness

They can't trust you before they know you.

This stage is all about driving traffic to your site through different sources and media (search engine optimization or SEO, paid advertising, banner ads, etc.). The awareness stage is about visibility and getting people to find you. You can achieve visibility through marketing and advertising, but be careful: users may trust you less if they feel they arrived at your site deceitfully.

Knowledge

When a visitor first lands on your site, you have mere seconds to convince him to stay, and that's when the knowledge stage begins. You must demonstrate your value proposition during this stage. Now that visitors are aware of you, it's a matter of convincing them that you offer a unique value, unmatched anywhere else.

Liking

As visitors get to know your business, they will decide whether to purchase from you. During the liking stage, you should address visitors' questions, such as "Do I know enough about what they do or have to offer?" and "Can't I go to a more well-known, established name and get these products or services?" If you succeed in moving visitors through the liking stage, you've gained them as customers, at least once.

Trust

Once visitors have purchased from you, it's important to ensure that they have a wonderful experience. Trust happens when users complete the shopping experience and successfully receive their product. Up to the point of having the product in their hands, visitors are still anxious about the purchase they just made. A good experience includes receiving the shipment in a timely manner, ensuring that the product is in pristine condition, and, if necessary, making an exchange or return as seamless as possible.

What will persuade and enhance trust in one site visitor versus the next varies tremendously, which goes back to the importance of personas. Many of these issues reflect on business operations beyond your website, but sites can demonstrate seven areas that enhance trust:

- Value proposition for the company, products, or services

- Continuity

- Congruency

- Social proof

- Membership/professional organizations or affiliations

- External reputation

- Design aspects

Value Proposition

Your value proposition says why a prospect should buy your product or service. What distinguishes your company from the rest of the competition? Customers always want to know the benefit of the product or service, but furthermore, they want to understand why they should do business with you and not with your competition.

Although a well-known company does not need to keep telling visitors who it is once they reach the site, it's important to maintain relevance by alluding to the value proposition throughout the page. Value propositions are especially critical for newer sites competing against bigger names. They provide a way to conquer the initial online anonymity. Once users identify who you are, what you provide, and what you can do for them, they will overcome their first set of confidence issues.

Many companies define themselves as having "the best customer service" or "the lowest prices." That's not an issue as long as you do indeed *uniquely* offer that value. You must truly stand out in that area among the rest of your competition. We tend to encourage clients to shy away from such overused terms since these are repeated values that many competitors offer. The value proposition must put you at a level that is above the rest. Online, visitors can easily compare sites to figure out whether you really are unique.

Every element on your website, from the home page to the product pages to site navigation, should support that value proposition. It's the message that you want your visitors not only to read, but also to experience throughout the site. Again, you are defining your company (not your products—there is a different value proposition for that) in a way that you'd like to be remembered by your site visitors.

Amazon.com offers a wide range of items. The site also offers community feedback and reviews on just about anything, positive or negative, throughout the site. Before many online shoppers make a purchase decision, they are likely to visit Amazon.com to comparison shop. The value proposition at Amazon.com could be that it is a community site, allowing you to purchase from a range of vendors, and get the feedback you need to make a more educated decision.

When Ebay.com was first launched, it was one of the first online marketplaces where items could be bought, sold, or traded. Users could successfully auction off items as large as a home (sold for $1) or as bizarre as the Virgin Mary Sandwich (sold for $28,000). There was little other value like that on the Web, and people came flocking as a result. The value that was being offered superseded any concerns users may have had about the site. Therein lies the power of a value proposition.

A well-stated value proposition throughout the site promotes visitor "confidence." It does not necessarily build your visitors' trust in your company. As mentioned earlier, confidence is only the second step toward the establishment of trust. If users have enough confidence, they will like you and make a purchase from your site.

Bluefly.com positioned itself as a company that offers only the latest high-end designer fashions. This is not enough to define the value proposition internally; it has to be present throughout your site. Bluefly.com does this beautifully, as you can see in Figure 4-1.

Figure 4-1. *Bluefly.com main home page*

Several elements on the main home page of Bluefly.com communicate the value proposition clearly:

- The website's tagline below the logo, "the ultimate hook-up for the fashion obsessed"

- The "New This Week" section allowing visitors to navigate to the latest items just released in the market

- The main image displaying the latest models from the fashion world

Every element points to that value proposition. What does this mean for Bluefly customers? Visitors to the site are well *aware* of what this site has to offer. There is very little chance that visitors will leave the site because they do not know what Bluefly offers—the company clearly states what sets it apart from other apparel stores. This clear value proposition serves another vague purpose: since it caters to the fashion-hungry, visitors to whom this doesn't apply will bounce off the site quickly. If a visitor does not fit within Bluefly's niche market, this will become apparent as soon as the visitor sees Bluefly's home page.

Figure 4-2 shows the main home page for Bookpool.com. The value proposition of the site is stated clearly in its tagline, "Discount Computer Books." Every image or incentive on the page drives the point that it is a discount computer bookseller:

- The main image of the site offers an incentive of a 45% discount on books by different publishers.

- The site allows visitors to browse through technical books on Windows Vista.

- The navigation panel on the lefthand side of the screen presents different categories of technical books.

Figure 4-2. *Bookpool.com main home page*

Compare Bookpool.com to Powell's Books' main home page in Figure 4-3. Visitors to the Powell's Books website have no indication of what distinguishes this bookstore from the competition. Why would a visitor, who hadn't encountered Powell's Books before, select Powell's over any other bookstore? The main home page does not communicate a clear value proposition. The only hint of a possible value proposition is the rather difficult-to-read tagline saying that the company was established in 1971. Is that enough for visitors who do not know Powell's Books to judge whether it is a reputable and trustworthy bookstore?

Figure 4-3. *Powell's Books main home page*

───── **NOTE** ───
The Unique Selling Proposition (USP) is not the same as the value proposition. The USP refers to what is unique and attractive about a specific product, whereas the value proposition is the overall benefit and value a customer will derive from purchasing from your company. Although they are different, they do work hand in hand: the USP for varying advertisements and landing pages will be aligned with the value proposition.

During your initial conversion analysis of a client's website, determine whether the site's value proposition is unique. If it is not, work with the client to come up with a value proposition based on their offerings and their customers' expectations and needs. If the client has a value proposition but it is not clearly stated on the site, focus your efforts on amplifying that value throughout the site.

For example, Zappos.com is one of the few companies that is able to differentiate itself from its competition through excellence in customer service. It is one of the few large ecommerce sites that displays the customer service phone number in the header inviting visitors to call 24/7 if they have any issues. When shopping for shoes online, customers are worried that once the shoes arrive they will not fit correctly or will not be comfortable. Zappos' unique value proposition addresses these concerns head-on: you can return an item within 365 days, and you get free shipping both ways.

Figures 4-4 through 4-6 show how Zappos reiterates its excellent customer service. Figure 4-7 shows the home page of Endless.com, a direct competitor of Zappos.com. This site lets you know immediately what it is: a "shoes and handbags" site, which is stated in the tagline. The name "Endless" refers to the fact that the company sells anything and everything that falls under the umbrella of shoes and handbags. So, how does Endless deal with the Zappos value proposition? Endless offers:

- Free overnight shipping on new styles
- Free return shipping
- A 100% price match

The free *overnight* shipping from Endless.com beats the free shipping from Zappos. com. However, the caveat is that overnight shipping is only available on new styles. Overnight shipping appeals to several personas, but it resonates very well with the spontaneous persona. Both sites offer free return shipping. Endless.com offers a 100% price match, which Zappos.com does not offer. Figure 4-8 shows the value propositions of the two sites against each other.

Figure 4-4. *Zappos.com main home page*

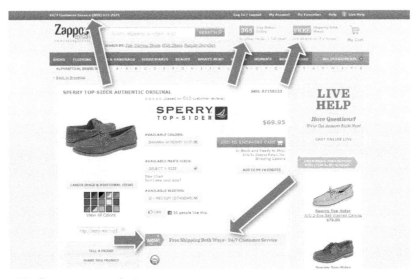

Figure 4-5. *Zappos.com product page*

Figure 4-6. *Zappos.com cart page*

Figure 4-7. *Endless.com main home page*

Figure 4-8. *Endless.com versus Zappos.com value proposition*

Like every element in optimization, a value proposition is a work in progress. Identify your value proposition and then test it to see its impact on your customers. Based on shifts within the market and changing customer expectations, you may need to readjust your value proposition to meet these changes. For instance, in 2009 many companies shifted their value to reflect the downturn of the economy. Wal-Mart has always been a company that "slashes" prices, so it was not much of a departure to bring that within the context of the economic downturn. Wal-Mart became the company that saves you money with a powerful value proposition: "Save Money, Live Better."

Defining Your Value Proposition

What drives a customer to make a purchase decision? When visitors arrive to your site, they could have come for a few reasons:

- They arrived by accident because they clicked on the wrong link or advertisement.

- They are browsing.

- They have a "problem" and your product will solve it.

It is rare for offline stores to have customers walk in "by accident." Customers walking through the door either are *browsing* and window shopping, drawn in by your sale sign or featured product, or are coming specifically to your store to fill a need.

Understanding motivation is key to creating a clear value proposition. By identifying what brings different customers to your site or store, you can adjust your value proposition to meet the needs of every customer. The value proposition should state a value your customers are actually looking for. You can determine this by conducting surveys and field studies of your market. Tapping into your market is the best way to understand what motivates customers to make a purchase.

Our client, RHDJapan, offers the widest selection of Japanese domestic market (JDM) auto parts on the Web. Visitors arrive at the RHDJapan.com website with a number of motivations:

- They are curious (browsing).

- They have a knack for building race cars (problem).

- They sell unique parts to customers (problem).

- They have a vehicle they'd like to improve but are unsure of what they need (browsing).

Once you've identified the motivation, it's time to evaluate your company: what value do you offer customers that no other competitor offers? If you have no distinguishing value, you are going to have a difficult time convincing visitors that you are better than the alternatives online or offline. Identifying your value proposition requires lengthy brainstorming discussions with key individuals within your company: C-level personnel, VPs, and marketing directors.

For RHDJapan, we discovered that the majority of customers were students, and cost was definitely an issue for them. Race car parts can get very expensive, so getting factory-direct brand-name parts from Japan at the lowest prices was a tremendous value to customers. Again, we do not recommend advertising "lowest prices" unless you really offer the lowest prices and can match a lower price offered elsewhere. Figure 4-9 shows how we communicated RHD's value proposition on the main home page, giving users more confidence.

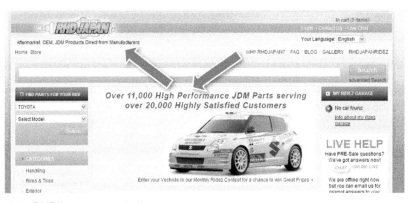

Figure 4-9. *RHDJapan.com main home page*

Value Proposition Matrix

As you work to identify your value proposition, evaluate it based on a scale of 1 to 5 in each of the following areas:

Exceptional

Make your value proposition stand out to be *exceptional*. This area evaluates the value proposition's originality as experienced by your customers, as well as within the marketplace. Overused value propositions, such as typical customer service, will get a score of 1. When Zappos first came out with its free shipping both ways, the company introduced an innovative value proposition to the marketplace that set it apart from the competition. Progressive Insurance positioned itself as the website that allows visitors to compare insurance quotes from different companies, which was novel and gave customers enough knowledge to develop a liking for and make a purchase from the company.

Uniqueness

How unique is your value proposition compared to your competitors'? Your value proposition should distinguish you in at least one area from the rest of the competition. Consumers consider several companies before making a major purchasing decision because of the commonality these companies share, but the one they select is often the company that offers the most unique value to them. When we launched Invesp in 2006, we competed with few conversion optimization companies. But we suffered from lack of uniqueness. When we found we were most successful working with ecommerce companies on complex conversion optimization problems, we hit gold because none of our competitors positioned themselves that way.

Excellence

How do you excel at your value proposition? Toyota's value proposition focuses on quality and reliability. The company delivered on this value until it had major recalls in 2010, which shook consumer confidence in the company and its products.

Desirability

How desirable is your value proposition to your customers? It is important to consider how relevant or desirable your value is to the various types of customers you have. The more desire you provide them, the more inclined they will be to purchase from your company. Netflix's value proposition of never charging late fees resonates well with consumers who are tired of paying late fees. Compare that clear value proposition to the number of times Blockbuster had to change the way late fees are calculated in the past few years.

Different visitors will be interested in different aspects. Browsers who are just looking around your site appreciate the originality of your value proposition. Visitors in the early stage of the buying cycle will most likely give the same weight to the different factors. Visitors in the later stage of the buying cycle will most likely give "desirability" and "excellence" more weight.

Evaluate your value proposition through the lens of your personas. What's the value for the individual persona versus the value for the entire market? Test the value proposition to understand how it will resonate best with each persona:

- Does it appeal to the impulsive persona? Is it a value the customer can act upon immediately?

- Does it appeal to the caring persona? How does it relate to other customers? Have other customers benefited from this value?

- Does it appeal to the aggressive persona? Is this value unique? Do other competitors offer something similar? Why is this value better?

- Does it appeal to the logical persona? What's so useful about this value? Will this value truly impact this person's conversion?

When evaluating your value proposition, you should also consider personas from the various buying stages.

Continuity

To understand visitors' motivations or their "intent," you must look at the keywords and ads that inspired visitors to click through to your site in the first place. Keywords are often loaded with meanings and particular motivations, so researching them is helpful. Companies build entire pay-per-click (PPC) campaigns on keywords that hold no relevance to what they offer. Furthermore, the keywords are important, but how relevant is your landing page to the keyword visitors used? Some companies use a single, general landing page for a variety of paid campaigns. Others use their main home page as the landing page. Funneling all sorts of personas—with varying motivations at different stages of the buying process—through a single common page usually results in a low conversion rate. The challenge is to cater the message and the unique *selling* proposition to satisfy various visitor intents.

Continuity is an important component of trust and is addressed by answering the following questions:

- What brought the visitors to your site in the first place?

- How did they get there?

- Where did they land?

- What did they see?

- Was there relevance to what brought them there in the first place?

Continuity refers to maintaining relevance and scent at every touchpoint visitors have with your website or campaign. *Relevance* and *scent* reflect a continuous theme on the different pages the visitor navigates through, such as the pages' look, feel, offers, and copy. Continuity becomes especially important when you have control over the ad that leads to the landing page. Both variables must work together to increase users' trust by assuring them that they have not landed on the wrong page and that your page is relevant to what they are looking for. But it does not stop there. As visitors navigate through your website, the same themes should continue from one section to the next.

Continuity is equally relevant to any marketing and advertising. If your company promotes a service or product using a television commercial or magazine ad, the continuity is important when the user responds to that advertisement. How is the message continued between the advertisement and the actual store? How relevant is the prospect's exposure to the ad? How relevant is the medium where the ad appears? Online marketing simplifies these processes because it provides greater control over how potential customers interact with your advertising and website. It also provides mechanisms to track actions to evaluate the effectiveness of advertisements and marketing efforts.

When visitors click on an online advertisement, they come with two emotions: *hope* that they will land on a page relevant to what they are looking for, and *worry* that the page will be a disappointment. Each of us can count the number of times we clicked on an ad and landed on a page that had nothing to do with the advertisement. Our research indicates that visitors judge the relevancy between the ad and the landing page in less than one second. The lack of continuity causes visitors to lose confidence in your site. Once they lose the scent of what you are trying to get them to do, once they do not see the relevance in your marketing campaigns, you have lost them, possibly forever.

How Do You Maintain Continuity in Online Advertising?

Conversion optimization goes well beyond a single landing page. It is an entire process that includes where the user came from, how the user got to your site, and what you will do to persuade the user to convert. Conversion optimization is about more than placing a button here and some text there; it's about having a holistic approach to optimizing your online transactions. Continuity is one of the ways to have that holistic approach to and outlook on conversion optimization. To maintain continuity in any type of online advertising, use the same creative elements in both the ad and the landing page. These elements include the headline, keyword, message, and images. Remember, the first step in establishing trust is generating *awareness*. The ad that you display is the gateway to further awareness about your company.

Figure 4-10 displays the PPC advertisements that appear when you search for the term "Dora Dolls." What do you think is the user motivation behind this search?

- The user could be interested in purchasing a doll.

- The user may want to see if these types of dolls exist.

- The user may want to find places where these dolls are sold.

- The user may want to do some comparison shopping.

Which of the ads in Figure 4-10 does a better job of capturing the attention of users interested in purchasing Dora Dolls? The first ad for Target.com seems the most relevant. The remaining ads bear some relevance to the term, except for the Toys R Us ad: nothing in this ad relates to the search term "Dora Dolls." The headline reads "Toys R Us Official Site," and the ad copy reads "World's Greatest Toy Store. Save big on toys and games." Perhaps Toys R Us is relying on its well-known brand as opposed to ad scent to convince visitors to click through to its site.

The Amazon.com ad uses a different approach. The headline reads "Dora Figure at Amazon.com." The ad copy states "Discover Amazon's new Toy Store Qualified orders over $25 ship free." The headline uses the word *Dora*, but the copy does not include the search term. Amazon.com compensates for that by including a free-shipping incentive to entice visitors to click.

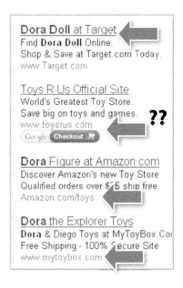

Figure 4-10. *PPC ads for the search term "Dora Dolls"*

Before we look at the actual landing pages, let's take a look at a different ad that Amazon.com uses. Figure 4-11 shows two different ads for Amazon.com, both for the term "Dora Dolls." Notice how the second ad flips the search term and displays "Doll Dora" instead of the term we searched for. Both ads use the same incentive of free shipping on orders of $25 or more. The first ad emphasizes an Amazon.com feature: "new Toy Store." The second ad is more relevant to users by emphasizing low prices.

Dora Figure at Amazon.com
Discover Amazon's new Toy Store
Qualified orders over $25 ship free
Amazon.com/toys

Doll Dora The Explorer
Low Prices on **Doll dora** the explorer
Qualified orders over $25 ship free
Amazon.com/toys

Figure 4-11. *Amazon.com ad for the search term "Dora Dolls"*

Figure 4-12 shows the MyToyBox.com landing page for the same search. The ad seems relevant and also includes the incentive of free shipping. However, the landing page is a different story. Although we see Dora items displayed on the landing page, the results do not directly relate to the term. The products on this page include Dora quilts, books, and even toy boxes, but no Dora dolls. So, although the ad is relevant, and the products on the landing are relevant to the term "Dora," they certainly lose scent for the term "Dora Dolls." The landing page has broken the cycle of continuity at this point.

Figure 4-12. *MyToyBox.com landing page for the search term "Dora Dolls"*

Figure 4-13 displays Amazon.com's landing page, which has a similar problem to the landing page of MyToyBox.com. Although Amazon.com's ad may have enticed the user to click through because of the free-shipping incentive, the lack of continuity on the landing page may result in a quick bounce off the page. The first six items on the page are "related" to Dora—Diego, Daisy, Dora furniture, etc.—but are not actual Dora dolls. Dora dolls didn't appear until the bottom section of the page. Amazon.com is expecting visitors to be patient enough and scroll down to find these dolls. As a general rule, the landing page should be relevant immediately. Figure 4-14 shows a new and updated landing page from Amazon.com for the same term. The new page maintains relevance and avoids the mistakes we pointed out in the original design by displaying the Dora dolls first on the page.

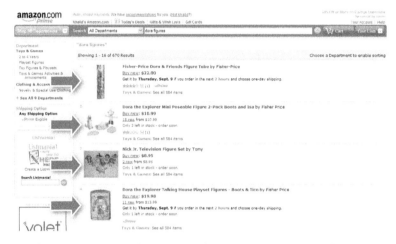

Figure 4-13. *Amazon.com original landing page for the search term "Dora Dolls"*

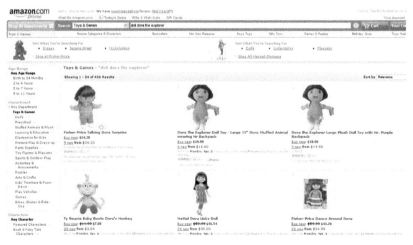

Figure 4-14. *Amazon.com new landing page for the search term "Dora Dolls"*

Finally, Figure 4-15 displays the landing page for Target.com. This page maintains the most relevance to this particular search term compared to the other sites. Target's ad displays the keywords searched for. The landing page continues the scent to enhance the user's confidence in the site.

Figure 4-15. *Target.com landing page for the search term "Dora Dolls"*

Relevance of ad content to keyword is important; so is the geotargeting of your ads. Displaying French ads for a US resident, for example, has little relevance. Figure 4-16 shows a banner ad targeting US residents that appeared on the lefthand panel of Hotmail.com.

Figure 4-16. *French ad targeting U.S. residents*

Scent does not end on the landing page. You must maintain the message throughout your site. Every site maintains a uniform design, because if each page had a different design, look, and feel, the site visitor would lose scent quickly. Your page is delivering a promise to the user; as the user clicks through to the next page on the site, you will need to anticipate what *the user expects* to see.

That is where personas play a key role when creating ad campaigns, landing pages, and entire sites. Ads must cater to specific personas, and your landing pages should address the issues that are relevant to that persona. Not all companies can create campaigns that target specific personality types, so the challenge is to make an ad and design a landing page that can address and maintain relevance to all your target personas. To do so, you should ask the following questions:

- Which continuity elements on a page cater to which personas?

- What will each persona expect to see as they click on this link?

- Will all personas even click on this link?

As visitors navigate through a site, continuity is as important, if not more so, than when visitors navigate from an online ad to a landing page. However, we spent most of this chapter reflecting on the continuum between ads and landing pages because there is often a lack of continuity within a site, and although it may be subtle, it is enough to lose a few potential buyers. Figure 4-17 shows the Bassett Mirror Company category page on the website of one of our clients, HomeGalleryStores.com. Analytics revealed that a large number of visitors were navigating to the mirror subcategory from this page. By following the continuity principle, the next page should show the same mirror that was displayed on the parent category page. Figure 4-18 shows the Bassett Mirror Company Mirrors on HomeGalleryStores.com, but the mirror that was displayed on the parent category page is nowhere to be found on this subcategory page. By merely adjusting the way items are listed on the subcategory page to maintain continuity, HomeGalleryStores.com increased its conversion rate by 10%.

Figure 4-17. *Bassett Mirror Company category page on HomeGalleryStores.com*

Figure 4-18. *Bassett Mirror Company Mirrors subcategory page on HomeGalleryStores.com*

The key is to ensure that whenever visitors click on your site, continuity doesn't stop.

Typical Problems When Maintaining Continuity

Here are some of the problems our clients run into regarding continuity:

Poorly designed ad campaigns

Ad campaigns should be monitored carefully to track what keywords visitors are using to land on the site. Adjust ad creative and landing pages to address user motives. Ensure that you geotarget your ads to the correct location where your offering is relevant. Finally, use negative keyword bidding to ensure that your ads are not displayed for terms that are not related to your offering.

Poorly structured SEO campaigns that drive visitors to the wrong pages on the site

Don't underestimate organic results. Ranking first in organic results for a term is a lot better than spending hundreds of dollars on a paid placement. The key is to attach the most relevant page on your site to the particular search term.

Using the home page or category pages as a landing page

Home pages are wonderful, but they are multipurpose pages, and therefore they lack focus. The more focused a landing page is on the actual objective of the user, the more likely that visitor will convert.

Using search results pages as the landing page

You might have noticed both Amazon.com and Target.com in the previous example used the search results page as a landing page for the term "Dora Dolls." Sites resort to this approach because creating a custom landing page for tens of thousands of terms is not feasible. Although we understand the logic, you should make certain this works for your site. Driving visitors to your search results page will only make sense if you know your internal search technology and search results will display relevant results. You can rely on the internal search to display results, but add logic to your system so that the search results page adapts its look and feel for users landing on that page from an external source.

Maintaining Continuity with PPC

There are two aspects to ensuring continuity to the message you are trying to communicate with your buyers: pre-site or landing page exposure, and post-arrival. To enhance your visitors' trust in your site, follow these rules:

- Ensure that the keyword used in a search is found in the ad, preferably the ad headline.
- Ensure that you maintain strong scent in the ad content to entice users to click through. Yes, the ad may include the keyword in the ad headline, but if the content does not maintain the scent and provide an incentive to click, the user may select your competition.
- Have the landing page relieve visitors' anxiety by maintaining the relevance of their search and having a strong scent throughout the page that supports the original search.
- Maintain site continuity as users click on text, images, links, and more. Resultant pages should reflect what the user clicked on.

Congruency

Up to this point, we have focused on providing visitors with scent and relevance by maintaining continuity from an ad to the landing page. But how harmonious are the different elements on the landing page? Is there a congruent theme and message throughout the page and on every page throughout the site?

Visitors move to the knowledge stage of building trust the minute they land on your website. If your landing page does not address their questions, you have not succeeded in building trust. *Congruency* means maintaining a single harmonious message within the same page while answering the personas' different questions. For the value proposition to transcend to visitors, every element on a single page has to support that value. Very often you'll find that a site will have many competing messages on one page, or you'll find a site in which the copy, images, and elements do not work together to fulfill the value proposition. The lack of congruency increases visitors' anxieties and leads to more *friction*. Friction results when two forces collide. Online, the two forces colliding are the visitors' anxieties and your landing page elements. The more friction that results from this collision, the more likely it is that visitors will abandon the site. It is impossible to completely eliminate friction, and every transaction will have some degree of it.

How can all the elements on the site support the present congruent message?

Every page on the site should serve two purposes:

- Support the overall value proposition of the site
- Move visitors toward the primary conversion goal for that particular page

When elements on the page work harmoniously toward these goals, you will achieve congruency. As you evaluate different pages on your website, you should ask the following questions:

- What is the primary conversion goal for the page?
- Do the different page elements (copy, images, and design) support the primary conversion goal as well as the value proposition of the site?
- What page elements are distracting visitors from the primary goal or from the value proposition?
- Do the different elements present a single congruent message?
- Are the different elements relevant to each other?

Figure 4-19 shows the organic results for the term "pest control." There is enough continuity from the search term to the description displayed on the search engine results pages (SERPs). Figure 4-20 displays the page we landed on when we clicked on the

ClarkPest.com organic result. Continuity is definitely lacking from the search results page to the landing page. The page is also not harmonious, as it lacks one consistent message throughout.

Figure 4-19. *Organic search results for the term "pest control"*

Figure 4-20. *ClarkPest.com landing page*

The page does not present a congruent message because:

- Although peace of mind and being a trusted family company are values that are important to visitors, they are not the prime motivation for the visit.

- The page is overwhelmed by the value proposition, which takes away from the actual service the site is offering.

- Although this company presents a wonderful value proposition, it is increasing friction because of the disconnect among the search, the service, and the messages suggested on the page.

Can those messages work harmoniously? Yes, but you don't want them to be competing and confusing the user. Again, congruency is achieved when all of the elements work together to support the value proposition and primary conversion goal of the page.

Your pages should be built to address visitor intent. The value proposition should tie in directly to the service or product you are offering. Figure 4-21 displays the landing page for Compel, a marketing and web design service. After an initial search for web design services on Google, Compel was listed as one of the first results in the area. The home page does not indicate what Compel offers. The headlines below the main image do not clearly indicate what the site is about. The words Conceive, Connect, and Compete are meaningless to a user looking for a design solution.

Figure 4-21. *Landing page for CompelInteraction.com web design services*

Product or service pages must maintain congruency as well. Every element on the page must reemphasize the importance of the product and service by giving the user the confidence to move through the conversion process. Figure 4-22 displays the different ways Zappos reemphasizes its commitment to unmatched customer care. Also notice how Zappos removed the left navigation panel on its product page to emphasize the product (primary conversion goal) and not take away from the overall value it is offering. Again, a value proposition has to support the main objective, which is ultimately to sell products on the site. Congruency lends credibility and authenticity to the value you are offering.

The Nike Shox product page, shown in Figure 4-23, displays the features, images, and a brief description of the product. All the elements on the page support one goal: to sell the shoe. You should use caution when attempting to cross-sell or upsell on product pages, since these promotional messages can distract the user from converting. Remember, there is no salesperson to convince the visitor that the product is right for her, so the page has to do all the talking. Congruency is essentially the salesperson attempting to convince the user that not only is the product offering wonderful, but the value is unattainable anywhere else.

Figure 4-22. *Zappos supporting the value without taking away from the product*

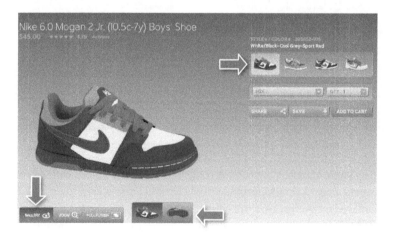

Figure 4-23. *Nike Shox product page*

Social Proof

Social proof refers to the influences that lend you credibility and authority within society; hopefully, but not necessarily, for a good reason. This phenomenon is especially important when people are not able to determine how to react to a specific person or entity, so they rely on the behavior of others to guide their actions. In many cases, your website visitors will evaluate your business based on how other people behave toward to you.

So, what are some social proof techniques that you can use on your website?

Number of clients

RHDJapan was serving thousands of customers internationally. We suggested that it use this as social proof to increase trust among new site visitors. Figure 4-24 shows the newly designed home page for RHD with the social proof as a main focus of the headline.

Visitors want to know they aren't the only ones out there buying from you. If you drive by a restaurant that is buzzing, as opposed to one that has one or two cars in the parking lot, which one are you more likely to want to try? Few people would be willing to give the latter restaurant a chance. The majority will rely on the social proof of the busy restaurant—"a lot of people must love this restaurant, and I want to experience that, too." This type of social proof appeals to the caring persona in particular. But ultimately, the majority of us have humanistic aspects to our behavior, which is why social proof is critical. If you have many clients or customers, list the exact numbers on your website and see what a difference this makes.

Figure 4-24. *Social proof for RHDJapan.com*

Newspaper and PR mentions

How many times have you seen these words on an ad or website: "As Seen In…"? If your company is mentioned on CNN, in the *New York Times,* or in any other industry-related or reputable media outlet, definitely mention it. This is excellent social proof, and it will gain you the trust of your visitors and future customers.

Expert status

In most industries, publishing research or speaking at industry conferences gives your visitors a boost in confidence in what you have to offer.

Celebrity endorsements

When the Google phone came out, Google ran a number of ads featuring very well-known artists and actors using the device. This gave the new phone a ton of social proof. People want to be like celebrities. If they see a celebrity using and enjoying your product or service, you can be sure you've gained their trust and confidence.

For a very long time, Jessica Simpson was the face of the skin care product Proactiv. For young teens, her endorsement authenticated the product so much that it became one of the most popular skin care products on the market. Of course, Jessica Simpson was endorsing the product because Proactiv was paying her good money to be its spokesperson. Does that mean anything to young teens? Not really; as far as they're concerned, her skin is flawless because she uses the product. Celebrity influence has a big impact on product success. Revlon, L'Oréal, and Garnier all feature celebrity spokespeople rather than no-name models to endorse their products. This type of social proof resonates well with customers who are more caring in nature.

Well-known customers

If you have a well-known client, don't hesitate to make that clear to visitors and prospects. Figure 4-25 shows how Google Analytics uses its list of customers as social proof for its service. Much like celebrities, if a large client trusts you, you must be a good company to work with. This type of social proof resonates well with the aggressive and logical personality types.

Figure 4-25. *Google Analytics clients*

Social media following

Social media websites, such as Twitter and Facebook, have increased in popularity over the past few years. These websites allow your business to interact with potential as well as existing customers. Having a large following on these sites can indicate how popular your business is. Placing prominently on your site the logos of sites you are involved with can lend credibility to your site. The same applies if your business has a blog with a large RSS following.

We would caution against implementing any of the aforementioned suggestions without measuring their impact on visitors. Ultimately, every website activity, change, or enhancement should directly impact the goals of the site, the strongest of which is to increase the bottom line. Blindly adding elements that you may think will enhance trust and build more confidence in your users is not enough. Remember, customer-driven changes should influence decisions.

Social proof is very often abused, as witnessed in the Dr. Oz debacle that occurred in 2009. The name of this well-known celebrity was being plastered all over weight-loss products because he had endorsed a specific ingredient that these products were using. The offending companies were using social proof, Dr. Oz's endorsement, to enhance trust in users and motivate them to purchase. Dr. Oz and Oprah ended up suing these companies over their claims.

The new age of digital photo editing and enhancement makes it even easier to plaster faces of celebrities on websites to try to promote and endorse products. Many times, these types of hoax companies get away with this practice since their products are not so popular, and it's virtually impossible to monitor all activities over the Internet.

Membership/Professional Organizations or Affiliations

Memberships and affiliations with professional organizations can improve the odds that visitors will trust you. Similarly, many ecommerce companies use services to ensure the security of their websites and their compliance with Payment Card Industry (PCI) standards. These services scan websites on a regular basis to ensure that all transactions will be safe and secure. Using a well-named security service brings comfort to your visitors. Adding these security icons and seals has resulted in large increases in conversions for some of our clients.

It's important to realize that you should not expect your visitors to do the digging and make sure you are a legitimate business. You can't expect them to look up the various memberships and professional affiliations you have with different organizations. You can't expect much from them because they have come with a purpose, and if you do not do all you can to address all of their concerns and remove anything that blocks their path, you will lose them as potential customers or clients.

It's key to realize that not all memberships will resonate well with users. Some of your customers may appreciate your affiliation with the Better Business Bureau (BBB), whereas others will associate this affiliation with a small business and would not want to work with your company as a result.

External Reputation

Your reputation can vanish quickly and brutally. A single blog or video can go viral in a matter of minutes. To maintain trust, you need to realize that recovering from a negative campaign is important. With everything published online, it takes a shopper a simple search of your company's name to see what others are saying about your service, products, or company in general.

What can you do about negative buzz? There are a few steps you should consider when trying to clean up a negative campaign:

Get to the root of it

Companies have never been under such scrutiny as they are today. Users now recognize that they have some power, and if something they say about you goes viral on the Web, they can negatively impact your reputation. If you've received negative comments about your company, it's important to get to the bottom of it and understand why clients or customers are reacting this way. Just being angry about the negative comments will not get you anywhere. Address any flaws in your products or services. The Toyota recalls in 2010 stirred up a lot of controversy. Toyota had always maintained a strong image, but that image quickly unraveled once news of the recalls got out. To clean up the damage, it launched a television ad campaign featuring its many happy customers (emulating Microsoft's "I am a PC" ads).

Get social

Many companies have moved into the social media space to mitigate complaints. Twitter allows companies to monitor any communication about them and address concerns immediately. The Facebook company page is another medium that can help you stay involved with the community. Companies are now hiring specialists to maintain a strong, socially connected image. One of the more recent successes has been with the Ford Motor Company, which has been able to successfully connect with customers like never before using social media platforms such as Facebook and Twitter. Ford's social media team is always monitoring and engaging the community in discussions around the company.

Get busy

Many times you'll find that negative comments about your company are coming from a dissatisfied blogger or some sort of discussion on a forum. It's important to set up alerts to receive notifications whenever anything is posted about your company. Also, visit these forums or blogs and interact with the community there.

Show members that you are not only aware of their concerns, but that you will handle the situation. Again, it's all about being present. The more customers feel you are not a big-shot corporation that couldn't care less about the little guy, the more you can deflate some of the anger and begin to connect with customers at an entirely different level.

Get ranked

Reputation management can be very expensive, online or offline. But to maintain trust, it's important to consider setting aside some of your budget to handle these matters. We recommend that you hire experts to take care of the damages for you.

The Perils of Social Media

The exploding social media industry is changing the way businesses interact with their customers. Twitter, Facebook, and MySpace are drawing millions of people into active participation—and when you find millions of engaged people, you'll find plenty of businesses trying to convince them to part with their money. For all the altruistic talk of companies connecting with human beings (that's the social aspect), the endgame is always going to be revenue (that's the marketing aspect).

Sometimes, however, the marketing and the social aspects end up colliding and failing. When this happens, we can all learn from and laugh at their mistakes. So, we compiled some of the biggest social media mistakes so you will know what not to do:

Not knowing your market

Many companies attempt to capitalize on a certain event that is in the news or that has gone viral on the Internet. Motrin thought it could capitalize on International Baby Wearing Week in 2008 with a YouTube video singing the praises of safe-for-nursing Motrin for alleviating the pains of toting a tiny tot. Many people saw it as "wearing your baby is bad for you, but Motrin is good for you." The ad, which was trying to be funny, struck the wrong chord with some mothers, and their reaction was explosive. These mothers found the ad disrespectful and insulting. The ad may not have been awful, but if the core market feels that it's wrong, something has to be wrong about it. Know your target market before designing a social media campaign.

Not being honest

Long before the "People of Wal-Mart" blog (which is real), the marketing brains at Wal-Mart thought their image would be better served with a fake blog called "Wal-Marting Across America." The blog featured the journey of Laura and Jim, a couple making a trip from Las Vegas to Georgia and parking for free at different Wal-Mart stores during the trip. Every Wal-Mart worker Laura and Jim interviewed seemed to love working for the company. It was great publicity for Wal-Mart. But what was supposed to be a home-cooked, feel-good story of American folklore turned into some awful publicity for the company and the blog when it was revealed that Wal-Mart had hired the bloggers and paid for their journey. Blogs are only effective when they are true and relate to the reader.

–continued–

Design Aspects

Design is subjective, especially to online users. You may have been certain that users would respond positively to a redesign, but you discovered quickly that the new design only confused existing customers and did nothing to motivate new customers. What you may find as an appealing design may not resonate well with your visitors. This is when taking a client-centric, visitor-focused approach will help you deliver a design that works for your potential clients. As you work through your website design to enhance trust, we recommend the following guidelines:

Start small

Start by making small changes on a page. You can use these changes to learn more about your visitors' behavior, and then build upon these changes with further improvements to the site. Changing too many elements on your website will leave you confused about what worked and what did not. Small iterative changes will produce more results in the long run than drastic measures. By following this approach, you will arm yourself with the knowledge necessary to make educated changes instead of randomly throwing together combinations.

Know when to redesign or not redesign

Many clients ask us whether they should focus on redesigning their websites or on using conversion optimization. Redesigning a website with no prior knowledge of user behavior has failed for a number of companies we talked to.

Test your design

Chapter 9 is dedicated to testing because it is an integral part of the optimization process. Conversion optimization remains part art and part science. Testing will allow you to validate whether your design is working for your visitors.

The following discussion highlights some areas of design that you must consider from a trust and confidence perspective.

Functionality and Usability

Having a functional website with a user-friendly design is integral in terms of allowing your site visitors to have an enjoyable site experience. As visitors go through the site, their confidence in your brand increases. To continue growing that confidence, the site must be user-friendly. When we conduct an initial review of a website, one of the first areas we consider is the general functionality of the site. If an area is not working properly, it must be addressed immediately.

Site navigation

Users can take different navigational paths around your website. You should measure the effectiveness of each path in getting the user to the end conversion goal. One user may utilize left navigation, while another uses top navigation, and yet another uses the search functionality. Users can get to their desired service or product page in several other ways. Site navigation is one of the biggest culprits when it comes to usability. It is also an area where you might run into technology limitations when attempting to change it. Maintain that everything works properly by:

Creating path scenarios
> Before conducting a usability study, it's important to create path scenarios based on analytics. What paths do users most commonly take to get to a conversion goal? Evaluate the paths along the way to determine whether the functionality is working properly. Common paths should have prominent placement for visitors to find what they are looking for faster.

Analyzing the search functionality
> Based on your vertical, 10% to 30% of your website visitors will rely on search functionality to find what they are looking for. If your search function does not display the most relevant results for visitors, you should consider removing it from the forefront of your page.

Ensuring continuity
> Continuity is crucial throughout the user's experience on your site, up until the user reaches the order confirmation page. Provide continuity from page to page by ensuring that any images or text your users click on appears in some way on the next page.

Placing elements in the right place

There are common areas where users expect certain elements, such as descriptions, images, benefits, and call-to-action buttons. Visitors expect links to be underlined in blue, for example. However, some sites try to do things differently and present an unorthodox layout, navigation, and design. It's important to measure the effectiveness of any changes and their impact on conversion. Online shoppers are generally unaccustomed to change, so when you present them with a different layout and design, they may not know what to do, which increases anxieties.

Other Design Factors

Here are some best practices that we like to consider early in the conversion process:

Whitespace needs balance
Too much or too little whitespace can have a similar impact on users. Space between elements on a category page can give a page an "unpolished" look, which will damage visitors' confidence in the site. Your goal is to have enough space so that a user can distinguish the different elements and you can avoid cluttering the page.

Product images are key ingredients to successful selling online
The image can convince site visitors either to move forward with their purchase process or that the product is not for them. Figure 4-26 displays an image of an ecommerce site offering engraved and personalized gifts. Would you purchase from this site if this was the main image on the home page? Do the gifts look like something you would present to a loved one? It's a matter of taste, but you can be certain that more optimized images and close-up options will build user confidence in the product.

Product presentation is central
Building user confidence has never been a more enjoyable challenge than it is today because of all the technological advances that allow companies to sell more effectively. Apparel stores have taken products to an entirely different level with their virtual models. A user can select her body type and size, and in some cases upload a photo of herself to model the clothing—all from the comfort of her home. Although the technology still has its flaws, it allows users to leave nothing about the product to the imagination. So, do not clutter your page with competing images. All elements need to work harmoniously to support the value you offer your customers. This pertains especially to landing pages that are standalone (i.e., the subscription or email capture happens within one step). Since there is usually one primary goal for such a campaign, competing messages can deter from the main objective of the page and the value you are trying to reiterate.

Avoid using flashing colors that distract visitors from the main purpose of the page
Figure 4-27 shows the main home page for Hasbro.com, the large toy manufacturer. Although flashy neon colors may work for Hasbro because of the products it sells, these colors can deter from the main objective for other websites. Can you determine by looking at Figure 4-27 what the designers of the site want visitors to do? The "Shop" feature, which might be one of the most important functions of the site, is crowded with too many competing elements.

Figure 4-26. *Personalized gifts product image*

Figure 4-27. *Hasbro.com main home page*

Increasing Conversion Rate by 400% Through Trust and Confidence

A mid-size telecommunications company provided electronic fax services via the Internet but was suffering from a low conversion rate. Its target market was small to mid-size companies in a variety of industries, including real estate and trucking services.

The main method used to advertise the service was online paid advertising (PPC campaigns, banner ads, and affiliate marketing). All of these ads drove traffic to a single landing page where visitors could sign up for the service. With a 0.9% conversion rate, the landing page was performing poorly. Our task was to help the client improve its conversion rate as quickly as possible.

–continued–

In our initial examination, we noticed that there were no elements of trust and confidence throughout the landing page. No value proposition was stated and upon entering the page, the user was bombarded with flashing images. There were no icons that showed the client's affiliation with the BBB, McAfee Secure, or VeriSign. The design did not even display that they received the Best Customer Service Award from the BBB.

The Invesp optimization team began to add elements of trust to the page one at a time. Adding a clearly stated value proposition under the company name resulted in an increase in conversion rate from 0.90% to 1.22%. Adding a statement that indicated the service received the Best Customer Service Award from the BBB caused the conversion rate to jump from 1.22% to 2.1%. Replacing the flash image used on the landing page with a static image that supported the value proposition caused the conversion rate to jump to 4.8%. Within the span of three weeks, the team was able to increase the conversion rate significantly by implementing the trust guidelines outlined in this chapter.

Clearly, the landing page suffered from a low conversion rate because of mistrust and low confidence. By continuing to optimize the landing page with the various elements of the Conversion Framework, our client continued to increase their conversion rate.

—— **DON'T FORGET!** ——

There is never a one-size-fits-all solution when it comes to trust. The placement and layout of trust elements is influenced by personas developed for a particular landing page.

CHAPTER FIVE

Understanding the Buying Stages

ALTHOUGH YOU HOPE YOUR WEBSITE VISITORS will buy eventually, many of them aren't ready to buy today.

Many website visitors are browsing, looking for information, comparing products, or simply killing time. The same applies offline. Not every consumer who walks into a store will end up buying something. Some people might be window shopping with no particular item in mind, while others might be looking for a good deal. And then there are those people who are ready to buy. Consumers typically go through these five stages before making a buying decision:

1. Need recognition

2. Information search

3. Evaluation of alternatives

4. Purchase

5. Post-purchase evaluation

Not every buying decision will go through these five distinct stages. If you get hungry in the middle of the night (need recognition), you might skip the information search and evaluation phases and move right to the purchase stage. The length of time it takes a consumer to go through these stages will vary based on a mix of internal and external factors.

Visitors in different buying stages require different sets of information and different styles of presentation to persuade them to convert. Visitors at the need recognition or information search stage are in the beginning of the buying funnel. They have not invested the time to determine the best solution for their need. The evaluation stage indicates that visitors are in the middle of the conversion funnel. Finally, visitors in the purchase stage are at the end of the conversion funnel. These consumers are most likely to convert if you present the right information to them.

Deciphering the Buying Stages Online

Before you can design your website or landing pages for each buying stage, you must decipher the actual stage of each visitor who lands on your website. It is easier to do this offline, where you have the luxury of interacting with the customer, asking questions, and analyzing the situation. Your options are limited online. A good starting point is to analyze keywords that drive visitors to your website and to decode their intent based on these words. You can then use the visitors' intent as a signal or an indicator of where they are in the buying funnel.

Both single keywords and generic search terms can be loaded with information. They can indicate that a visitor is at an early or late buying stage, or not in a buying stage at all. Other searches might be a lot easier to decipher. Table 5-1 shows the possible intent of visitors when they land on a website after searching for the term "laptop." A visitor could be looking for product evaluations or reviews, or he might be ready to buy. In each case, the visitor is in some sort of a buying process (mid- or late-stage). The visitor could also be searching for the history of laptops or the latest in laptop technology news, both of which indicate that he is not in any type of a buying process.

Table 5-1. *Possible visitor intent breakdown when searching for the keyword "laptop"*

Perceived intent	Type of intent	Actionable
Product evaluation	Ecommerce	Yes
Laptop technology	Knowledge	Maybe
Laptop history	Knowledge	No
Laptop reviews	Ecommerce	Yes

If the visitor gets to the site by searching for a less generic term, such as "laptop reviews" or "laptop history," you do not have to do a lot of guesswork. The visitor is letting you know what he is looking for. A search for "laptop reviews" indicates that the visitor is in the evaluation of alternatives stage. A visitor with a search term such as "cheap laptops" might also be in a purchase stage, although he is obviously price-sensitive. Finally, there is a very good chance that a visitor who lands on your website after searching for a particular model, "Dell Latitude 8200," might be in the purchase stage of the buying funnel.

During conversion optimization projects, we use software to mine analytics data for new keywords and for opportunities to understand visitors' motivations when they land on the site. It is typical for a website to have thousands if not hundreds of thousands of keywords that drive traffic to it. The task of analyzing keywords can be challenging, but here are some guidelines:

- Create a list of keywords that drive large amounts of traffic to your website (high-volume keywords). The number of visitors a keyword should bring for it to be considered a high-volume keyword depends on your site. For some websites, a high-volume keyword can bring 500 visitors per month. For others it can bring 50,000 visitors per month.

- Focus on the top 100 keywords for your website. For many websites, 80% of their traffic comes from 20% of their keywords. This second list of keywords is another goldmine in determining visitor intent.

- Segment your keyword lists by visitor intent, bounce rates, and time spent on site.

Do not aim for 100% accuracy. Deciphering visitor intent is a qualitative area of research. Your goal is to look for general trends to understand what brings visitors to your website.

No companies spend more time analyzing visitors' intent based on keywords than search engine companies. The quality of search engine results pages (SERPs), and therefore the quality of the search engine itself, depends on providing relevant data to the term a person searched for. Search engines use complex algorithms to decode visitor intent based on linguistics. They also have the advantage of monitoring what search results people are clicking on when they search for a particular term. If people regularly click on a particular result when searching for a term, the engine creates an association between this type of result and the search term.

Table 5-2 shows the breakdown of the type results that search engines display for the term "laptop." When a person searches for this term, Google takes this as an indicator of an intent to buy a laptop. In this case, Google SERPs are heavily tilted toward ecommerce, showing eight ecommerce websites out of the 12 results on the page. Bing, on the other hand, splits the results evenly between review and ecommerce websites. The Yahoo! SERP divides the results equally among ecommerce, review, and general knowledge websites.

Table 5-2. *Breakdown of types of sites based on the big three search engines*

Type of site	Google	Bing	Yahoo!
Ecommerce	8	9	3
News	1	0	0
Reviews	2	10	4
General knowledge	1	2	3

In the following sections, we will cover how you can improve your website to cater to visitors at each buying stage. As you read through each section, keep in mind that a wealth of information creates a poverty of interest. Your goal is to provide the right amount of information for each stage, and nothing more.

Need Recognition

During the need recognition stage, consumers realize they have a specific need or want due to an internal or external stimulus:

- An *internal stimulus* is based on the consumer's internal system. For instance, when a consumer becomes hungry or sleepy, or if her laptop breaks, the consumer recognizes that she must do something to satisfy her need (get some food, take a nap, or buy a new laptop).

- An *external stimulus* is based on external factors which cause the consumer to recognize a specific need or want. Late-night advertising of fast food, weight-loss products, or money-making schemes is aimed at stimulating potential consumers to recognize a specific need.

Although marketers can do very little about internal stimuli, most types of advertising are designed as external stimuli for consumers to recognize a need. Also, in some instances, social pressures or norms stimulate consumers to recognize a need or want. High school or elementary school students are stimulated by the social pressures of their peers to own particular items. Apple's products, such as the iPhone and iPad, are successful because of their social acceptance as being "cool" products. Of course, the quality of these products also positioned them to enjoy great success.

On the Web, banner advertising plays a role in stimulating consumers to recognize a need. As people browse online, banners that relate to the content they are viewing can spark them to recognize a need. Selecting the right medium and how relevant the banner is to the content will have the most impact on the banner's effectiveness. Figure 5-1 shows a banner advertisement on the popular social website Digg.com for Omniture, the enterprise analytics package. The banner advertises an Omniture white paper titled, "Can You Quantify the ROI of Social Media?" Although the topic is important to those who work on social media strategy, it is difficult to see how this paper will be relevant to 99.99% of the visitors to Digg.com. Yes, Digg.com is a social media website, but the average Digg.com user is in his 20s, either a college student or a recent graduate. These visitors usually come to Digg looking for quick news updates. Do you think Omniture is getting great ROI on this particular social media advertising?

Figure 5-1. *Omniture advertising on Digg.com*

Ecommerce companies with large customer databases can be sitting on a wealth of information with the unique ability to create external stimuli. Customers provide insights to items they are interested in either explicitly or implicitly. Examples of using customer data in email campaigns include the following:

Customer-expressed preferences

A customer might let an ecommerce website she has shopped on know that she is interested in a particular category of items. Figure 5-2 shows the user profile preferences that Amazon.com offers to its users. By letting Amazon know you are interested in a particular topic such as marketing, you are allowing them to create a need for you. When the site receives new books on marketing, it can alert you of the new arrivals.

Customer purchase history

Based on a customer's purchase history, a website can determine that the customer would be interested in a particular product. If you bought the latest technology item from a particular website, and that website now offers a complementary or similar item at a discount, the website can notify you.

Customer-implicit preferences

A particular website can use business intelligence software or methods to determine what information a customer is interested in. If you visit an ecommerce website multiple times, and on every visit you navigate to the same category and examine the same item, the website can use that information to send you a special offer for that line of products. It can also use the same information to display these items on the website on your next visit. For instance, an apparel store can look at buying trends and decide that a particular segment of its customers is always interested in buying new lines of clothes as they become available from designers.

Figure 5-2 shows email preferences on Amazon.com. When a customer tells Amazon she is interested in a particular topic, she is allowing Amazon to stimulate her needs when a new item arrives or if items go on sale.

Figure 5-2. *Email preferences on Amazon.com*

CASE STUDY

Stimulating Customer Needs

The analytics team at a large hotel chain spent an extensive amount of time researching the behavior of customers who buy vacation packages. The team noticed that most customers will start searching for a hotel package six weeks prior to making their final purchase decision. Aware of buying stages customers go through, the team decided to use this data to their advantage. They figured that if they have a way to bring potential customers to their site five to six weeks after their initial search, the customers will be more likely to convert.

Acting on that data, the hotel chain contracted with a large content network to target these customers through banner advertising. To average consumers, there was no relation between the content network and the hotel chain. When customers searched on the hotel website for a vacation package, the chain would use a cookie to flag the customer records. As customers navigated to sites in the content network, these sites checked for hotel chain cookies. If a visitor had one of these cookies, and five weeks had lapsed since the visitor searched for the package, vacation banners for that hotel would appear on the content network website. Customers thought it was coincidental that these ads appeared and were unaware of the amount of behavioral research that went into these banners.

These banners did a great job of stimulating these customers and reminding them of the vacation package they had searched for at a discounted rate. This plan had a great impact on the chain's bottom line and resulted in a large increase in its conversion rate.

–continued–

Although this strategy worked well for the hotel chain, a 2008 Harris Interactive poll found that many U.S. consumers "are skeptical about the practice of websites using information about a person's online activity to customize website content." * For example, "A six in ten majority (59%) are not comfortable when websites like Google, Yahoo! and Microsoft (MSN) use information about a person's online activity to tailor advertisements or content based on a person's hobbies or interests." †

Marketers will have many options to reach customers and stimulate their needs as technology continues to evolve. Although this represents a great evolution in marketing, we must be aware of privacy concerns consumers will have.

---

* *http://www.harrisinteractive.com/vault/Harris-Interactive-Poll-Research-Majority-Uncomfortable-with-Websites-Customizing-C-2008-04.pdf*
† Ibid.

Information Search

During this stage, customers are gathering information about different products and services that meet their needs. They have not committed to a particular product; they are also not focused on specific solutions or product specifications. At the same time, these customers might have preconceived notions about particular brands that can influence their final buying decision later on.

Visitors in the information search stage use general terms to express their needs when using search engines. Their searches do not use specific branded terms. Can you decipher a visitor's intent if he searches for the term "laptop"? The search term that visitors use during this stage of the buying funnel might not clearly indicate what they are looking for. As we noted earlier, a visitor might be considering buying a laptop and wants to see his options. He might also be interested in learning about the latest in laptop technology or learning when the first laptop was sold. This demonstrates the complexity of deciphering a visitor's buying stage when he lands on your website.

In traditional marketing, manufacturers focused on capturing visitors' interest during the information gathering stage. Since customers have not committed to a particular solution, getting your brand into the realm of consideration is a good first step toward convincing potential buyers to consider you. Since the information search stage is still early in the buying process, many online retailers do not focus on it. Conversion rates for visitors in the information search stage are typically lower. For that reason, most retailers design their websites to capture visitors who are done with the information search stage and are at a later stage in the buying process. Satisfying customers during the information search stage requires an investment, and some of these customers might not be ready to make a final decision for months. Even worse, some of these customers might convert on a competing website, which means you contributed to a competitor's sales cycle. Although we understand these concerns, allowing your competitors to dominate this stage can be an expensive mistake. Your goal during the information search stage is to do the following:

- Influence the criteria the prospect will use for buying.

- Get the prospect to start thinking of specific brands you carry that meet the purchase criteria.

- Develop a value proposition for your business with the potential customer.

If you provide consumers with information that helps them make a decision, there is a good chance you can capture them as customers when they are ready to convert.

How do you cater to visitors in the information search stage? The simple answer is that you provide them the information they are looking for. The challenge is to determine the actual information visitors need. There are several techniques you should follow to help capture visitors' interest in this stage.

Buying guides and wizards

We have highlighted how search engines decipher the information searchers are looking for. Look for insights by analyzing the different results the search engines provide. Not all the results are designed to help buyers move farther along in the buying cycle. So, you should determine which of the first 20 results on the SERPs are helpful to buyers. Taking clues from this will get you started. When examining the Google, Bing, and Yahoo! SERPs for the search term "laptop," we noticed these engines determined that people needed information on the following:

- Ecommerce website to place orders

- Product reviews to determine which laptop is a good fit

- Buying guides to find the right laptop for their needs

- Laptop history and general knowledge regarding them

- News about the latest in laptop technology

For this particular search, customers in the information search stage will value buying guides the most. There are, of course, many ways to design these buying guides to meet different customers' needs.

Creating the buying guides for your website will depend on the personas you are targeting. A methodical persona will more likely need comprehensive guides that explain how to choose the right product. These people are not looking for shortcuts, preferring to have something they can print and take their time analyzing. However, these types of detailed guides will not work with a spontaneous persona. These people need information that answers their questions quickly. Humanistic and aggressive personas might need a mix of the two. So, it is important to develop an appropriate guide for each persona. Finally, the more expensive your solution is, the more details visitors will need in helping them choose the right product or service.

Figure 5-3 shows Dell's organic landing page for the term "laptop." The page is well designed for visitors in a late buying stage. However, there is nothing on the page that addresses visitors who are in the information search stage. The page assumes visitors know what they are looking for and that they are ready to convert.

Figure 5-4 shows Best Buy's organic landing page for the term "laptop." Although most of the page is focused on visitors in a late buying stage, two areas of the page are targeted at early stage visitors. The "Know Before You Buy" and the "5 Features to Consider" areas are in the middle of the page and occupy an important part of the page real estate.

Figure 5-3. *Dell.com landing page for the term "laptop"*

Figure 5-4. *BestBuy.com landing page for the term "laptop"*

Figure 5-5 shows how one of our clients, Massage-Tools.com, provides a textual guide for the methodical persona. This guide provides a lot of the details and methodology you need to follow to select the right massage table for your needs. Figure 5-6 shows how Massage-Tools.com used a guided widget to allow the spontaneous persona to find the right massage table. These types of tools are designed for people with a spontaneous persona who are looking for a quick way to find the information they need.

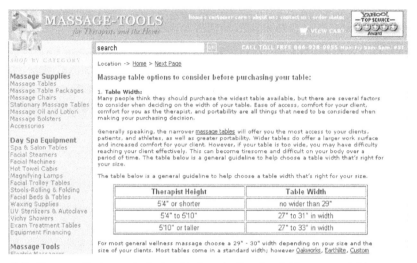

Figure 5-5. *Massage-Tools.com textual guide to selecting the right massage table*

Figure 5-6. *Massage-Tools.com wizard to selecting the right massage table*

When designing wizards or guided selling tools, you should pay close attention to the options visitors have to select to find the best fit for their needs. Massage-Tools.com initially provided visitors with many options based on customer feedback. For example, visitors could select to view massage tables by price, brand, table width, table height, and frame material, among many other options. This type of design, although comprehensive, left many users more confused. Our recommendation is to start with no more than four options on the wizard. You might also consider providing two types of guided wizards—a simple wizard for people who are looking for a quick answer and an advanced wizard that offers experienced visitors more control over the features.

Figure 5-7 shows a TV buying guide from CNET. The page is designed to meet the different needs of the different personas. Understanding that budget is a major factor, the middle section of the page allows visitors to see what TVs they can afford based on their budget (LCD, CRT, plasma, etc.). For the spontaneous and aggressive personas, the page displays a list of best-selling products divided by type of TV: "Best 5 HDTVs," "Best LCD TVs," "Best cheap LCD TVs," and so on. For those looking for more details on what to consider when buying a TV, the navigation panel on the lefthand side of the screen provides a large number of guides based on budget, HDTV basics, features and connectivity, and more.

So, how do you implement a similar buying guide for your business? Here are the steps you should follow:

1. Identify the major features visitors are considering when buying an item. In the case of CNET, the major features included price, type of display (LCD, plasma, etc.), and size of display.

2. Determine possible further breakdowns *within* the major features groups. In the case of CNET, the second level of breakdown allows customers who are within the price range (major features group) to view the types of displays (LCD, plasma, etc.) within that budget.

3. Consider creating different ways to satisfy the different personas for each major and subset features group. Aggressive and spontaneous personas are looking for top sellers in each group. Methodical and humanistic personas are looking for more detailed feature information.

4. Create detailed editorial guides that explain product features, as well as their advantages and disadvantages.

5. Ask customers (both existing and potential) to provide insights regarding what features are the most important, what features are the most difficult to understand, and the best way to present information for consumption.

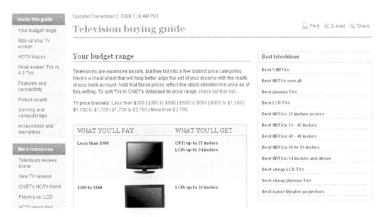

Figure 5-7. *CNET.com TV buying guide*

Self-actualization

Both the buying guides and product wizards focus on product features. Another way to connect with customers is via self-actualization. Using this approach, you will give visitors a list of possible selections to identify who they are and what brought them to your site. When a user selects the option that best describes her, she is committing to a certain path in the site. By identifying the visitor's specific needs, you will be able to tailor the messages and copy on the site to satisfy those needs. Figure 5-8 shows how IBM uses this strategy on its home page by providing visitors with a list of possible industries and roles, so they can select the one that best describes them: Government, Investors, CIOs, Journalists, and so forth. When the visitor selects her industry, she is taken to an appropriate page that provides her with the information she needs.

What IBM can do for...

Industries ▸	A smarter planet	Investors
Government	CIOs	Journalists
K-12 and higher education	CFOs	Job seekers
Small and medium business	IBM Business Partners	Developers

Figure 5-8. *IBM's use of self-actualization on its home page*

Need identification

Focusing on product or service benefits is a great way to connect with visitors. Similar to self-actualization, you will ask visitors to identify which of your offer benefits relates most to them. You will then direct these visitors to specific pages that answer their questions. Since you know the need these visitors are looking to fulfill, your copy, design, and overall online message will be fine-tuned to them. The persona development stage includes needs assessment analysis, whereby the design team will identify the different needs your service provides for your target market. Figure 5-9 shows how the IRS identifies different needs a visitor might have when he visits its site. Although there might be many reasons a person would visit the IRS site, the design team focused on the more popular items people ask for on a regular basis. Besides providing visitors with a better website experience, the IRS is able to minimize the number of inquiries to its calling centers.

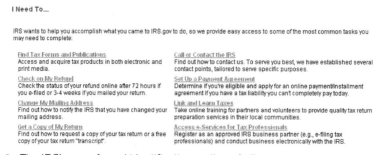

I Need To...

IRS wants to help you accomplish what you came to IRS.gov to do, so we provide easy access to some of the most common tasks you may need to complete:

Find Tax Forms and Publications
Access and acquire tax products in both electronic and print media.

Check on My Refund
Check the status of your refund online after 72 hours if you e-filed or 3-4 weeks if you mailed your return.

Change My Mailing Address
Find out how to notify the IRS that you have changed your mailing address.

Get a Copy of My Return
Find out how to request a copy of your tax return or a free copy of your tax return "transcript".

Call or Contact the IRS
Find out how to contact us. To serve you best, we have established several contact points, tailored to serve specific purposes.

Set Up a Payment Agreement
Determine if you're eligible and apply for an online payment/installment agreement if you have a tax liability you can't completely pay today.

Link and Learn Taxes
Take online training for partners and volunteers to provide quality tax return preparation services in their local communities.

Access e-Services for Tax Professionals
Register as an approved IRS business partner (e.g., e-filing tax professionals) and conduct business electronically with the IRS.

Figure 5-9. *The IRS's use of need identification on its website*

Figure 5-10 shows how Xerox allows visitors to select the benefit or need that best matches what they are looking for. For example, a visitor may need to increase productivity, reduce operational costs, or provide superior customer service.

Figure 5-10. *Xerox's use of need identification on its website*

Evaluation of Alternatives

Visitors in the evaluation of alternatives stage are getting closer to the conversion point. They decided that they *do need* or *want* the product or service you offer. However, they have not selected the vendor they will use or the particular product that will fulfill their needs. A higher percentage of them will convert compared to visitors in the earlier stages of the buying funnel. The question is, are they going to convert on your website or on another website?

You will again look for linguistic cues from visitors to determine whether they are in the alternative evaluation stage. These visitors are likely to:

- Use multiple keywords in their searches.

- Move away from general, broad terms to more specific, qualified terms.

- Search for particular brand names. Instead of searching for "laptops," visitors might search for "Toshiba laptops."

- Search for a specific product model.

- Search for product reviews.

These potential customers are not looking to buy a product; they are looking to buy value. They are assessing two main elements. First, they are looking for the best product or service to fill their needs. Second, they are looking to do business with the best company that provides the particular product or service. To persuade visitors during this stage, you need to present them with the best combination of:

Product benefits
    Why this product is best suited to meet their needs

Vendor benefits
    Why your company is best suited to meet their needs

If visitors can buy the same product from different vendors, the emphasis shifts from the product benefits to the vendor benefits. Several of the techniques we discussed in Chapter 4 will persuade visitors to do business with your company instead of the competition.

The type of information your website needs to provide visitors during this stage will vary based on the type of transaction the visitor is going to complete on the site. In business-to-business (B2B) complex sales, the visitor is looking for product or service demos, white papers, or case studies. In business-to-consumer (B2C) sites, the visitor is probably looking for product information, technical specs, price comparisons, and shipping information.

Evaluation of alternatives: The search for a VoIP system

Let's look at a real-world example to demonstrate the issues visitors deal with when evaluating alternatives. Invesp had moved to a new office and decided it was time to upgrade to a new phone system. After researching the options, we decided to go with a VoIP system.

Figure 5-11 shows Google's SERP when we searched for the term "voip telephone comparison." Initially, we were unsure which of the different manufacturers and models would best meet our needs. Unfortunately, none of the results displayed on the page answered our questions. Two of the top three pay-per-click (PPC) results (CudaTel and Avaya) offered particular brands and no real way to compare the different alternatives from various manufacturers. The other result from the top three PPC results, ShoreTel, seemed to answer our question directly. However, clicking on that result took us to the landing page displayed in Figure 5-12, where ShoreTel offers a report that compares the top 11 VoIP vendors. Although this is exactly what we were looking for, the report was only available if we submitted our contact information. We were not ready to hand out our information to ShoreTel. So, we went back to the SERP looking for other options. The rest of the PPC results did not answer our question. AT&T's paid ad offered "DVR, HD Channels," which did not relate to our search query. Google's organic results did not resolve our problem either. Although we were searching for a VoIP phone system, the page displayed VoIP providers—not exactly what we were looking for. So, we had to ask friends and family what phone systems work best for them.

After further research, we decided that the Cisco 7960 was the best option for our office. We again went to Google to find the best website from which to order the phone. Figure 5-13 shows the top Google PPC results when searching for "cisco 7960." When selecting a website from which to buy the Cisco phone, the features that mattered the most to us were store rating, unit price, shipping cost, and delivery time.

Figure 5-11. *Google's SERP when searching for "voip telephone comparison"*

Figure 5-12. *ShoreTel's landing page for the term "voip telephone comparison"*

cisco 7960   **Search**

About 262,000 results (0.31 seconds)   Advanced search

Cisco 7960G IP Phone $119   Sponsored links
www.TelephoneGenie.com   1 Year Warranty, Quantity discount available, in stock!   Google Checkout

Cisco 7960 IP Phone $128
telecombiz.com/Cisco_7960   Cisco 7960 IP Phone On Sale Now In Stock. Free Shipping.

Cisco 7960G IP Phone $128
www.AtlasPhones.com   Cisco 7960G Telephones On Sale Buy from the Trusted Source Today!

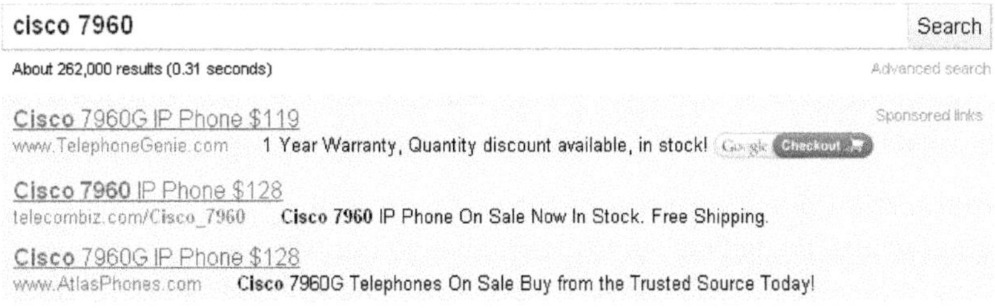

Figure 5-13. *PPC results when searching for a Cisco 7960 phone on Google*

We examined the first three vendors listed on the page. The first result, for TelephoneGenie.com, brought two additional features to our attention: warranty and quantity discount. Both of these features were important to us in making a final decision. Table 5-3 compares the availability of information on the six features we were concerned with among the top three vendors listed on the PPC results. The table shows that TelephoneGenie.com and TelecomBiz.com, the first two results listed, do a much better job of selling the stores' features and convincing us to click on their respective ads. TelephoneGenie.com has four of the seven features we were considering. TelecomBiz.com has three of the features we were considering. Finally, AtlasPhones.com has only one of the features we were considering.

Table 5-3. *Comparison of store features by the top PPC results for the term "cisco 7960"*

Store	Store rating	Unit price	Shipping cost	Delivery time	Warranty	Quantity discount
TelephoneGenie.com	NA	Yes	NA	Yes	Yes	Yes
TelecomBiz.com	NA	Yes	Yes	Yes	No	No
AtlasPhones.com	Maybe	Yes	No	No	No	No

Searching for alternatives: Differentiate or die

Our search online for a Cisco phone, and the PPC results we received, demonstrate a real problem many ecommerce websites suffer from. Can you tell the difference between Amazon.com and Books.com? How about the difference between Walmart.com and Target.com? OK, so the colors aren't the same and they aren't operated by the same company, but how about at a deeper level: are they that different?

Much has been written about positioning since the concept was introduced to the world of marketing in the early 1970s. You hear about positioning so many times that the word can almost become meaningless. Yet, with thousands of ecommerce sites offering very similar product lines and looking almost identical, either these sites are ignoring this very simple marketing concept, or differentiating themselves is much more challenging online.

Back to basics

The following principles are essential when defining your positioning:

Your site must offer real benefits to potential customers
> It is not about your business, your experience, or who you are. It is about how your customer will benefit by using your product or service.

The benefits must be difficult for your competitors to offer
> In other words, the benefits must be unique to your site. This is much more challenging with technology nowadays. Less than a day after Amazon.com offers a new service, many ecommerce sites will copy the new idea. Many ecommerce

sites suffer from "me-too" syndrome. Catalog listings look very similar, product pages are designed the same way, and visitors expect to see product reviews in every ecommerce site.

The benefits must be of great value to potential customers
The benefits must be strong enough to convert a site visitor into an actual customer.

Your site must be able to convey your unique benefits to your visitors
It is great that you know what sets you apart from your competition; now make sure every visitor to your site knows what is different about you. Focus on the unique benefits you offer to clients that they need or must know about.

You should be selling more than products

At a very basic level, ecommerce websites in the same vertical market sell the same products. It is very difficult, if not impossible, to differentiate them based on the product itself. Instead, any successful ecommerce site must resort to using other methods to establish its unique value proposition. To start on the right track, you need to understand what customers are really buying from your site. If you think that the online shopper is buying just a product from your site, you will struggle in the best-case scenario and fail in the worst-case scenario. When a consumer buys something from your site, he should be buying more than the product itself. He might be buying the comfort of a 100% satisfaction guarantee, or a fast shipping policy at no extra charge, or even the unbiased product reviews your site offers. You need to spend time understanding whatever the customer is really buying from you; then design your site to clearly convey that value to your visitors.

How can you stand out from the competition?

The following strategies can help set your operations apart from the competition:

Specialize
Hundreds of ecommerce sites sell books online. Although Amazon.com is the leader in selling books, many engineers or developers would rather order from Bookpool.com because it focuses its services on technical books. Internet marketing news and discussion forum Sphinn.com will not compete with Digg.com, as Sphinn.com's focus on the search marketing industry is what propelled it to success.

Establish a community around your site
If you can establish some sort of community around your site, you can be sure that consumers will come back to you again and again. Apple has been very successful in establishing a community among its users. Sometimes it is a lot easier to tap into an established community. Imagine an ecommerce site that allows you

to view what people who live in your city or work at your company are ordering. The site is not creating a new community; it is tapping into an existing and established community.

Get creative supporting services

When I (Khalid) ran Quill Books in the late 1990s, we focused our services on selling books to university professors. We doubled our sales in one month when we offered next-day delivery for the same price as regular shipping. Of course, I would not recommend doing this without a full financial analysis. In our case, I had worked out a deal with FedEx to allow us to provide such a service. When we offered this supporting service, our sales skyrocketed.

Price

Price is a difficult strategy to differentiate your business online or offline. However, you cannot ignore all the price comparison tools available online that allow consumers to compare product prices from different ecommerce sites. If you have the capital and margins, you might be successful at creating an ecommerce site that competes on price.

Focusing on product benefits

It is difficult to focus on product benefits or features when competitors offer the same products. But it is not impossible. You can do several things to draw visitors' attention to product benefits:

Product description

Most ecommerce websites use the standard product description provided by manufacturers on their sites. As a result, visitors find the same uninspiring descriptions as they navigate from one site to the next. Although this is a cost-effective approach, it does not take into account how different personas react to different types of copy. We do not advocate rewriting all of your product descriptions, but it is a wise investment to create custom descriptions for the top-selling products on your website.

Product images

This is another chance to move away from the standard images manufacturers provide for their products. Product images that show the product from different angles with great detail have a direct impact on conversion. Again, you do not need to take new pictures of all your products. Start with the top-selling products and analyze the impact the new images have on your bottom line.

Product videos

If you are a B2C site, consider utilizing videos if your products lend themselves to physical demonstration. For example, Skis.com offered the same ski equipment as many of its competitors. However, Skis.com took a unique approach to selling these items. Each year, it asked its staff to shoot videos of themselves using the new equipment, and the results have been great. Of course, you need to consider any technical requirements for supporting video, such as bandwidth issues, video format, and server utilization.

Purchase

During the purchase stage, visitors will take the steps to convert on your website. The good news is that many of these visitors are willing to put up with many of the headaches and hassles a website throws their way. For an ecommerce website, the visitor will add item(s) to the shopping cart and go through the checkout process. For a lead generation website, the visitor will click on the contact page and start filling it out.

Only 10% to 20% of website visitors are in the purchase stage. They are highly motivated to complete the buying process. Since these visitors require the least amount of persuasion to convert, they *should* have the highest conversion rate among the different buying stages. However, these visitors might abandon your website due to a process breakdown, usability issues, lack of trust indicators, or increased level of fears, uncertainties, or doubts (FUDs). For now, it is important to know that it is typical for unoptimized websites to convert into customers only 10% to 15% of visitors in the purchase stage. Optimized websites, on the other hand, can convert anywhere from 50% to 60% of these visitors into customers. To put things into perspective, a study by A.T. Kearney states, "Only 2 out of every 10 attempts to make purchases online result in a sale."*

Post-Purchase Evaluation

We all have been there. You get excited about finding an item, you order the item from an online store, and before the item arrives, you start getting buyer's remorse. This post-purchase dissonance is a typical feeling of regret and remorse that takes place after many purchases. These feelings are exaggerated the first time a customer places an order with a website. The customer does not know the site, or whether the company is going to deliver the order on time, or at all.

* *http://www.usabilitynet.org/management/c_business.htm*

Although this stage of the buying process does not have an impact on the conversion action that just took place, it does impact the possibility of the customer placing future orders with your website. There is also the possibility that the customer will cancel the order or return the item. The consumer could also spread bad word-of-mouth feedback about your business. Since customer retention is an important goal for most businesses, it is important to pay close attention to this stage of the buying funnel.

When a visitor places an order with your website, she has two different types of expectations:

Product expectations

These expectations include product quality, benefits, and features.

Service expectations

These expectations include delivery, customer support, refund policies, and other post-purchase activities.

There are three possible outcomes when a customer compares her expectations with the benefits of the product. These are:

Satisfaction

If the received benefits (product and service) exceed the customer's expectations, the customer will be satisfied and *is likely to do business with your website in the future.*

Neutral

If the received benefits (product and service) meet or match the customer's expectations, the customer will be in a neutral state and *might do business with your website in the future.*

Dissatisfaction

If the received benefits (product and service) do not meet the customer's expectations, the customer will be dissatisfied and *most likely will not do business with your website in the future.*

Since the post-purchase evaluation impacts the possibility of getting future business, you should aim—at a minimum—to get the customer to the neutral state.

Most companies are aware of the need to address customers' post-purchase expectations through reasonable return and exchange policies and customer support. It is equally important to address these concerns through careful messaging. Customers are highly aware of your communication with them during this stage. Offline, many companies use follow-up calls to ease the minds of customers. We do not generally recommend that approach online, since most customers expect a certain level of privacy and do not expect to receive a follow-up call from an online retailer. It is best to follow up on online transactions with emails designed to fulfill each of the following points:

Order confirmation email

Telling the customer the order was received and when it will be shipped

Order shipment email

Alerting the customer that her order has been shipped and when to expect it to arrive

Order alert email

Alerting the customer about any problems with the order, such as a delay in shipping, payment problems, out-of-stock items, and so on

Item rating email

Asking the customer for feedback on the item she ordered

Transaction rating email

Asking the customer for feedback on the transaction

Order status emails (confirmation, shipment, and alert) are standard and self-explanatory. The item rating email provides excellent insight into the customer's experience with the items she purchased from your store. Not every product bought by a customer will be used. An unused product or a product that fails to meet the customer's quality expectation will negatively impact future purchases from the customer. Transaction rating emails are your chance to review any possible issues the customer had with your store's performance. They also allow you to show customers your commitment to customer service. Mistakes in fulfilling orders will happen to the best of companies; it is how you react to the mistakes that will set you apart from your competition and bring customers to you for future business.

Figure 5-14 shows an email from OvernightPrints.com, apologizing for a mistake in shipping an order we had placed with the site. In this case, we asked for next-day delivery of the item. Due to a mistake on their side, the order was delayed and would arrive three days late. The email is a very good first step in the right direction. However, OvernightPrints.com only refunded the difference in shipping costs between next-day delivery and two-day delivery. That is not good enough for an upset customer. It would have been better if OvernightPrints.com had shipped the delayed order for free. When a mistake happens, you have to go above and beyond the absolute minimum.

Dear Khalid,

In reviewing your account our records show that your order was shipped on **June 4, 2010**. Your UPS tracking number is 1Z69F7970170482172. Please note that you can also track your order by logging into our website under Track My Orders, using your email address and invoice number. This will allow you to not only retrieve your tracking number, but also track your order directly from the UPS website as well.

We also apologize for the inconvenience and the delay of your order. Due to the delay, we will request a store credit in the amount of $123.69, which is the difference between Next Day Air and 2nd Day Air since the order is arriving one business past the expected delivery date of June 4, 2010.

Figure 5-14. *Apology email from OvernightPrints.com*

Complexity of the Product and the Buying Funnel

How fast a potential customer moves through the buying funnel defines the length and complexity of your sales process. Some purchases take very little time or financial commitment, and the process is completed in a matter of minutes. It's almost like stopping at a convenience store and grabbing a soda. However, in complex B2B sales or high-value consumer ticket items, the process may take months or sometimes years before it concludes. Most sales are in between these extremes.

Focusing on the buying funnel in conversion optimization is important, but it must be accompanied by an analysis of the complexity of your product and the investment (financial and time) your solution requires from customers. The higher the investment required by the customer, the more attention you have to give to the buying stages. There are three different problem levels that customers face, which vary based on the financial investment required. These are:

Minimal problem
> Buying decisions for these types of products are made quickly and in a routine fashion. Most of these products require a minimum investment from the buyer. If your product falls into this group, you should focus your efforts on the purchase and post-purchase stages.

Limited problem
> Buying decisions for these types of products will involve a more extensive search from the customer. These products also require a moderate investment from the buyer. You should focus on the information search and later stages of the buying funnel for these types of products.

Complex problem
> Buying decisions for these types of products will involve a large investment in time and money. Buyers will go through all the different stages of the buying funnel for these types of products, so you need to make sure you address each buying stage.

Different Names, Same Buying Process

We used the term *buying funnel* in this chapter to describe the different stages a buyer goes through before making a purchase. Marketers, customer relationship management (CRM) experts, and sales specialists use a variety of names to describe the same process. As you read through literature on the topic, you will find the same process referred to as *AIDA*, *customer life cycle*, or *sales cycle*. Here is a brief description of each of these methodologies.

AIDA

In 1898, the advertising and sales pioneer, Elmo Lewis, developed the AIDA funnel model to explain the mechanisms of buying. The model outlined the hierarchical process that buyers follow when purchasing a new product or service. The stages of AIDA are:

- *A*ttention (need recognition stage)
- *I*nterest (information search stage)
- *D*esire (evaluation of alternatives stage)
- *A*ction (purchase and post-purchase evaluation stage)

Customer Life Cycle

Marketing experts Jim Sterne and Matt Cutler developed the steps buyers go through to convert using the following stages:

- Reach (need recognition stage)
- Acquisition (information search and evaluation of alternatives stages)
- Conversion (purchase stage)
- Retention (post-purchase evaluation stage)
- Loyalty

Customers go through these steps in a cyclical fashion, moving from one stage to the next until they reach the loyalty stage. Creating loyal customers is the goal of conversion optimization; it is about keeping customers happy, engaged, and coming back to your store.

DON'T FORGET!

- Successful conversion optimization requires looking at each buying stage through the lens of personas. Create a large matrix that shows how to satisfy the different types of personas coming to your website at the different buying stages.
- Although you have to provide different types of information for each buying stage, how this information is created and presented must appeal to the various personas.

CHAPTER SIX

FUDs

IT'S EASY TO PUT CUSTOMERS OFF.

Imagine that as you walk into your local supermarket to purchase some cheese, a store representative jumps out at you, greets you, and asks if you have any questions that he can answer. Would you find that to be helpful or creepy? Then, as you select your cheese, he asks if you would like other kinds of cheese, or maybe some pizza dough to go with the cheese. Are you feeling the pressure yet? When you get to the register, the cashier says that you must become a member of the store to purchase the cheese. And just as you think it's all over, the cashier asks for your phone number, address, business name, and a few more personal details to complete the purchase. Why should the store retain sensitive customer information? By now you are completely spent and full of anxiety. Is this a typical sales experience?

Online, it is.

Offline, you are not likely to encounter such aggressive sales tactics. Of course, we may all be able to relay a story about a horrible experience with a pushy salesperson. A friend experienced it firsthand at a fitness center. They placed her in a room and put a lot of pressure on her to sign up for a membership. They left the room several times to "negotiate" a new price and then applied lots of pressure in hopes that she would sign a costly, non-negotiable or reversible membership with them. Not only did this experience give her a lot of anxiety, but it also made her hate the fitness center, vowing never to return.

This experience is all too familiar for online shoppers. Do these aggressive tactics work? Believe it or not, many times they do create a positive uplift. It's important, though, to always look at your website from a holistic perspective. Looking at a short-term uplift only can be detrimental to the growth and success of your online initiatives. So, although some of these aggressive tactics may work with a percentage of visitors and lift revenues from new visits, it's likely that they will lower the number of repeat customers who will probably never return because of a "bad experience."

We describe users' bad experiences as *FUDs*, which is an acronym for fears, uncertainties, and doubts. Every time a user questions her experience with you or is surprised by an element you present to her, she is experiencing FUDs, which can result in her abandoning the sale. FUDs are the site elements or experiences that can increase visitors' anxieties, deflate confidence, and result in a complete loss of trust of the site. Some of the questions users may have include:

- Will I like what I buy from this website?
- What if I don't?
- Will this service give me the results I am looking for?
- Is this worth the investment?
- Is my information safe?

So many questions, so many concerns—and a successful site will address all of them. FUDs create holes in the conversion funnel. Any sales transaction can be pictured as a funnel that users are sifted through. Along the way, however, many abandon the conversion funnel because of holes or FUDs they experience.

Offline, if a customer puts something in his cart, he is likely to purchase it from your store. At a psychological level, he has "committed" himself to making a purchase by putting something in his cart. This is not the case online. Many ecommerce companies experience high abandonment rates after a user adds an item to his cart. So, what is the difference? FUDs very often go into effect online once the user is more serious about the purchase. Adding an item online does not have the same psychological commitment as placing an item in a physical cart.

Offline, users may experience FUDs as soon as they walk into the store.

What are FUDs exactly?

Fears
    Relate primarily to security and privacy concerns

Uncertainties
    Relate primarily to the usability of the site, navigational errors, and site failures

Doubts

Relate to the questions and concerns users have about the product or service they are planning to purchase

Building visitors' confidence and trust reduces some of the FUDs they could experience early in the purchase process. And on the flip side, FUDs can retract from any progress you've made building confidence and trust within your visitors.

The Buying Decision and FUDs

Visitors begin to consider perceived risks of purchasing a product or doing business with a company early in the buying stages. During the persona creation process, these risks are outlined and considered from the user's perspective through drawn-out scenarios. These risks vary based on the following factors:

Price

The more expensive the product or service is, the greater the perceived risk the user will experience.

Anxiety about the product

The user questions the quality of the product, as well as whether the product will satisfy his need or want.

Anxiety about the company

The user questions the authenticity of the company, as well as its ability to deliver.

Confidence

The less anxiety the user experiences with the overall design and usability of the site, the more confident he will feel moving forward with the buying process and overcoming FUDs.

These risks are reduced by consumer buying behavioral patterns, which include:

Transaction abandonment

It is important to consider the cart as the turning point for visitors in the online buying process. Learning from certain user behaviors and tracking that user at a later time via email can help tremendously. For example, if a user abandons your site, but within 24 hours you follow up with an email reminder of what the user had in his cart, this allows the user enough time to mull over the prospective purchase instead of completely forgetting about it. In Chapter 7, we will discuss additional tactics you can use to get users back to the cart.

Information gathering

Providing visitors with a means to research a product so that they can understand what features they should be looking for and what options to consider can help remove some visitors' concerns.

Defaulting to a more well-known brand name

This goes back to the idea of offering your customers a great value proposition because, ultimately, they are not buying the product but rather the entire package. If you have nothing unique and valuable to offer them, they will, without hesitation, default to a more well-known brand name. This is especially apparent when users are making a big financial decision. Going with a no-name company is a risk that many users are unwilling to take unless you offer them a value they cannot pass up. Also, if your product has added benefits over the competition, presenting users with a comprehensive benefit comparison chart can provide comfort and confidence in the product.

Providing warranties

The more warranties you provide, the more likely the user will have the confidence to move forward. Fragile items, expensive items, electronics, and home furnishings are all products that will prompt user anxiety during the awareness stage. Countering this anxiety by providing warranties for delivery, service, repair, and returns gives users the confidence to continue.

Getting "Personal" with FUDs

During the persona creation process, you should consider what motivates a prospect to make a purchase or sign up for a service. More importantly, you should consider what would stop a prospect from moving forward with a conversion. What concerns are visitors fueled with upon entering the site?

Visitors can experience different FUDs as they move through a site. A visitor's initial concerns when entering a site can be either alleviated or aggravated as the buying process continues. Every visitor will experience a certain amount of friction, but you can reduce these concerns significantly. Anything that causes a visitor unease, anger, frustration, annoyance, or confusion results in another lost conversion.

Dealing with FUDs requires countering the objections users have throughout the buying experience and dealing with elements that cause friction and anxieties. As we discussed in Chapter 4, building trust first requires building confidence. FUDs are the elements throughout the site that can build anxiety and destroy confidence. Figure 6-1 is an overview of the "circle of trust."

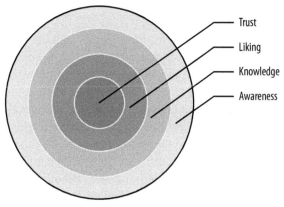

Figure 6-1. *Circle of trust*

Personas and FUDs

What raises anxieties in one persona may not phase another, which is why it is important to understand your visitors and create personas that best represent them. Every page on your site can be addressed from the persona perspective. We can look at best practices for days, but if you do not address issues on the site from the perspective of your customer base, best practices are meaningless and, when applied, will not have a strong impact.

An online retailer came to us with questions about their higher-than-usual abandonment rates. After studying their market, we created four personas and began to probe deeper into the questions and anxieties these personas would have on the site. Three of the four personas had major concerns about the privacy policies and overall security of the site. We countered this FUD by including assurances on the page. This assurance helped the retailer reduce cart abandonment rates by close to 35%.

Another retailer came to us only weeks later complaining of the same high cart-abandonment rate. Although they offered similar products, they were more of a niche retailer that appealed to only a specific type of buyer. Additionally, the items they carried were more expensive. The personas for the two clients were entirely different, yet this client insisted on including similar assurances on their site. Within weeks the client saw a drastic drop in conversion rates. The assurances only enhanced anxieties because visitors started to question the security of the site.

Fears

Fears deal directly with financial, security, form, and overall site errors. Although purchasing online has become more widespread in recent years, users are still anxious about site security before placing an order. Users may be confident in the site, but when it comes to entering credit card information online, their confidence in the company begins to waver a bit and must be reinforced during this process. We've all heard of or maybe even know someone who had a bad experience buying from the wrong place or providing her information to the wrong company. It's still an online transaction, and many users believe hackers can access their information. As online usage has increased over the years, so has online fraud. And although there will always be a degree of anxiety or friction in this regard, dispelling these fears head-on can have a positive impact on site conversion rates.

In a down economy, a common fear is the affordability of items and ease of return. Some companies caught on to this fairly quickly. Hyundai, the Korean auto company, countered this FUD head-on by offering a job loss protection clause to buyers. To ease the fear of making a large investment in the shaky job market of 2009, the car company reassured buyers that if they purchase a car, but later lose their job, they can simply return the car without having an effect on their credit score. The program offers a safety net of $7,500 for car buyers in case they encounter issues due to the rough economy.

As a result of this assurance program, Hyundai saw a spike in sales. It successfully understood the questions potential customers had and provided them with an apt solution to counter their fear.

Sears and Kmart understood that fears increased in a down economy as well. As a result, they increased the effectiveness of their layaway programs, which allow buyers to select items they need and pay for them over time. These companies had scratched their programs in 2006 but revived them in 2008, just in time for the holidays, to address cash-strapped consumers and recent drops in sales. Their strategy paid off. Shoppers could basically buy a large quantity of gifts and pay for them incrementally throughout the year, many times at a low interest rate. Additionally, the companies are now trading gold for cash in an effort to increase sales. At the time of this writing, gold prices are soaring, and consumers remain strapped for cash to purchase items. So, Sears and Kmart customers can now bring their gold to these stores and trade it for cash to purchase items. Since gold prices are so high, it's a win-win situation for Sears and Kmart. They are getting a good return on the gold and are gaining more customers by providing them with cash to purchase items from their stores.

Site errors and 404 errors

Regular quality assurance reviews of your website can ensure that you do not experience unfortunate consequences due to changes on your site. Any code change in a site can impact another part of the site in some way. Consistently reviewing overall site functionality is important. Some common site errors include:

Navigating through a site and then coming across a 404 error page will not go over well with online shoppers. You can be certain that they will have lost some confidence in your site. In early 2007, Motorola.com released its first ecommerce website on a new platform. Although the client team spent months developing the new site, they underestimated the server capacity required to handle all the site traffic. As a result, the site went down within four hours of going live, costing Motorola thousands of dollars in immediate revenue and a loss of user confidence in its ecommerce operation.

Long forms with too many unnecessary fields

Visitors consider lengthy forms, such as the one displayed in Figure 6-2, to be intrusive. It's not too difficult to get an email address from visitors, but the moment you start asking for more information, you will see a significant drop in conversions. We understand that an email address in many cases is not enough to capture all the information needed to follow up with a potential customer; however, you should limit forms to the minimum number of fields you need.

Many times ecommerce companies would like to increase their email subscriptions, and although this is not a problem in itself, if it competes with the overall goal and objective of the page, it becomes a FUD. This is where the idea of congruency on a page is crucial—there should be one primary goal to any single page on the site. Other secondary goals can be identified without directly competing with the primary goal. Figure 6-3 shows an attempt by an online retailer to increase email subscriptions by placing the email subscription box within the checkout process. Of course, visitors who go through the checkout are going to provide an email address to the retailer anyway.

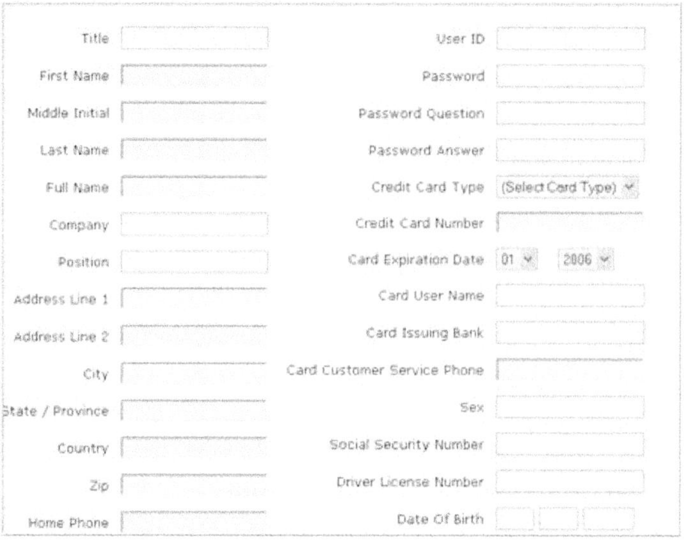

Figure 6-2. *Excessively long form, a cause of FUDs*

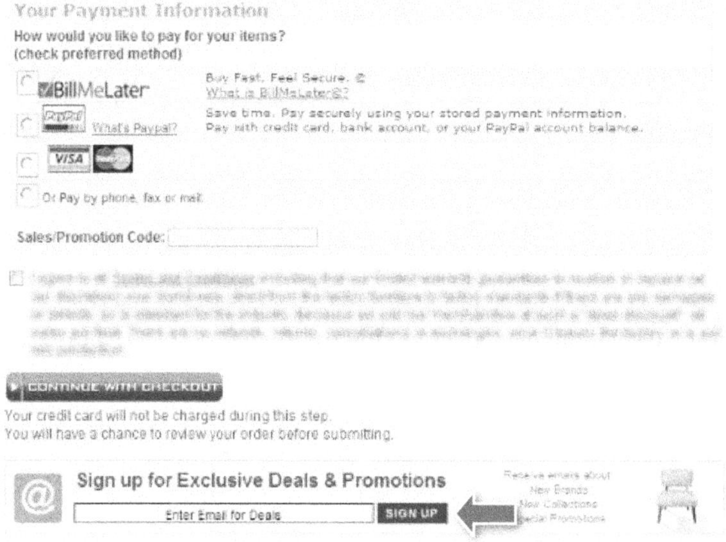

Figure 6-3. *Email sign-up on the payment page of an ecommerce site*

Forms and sign-ups have an impact on FUDs because this is the point where the user includes his personal information. Sensitivity to this issue is very important to decrease any fears users may have about giving out their information. It's important to reduce the number of fields and try to be conscious of where you ask for information from the user.

Security

Giving visitors a sense of security increases their confidence in the site. It also reduces any fears or anxieties they may feel about the authenticity of the site in general.

A client that sells high-end furniture online suffered from low conversion. They are one of the largest furniture stores online, but they are still relatively unknown, so they do not have the brand recognition that eases establishment of trust. However, the company carries a wide range of brand-name furniture that customers would be familiar with.

Their conversion rate was hovering at around .15%. Our team looked at the site and prioritized it based on the most effective areas of optimization (those requiring the smallest amount of effort). The checkout was pinpointed as a prime area for optimization.

It was apparent that people felt unprotected on the site because no form of security was in place. People can protect themselves in the absence of any third-party monitoring of web information. There are some standard security protocols for making web purchases safer; principal among them are Secure Sockets Layer (SSL) certificates, which are designed to ensure the security of web servers. When you visit an SSL server, it places a small lock icon in the bottom-right corner of the browser window, and the URL in the address bar begins with *https:*. The client made certain that their visitors would realize the security of the site.

Browser compatibility

Data provided by Net Market Share (*http://www.netmarketshare.com/*) shows that as of May 2009, Internet Explorer controlled close to 60% of the browser market share, while Firefox controlled 25%. Meanwhile, Google Chrome has been gaining in popularity and holds 7% of the market share. So, at a minimum, your site or landing page needs to support both IE and Firefox.

You can examine analytics data to get a breakdown of the browsers visitors use to get to your website. Beyond browser compatibility, you need to check how your design looks on different operating systems. Several commercial services are available that allow you to view your web design on any browser or operating system.

Tom Dahm from NetMechanic gives an excellent explanation for issues that cause browser compatibility problems:

> Your Web browser is a translation device. It takes a document written in the HTML language and translates it into a formatted Web page. The result of this translation is a little like giving two human translators a sentence written in French and asking them to translate it into English. Both will get the meaning across, but may not use the same words to do so.

Additionally, when you are dealing with browsers, you also need to view your site in the most popular resolutions. Also, what falls below and above the fold on your website? These are issues that you must address because, if you ignore them, they can lead to an increase in FUDs.

Uncertainties

Uncertainties lie within the site's overall usability. The less user-friendly your site is, the more uncertainty visitors will experience while navigating the site. Site usability goes back to the importance of page and business process flow. In the following subsections, we will discuss uncertainties, as well as focus on the importance of the overall navigational structure of the site, which will enhance the user experience.

Bounce-around effect

The bounce-around effect measures how much bounce-around is happening on a given navigational path on your site. It measures how many of your visitors seem disoriented and unable to locate the page they are looking for.

A typical linear navigational path may be home page→category page→product page→ checkout (see Figure 6-4). Of course, people do not navigate around your website in a linear fashion (see Figure 6-5). You can, however, expect the majority of visitors to follow general paths if they find the information they are looking for. Users who are impacted by the bounce-around effect find themselves going back and forth between different pages on a site for a better sense of "what to do next" and "where to go from here."

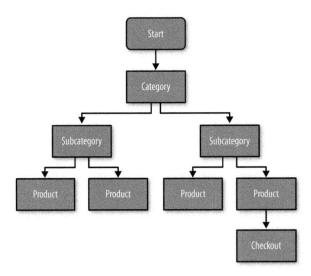

Figure 6-4. *Linear ecommerce path*

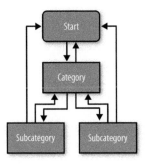

Figure 6-5. *Nonlinear ecommerce path*

The Case of the Confused Visitor

A client had been selling personalized bedding for years and relied heavily on sales during the holiday season, since they could not generate enough revenue during the rest of the year. The client received a good number of customers to the site, yet they were unable to convert some of these customers. Our team began this project prior to the holiday season. The team first gained a better understanding of the target market. They then proceeded to look at their analytics and specific metrics, including the bounce-around effect. It was clear that users were unable to find the products they were looking for. The pages were not filtering users effectively to their end objective. The category pages were designed with no type of filtration, so users ended up going back to the home page over and over again, until they finally exited the site.

The team determined that the bounce-around was more prevalent once the users reached the subcategory level of the site. The team created a filtration system that helped visitors reach their target pages faster. As a result, user confidence went up, and flow from category pages to product pages increased by 40%.

Visitors' inability to locate the call(s) to action

Call-to-action buttons must be clearly visible as well as easy to use. Requiring users to complete too many steps and to make too many movements throughout a site will result in lower conversions. The inability to locate calls to action is a problem that manifests itself in many different forms. Some sites are so unorganized that you cannot find the company contact information. A friend recently signed up for the Geico .com emergency car service. Unfortunately, within a week of starting the service, her car broke down and she needed to be towed. Luckily, she was close to home and was able to access her computer. She searched for 20 minutes on the Geico website for the emergency roadside number and could not find it.

On ecommerce sites, this problem takes a different shape. Some sites use "Add to Cart" buttons that are too small to notice. Sometimes other buttons are competing with the main call-to-action button. On NewEgg.com (see Figure 6-6), the product page offers a variety of call-to-action buttons. These include "Add to Cart," "Add to Wish List," "Email This Page," "Print This Page," and "Price Alert," which are all valid options. However, in cases such as this, the "Add to Cart" button must stand out.

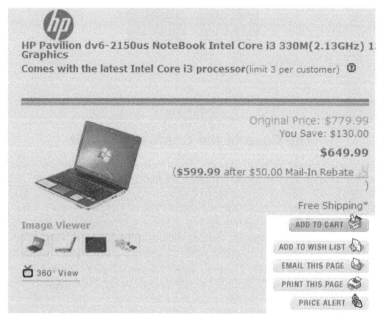

Figure 6-6. *Too many calls to action, which compete against each other and confuse the user*

Figure 6-7 shows another example of a call-to-action button that is difficult to find and use. The "Add Selected Products to Cart" button is at the top of the page, and users must enter the quantity of the product they desire and then scroll up to add the product to their cart.

Figure 6-8 shows an example of a site that has a hidden call to action. The call to action is far below the fold and is the same size as other elements. Because of these issues, visitors can miss the call to action completely (it's at the bottom right and is labeled "Add to Basket"). Remember, the call to action is the most important element of the page, so it must be visible enough to draw users' attention.

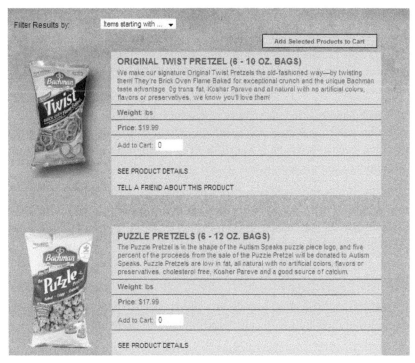

Figure 6-7. *A call-to-action button at the top of the page*

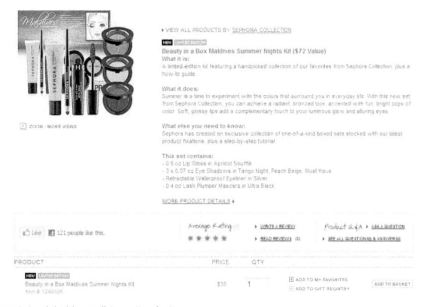

Figure 6-8. *A hidden call-to-action button*

Widgets and tools

Providing users with widgets and tools that can sort information and compare products is helpful and may enhance the overall user experience. However, this is only possible when the tool works and is easy to use. We find that many tools and widgets that are *intended* to help users end up confusing them.

A client of ours had provided his visitors with a tool that would compare the different products on his site. This widget was designed to help visitors decide which products best meet their needs. However, it was difficult to understand, and it did not use the categorization and comparison factors the visitors were looking for.

Search functionality is another example of a tool that can cause visitor confusion when the results are not precise and are unoptimized to match the search criteria. The point of search is to ease the purchase process for users by locating products faster, and this is only possible when the results are precise.

Doubts

Users have objections and questions about a site and its products. If you do not address these questions immediately, you can create doubts and more holes in the sales funnel.

Discount codes

Anything that distracts visitors from the main objective of the page is a potential FUD. Discount codes raise doubt in users since they will question where and how they can get a better deal. Figure 6-9 shows how Carters.com displays a promo code box in the first step of the checkout process, and Figure 6-10 shows the second step of the checkout process. Notice how the promo code box is displayed yet again, before the billing information boxes. We found it striking that an asterisk appears above the promo code box, indicating that this is a "required" field. This can cause users to question whether they have missed something.

Many times discount codes are the culprit behind the high abandonment rates that plague websites. Upon seeing a box for a discount code, a web-savvy customer will likely be prompted to search for the code. This abandonment results in a loss of hundreds of thousands of dollars and potential customers. However, discount codes can increase conversion tremendously, so, it's important to consider their placement carefully. It's also important to have the flexibility to remove the discount code box when you are not running any promotions for the site.

Figure 6-9. *Carters.com promo code box appearing in the first step of the checkout process*

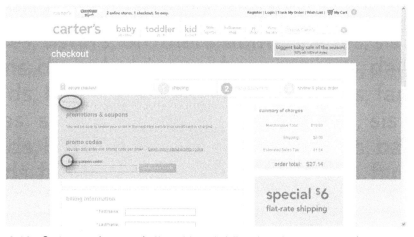

Figure 6-10. *Carters.com's second attempt to get visitors to enter a promo code*

Some companies feel that discounts should be included automatically, whereas others believe asking customers to input promo codes will allow them to better track some of their marketing campaigns. Regardless of the approach you take, the promo code box should not distract from the conversion goal, nor should it raise questions among users.

Using FUDs to Increase Conversions

Scuba gear companies use FUDs well. They make it seem as though your life is at risk if you buy the $30 gear instead of the $130 gear. The reality is that expensive gear can be better, but are there any statistics proving that $30 gear (which meets safety regulations) results in a greater loss of life? When you walk into these shops, the salesperson almost pointedly asks, "How much is your life worth: $30 or $130?" You're not going to be cheap when your life is on the line, right?

The use of FUDs is a tactic that has helped mount the most aggressive marketing campaigns to win customers over. IBM first used FUDs to show customers that "good things" would come to them from IBM, while bad things awaited them if they went with competitors. We see FUDs used all the time on commercials and in marketing campaigns. For example, many cleaning product companies, such as Clorox and S.C. Johnson, use FUDs to scare customers into believing that "other brands" will not remove germs, whereas their products will. In the early 1990s, Pampers launched a campaign titled "What was your baby's worst diaper experience?" Every parent can relate to an awful diaper experience, and tying that experience to a specific competing brand helped raise FUDs in customers from ever considering Pampers' competitors.

Like any marketing tactic, the psychological implications behind the use of FUDs must be strongly considered. Manipulating consumers' feelings, justly or unjustly, can often be considered unethical, which is why companies must use this tactic with caution.

CHAPTER SEVEN

Appealing with Incentives

WHAT DOES IT TAKE TO BREAK CUSTOMERS from their usual patterns and bring them to new places?

If you had the option of purchasing groceries from a store that is located in the next town but whose prices are 50% lower than your local grocer, would you make the trip? If the discounted store was not as organized and clean as the local grocer, yet provided the same quality products for a lot less money, would you still go there?

Offline, customers strongly value convenience, but they can be convinced to go out of their way for a deal. For example, if I (Ayat) am preparing dinner and I realize I need a small grocery item, it is unlikely that I will purchase the item from my local Wal-Mart, which is approximately 15 minutes away from my home. I'll rush to my local grocery store, which is two minutes away, even though the prices there are substantially higher than at Wal-Mart. However, I will pencil in a day to do my weekly or monthly shopping at Wal-Mart or Costco to take advantage of the savings these stores offer.

Customers are also willing to drive some distance to outlet stores, which are often located on the outskirts of large cities, to get good deals on the brands they love. Customers who may never otherwise shop at Macy's fill the store during its semiannual "One-Day Sale." Again, although convenience is big offline, incentives will drive customers to go the extra mile (no pun intended).

Incentives can change customer behavior. Incentives not only break loyalty, especially in a recession, but they also can overcome the FUDs described in Chapter 6. Even if you may have some glaring FUD-creating elements on your site, adding a few incentives could stimulate site visitors to ignore the mistakes and move forward in the conversion funnel.

Consider how you would respond to incentives when faced with a large purchase decision. Say you have to make a quick decision on a notebook computer. You've done your research and selected the best brand and features to meet your needs. Now, the decision comes down to *where* you will make the purchase. You have two choices:

- A well-known store, Best Buy (Figure 7-1)

- A virtually unknown store, Prostar.com (Figure 7-2)

Prostar.com is more amateurish in its general design and appeal. Also, the website contains some FUD-causing elements. However, Prostar.com is offering a 25% discount on the make and model you are considering.

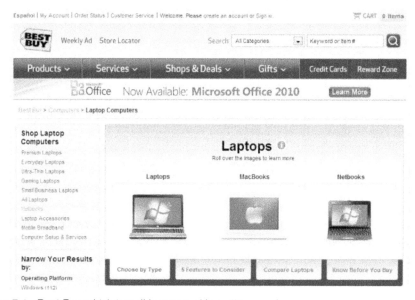

Figure 7-1. *Best Buy, which is well known and has site appeal*

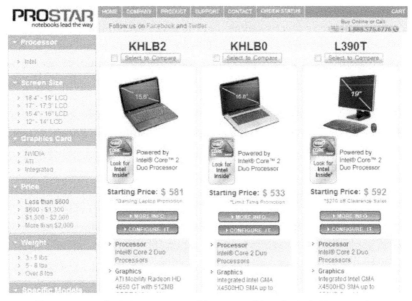

Figure 7-2. *Prostar.com, which is not very well known and has limited site appeal*

Which store would you select? What are you willing to overlook for an incentive? Our research shows that about 75% of customers will even overlook some security issues when presented with a compelling incentive.

Does this mean that all the concepts we have discussed in this book are meaningless if an incentive is present? The reality is that you can increase conversion rate tremendously just by offering incentives on your site, but this may not be the best "business decision" in terms of giving you a strong ROI. You need to position and present incentives in a way that gives customers great value without overlooking the benefit that you will get. By following all the concepts we've discussed in this book and positioning incentives correctly throughout the site, you will not only achieve but also surpass the results you are looking for.

What Are Incentives?

Incentives come in many forms, but all types of incentives offer some sort of *financial* gain for the customer. Incentives include:

- Lower prices and greater savings

- Freebies

- Buy one, get one free opportunities

- Product bundling

The ease of comparison shopping and accessibility to multiple stores has weakened the phenomenon of store loyalty online. For the majority of online shoppers, determining which store offers the better overall deal will drive their purchase decision. In Chapter 8 we discuss tactics that can help you promote store loyalty. However, we've found that a "good deal" has a stronger influence on the buying decision, especially during a time when every dollar counts. It's important to remember that the user tends to select the better bundled site experience from entrance until checkout, and incentives enhance an otherwise average site experience. Customers are unpredictable, and sometimes it's external factors (beyond your control) that result in contradictory motivations to regular buying patterns.

Incentives are, as defined in most dictionaries, "an expectation for customers to behave a certain way." Essentially, they are factors that motivate and persuade buyers to take action and make a purchase. Incentives come in all forms and sometimes even appeal to the buyer's moral sensitivity. For example, when Haiti was devastated by an earthquake in 2010, many ecommerce companies pledged that a percentage of their customers' purchases would go toward aiding victims of the quake. This type of incentive persuaded customers to make the purchase, not only in order to satisfy the need they had, but also because it was a *good* thing to do. Moral incentives tend to help remove guilt a customer may be feeling about a purchase because by making the purchase, the customer will be "donating" to a good cause.

Although some online incentives are designed to appeal to customers' morals, most provide customers with some form of financial compensation. Offers of "free shipping" and "10% off your purchase" provide money-saving opportunities. Some incentives offer added value to a purchase, such as "buy one, get one free." Stores use incentives to achieve any the following goals:

Store promotional incentives

The goal of these incentives is to encourage customers to select your "store" instead of your competitor's. This is the main reason for incentives, and it is most prevalent during the holiday shopping season and other seasonal events. The key for most stores is to determine how to outdo their competition by offering a more lucrative offer. Also, restaurants use this incentive during slow times of day, when they experience the least amount of foot traffic. Subway, for example, discounts subs during the dinner hours because the restaurant receives little foot traffic at that time of day.

Product promotional incentives

These incentives encourage customers to select one product over another. For example, many large superstores, such as Wal-Mart and Target, incentivize their generic-brand products with lower pricing over brand-name products. Because every penny counts due to the economic downturn, customers are drawn to generic brands.

Store clearances

This type of incentive is commonly used when companies want to move older merchandise out the door to make way for new products. Of course, it's important that the discounts make sense, especially when you're promoting to a broad audience. For example, a local expensive furniture store was planning a remodel and decided to conduct a closeout sale. As its products typically cost more than $20,000, a discount of 50% did not feel like much of an incentive for the broader general market. The sale was supposed to end within a week; at the time of this writing, months had gone by and the company still had not been able to move its expensive merchandise.

Word-of-mouth marketing

Companies provide incentives to create buzz about their offerings. This is especially apparent with companies that are just starting out. They will offer very low prices and special free gifts to get people in the door, and then again if those visitors refer their friends and family. Many telecom companies use this type of incentive to increase their popularity and reach. HandbagHeaven.com offered 30 lucky customers free handbags when it first opened its doors. The promotion got a lot of buzz and interest from users on social networks.

Incentives Versus Value Proposition

Some companies make the mistake of assuming that an incentive is the unique value they are providing to their customers. What they fail to recognize is that value proposition goes deeper than an incentive of free shipping or a 10% discount. Value proposition defines your company, and the incentive complements that value. For instance, Zappos.com, shown in Figure 7-3, is well known for its customer service, and its incentives of free shipping and a 365-day return policy feed into the customer service value it provides and markets to its customers.

Figure 7-3. *Zappos.com incentives, which match its overall value proposition*

Value proposition refers to the way a store positions itself in a growing competitive market. As a company, what value do you provide your customers? Stores cannot define their value only with incentives, but incentives are a part of the equation, enhancing the customers' experiences and persuading them to complete a purchase. However, it's the value proposition that first reels in visitors to the site and piques their interest.

Positioning Incentives

Incentives vary tremendously, and as we mentioned earlier in this chapter, companies use them to achieve certain goals.

Membership-Only Stores

Membership-only websites allow visitors to buy items at discounted prices after they join. Although this concept has existed offline for many years, websites such as Ideeli .com and DollarDays.com are successfully experimenting with it online. Both websites require interested prospects to become members before they can purchase items offered on their sites. Forcing visitors to join a website increases the visitors' FUDs, and many may opt not to register because of this contingency. However, both of these online stores offer products at discounted prices, so people looking for a bargain may overlook the fact that they have to register to make a purchase.

Ideeli.com, shown in Figure 7-4, does not allow visitors to view products or any "sales" it is offering prior to becoming members. The store relies heavily on referrals to grow its membership base and has applied the concept of incentives to customer referrals as well. Since it is a membership-only site, Ideeli.com allows users to upgrade their membership, for a monthly fee, to gain prime access to its sales. DollarDays.com, shown in Figure 7-5, allows visitors to view its products prior to becoming members. However, pricing information is reserved for members only. This provides a little flexibility for new users who are unsure of what the store offers.

Figure 7-4. *Ideeli.com, a website that offers discount prices; site visitors must be members to view products and pricing information*

Figure 7-5. *DollarDays.com, another website that offers discount prices; site visitors who are not members can view products but not pricing information*

Newport-News.com, shown in Figure 7-6, is a website that allows all visitors to view products and pricing information. However, visitors who pay a $25 membership fee become members of The Club, which offers "exclusive benefits" such as 10% discounts on all orders, 20% discounts during certain times of the year, and access to private sales and promotions. This tactic allows the store to benefit from customer loyalty, receive up-ticks in sales during benefit periods, and still cover its costs thanks to the membership fee it charges.

Figure 7-6. *Newport-News.com, which charges a $25 membership fee to visitors who want to receive "exclusive benefits"; the revenue it generates from the membership fee covers some of the benefits it provides to members*

Are membership requirements a FUD? There is no doubt that restricting visitors' access to your site's products and/or pricing information causes an added FUD. So, how do these sites succeed? Consider an offline store, such as Costco or Sam's Club, which offers discounted products sold in bulk. However, they require that you become a member (for a fee) prior to purchasing from their store. These stores succeed because of the incentives, or very often the "perceived" incentives, and value that customers receive as members.

Does this mean that as long as you offer incentives, FUDs are insignificant? The reality is that answering users' questions and reducing their anxieties is still key to any successful transaction. But incentives do help.

Bundled Prices

Specific niche retailers have been using the strategy of bundling several products for sale into one combined product for years. For example, fast food companies reap the benefits of product bundling with their "combo meals." For customers, purchasing each item—sandwich, drink, and fries—separately is more expensive than purchasing them as a bundle (the lower price is the incentive). For these restaurants, selling several items at a discounted price results in higher profits.

Some software companies apply this strategy as well. For example, Microsoft bundles Word, Excel, PowerPoint, and more into its Office suite. Also, companies in the cable and dish network industries tend to bundle many channels into a single price or package. This product bundling is often referred to as a *package deal* or an *anthology*.

Bundling is most successful when:

- The cost per unit decreases as the production scale increases. So, for instance, as a fast food restaurant produces more hamburgers, the cost per burger decreases because the cost of purchasing the beef in bulk is lower.

- The cost of promoting the product is reduced, although the number of products being promoted is increased. Promoting the entire Microsoft Office suite, shown in Figure 7-7, is less expensive than promoting each product separately.

- Customer acquisition costs are high. The more expensive it is to acquire customers for a specific product, the more beneficial it is for you to increase your average order value by bundling products for them.

- Customer satisfaction is high. As customers become more satisfied with the overall simplification of the purchase decision through bundling, they benefit from the joint performance of the combined product.

Figure 7-7. Microsoft Office, a software bundle that offers six programs for the price of two; an enticing deal even if you are looking for only one program

Companies such as OrientalTrading.com (see Figure 7-8) thrive on product bundling because their products are high-volume and require a low marginal cost. However, bundling is most effective with "digital" or software products where the marginal costs are close to zero. HubSpot.com, an online marketing software as a service company (see Figure 7-9), has found great success in bundling its online marketing services targeted for small websites. Many companies offer customers the option of purchasing products separately or as a bundle, but HubSpot.com restricts its offering to "pure bundling"—no single product purchases are allowed.

Figure 7-8. *OrientalTrading.com, whose high-volume and low-marginal-cost products are ideal for bundling*

	Small	Medium	Large
GET FOUND			
Website Management	Required*	Optional	Optional
External Website Support	✓	✓	✓
SEO Tools	✓	✓	✓
Business Blogging	✓	✓	✓
Social Media Engagement	✓	✓	✓
Email Marketing	✓	✓	✓
CONVERT			
Prospect Identification	✓	✓	✓
Landing Pages	✓	✓	✓
Lead Segmentation	✓	✓	✓
Lead Grading	✓	✓	✓
Lead Nurturing Campaigns	1	5	100
Lead Tracking	✓	✓	✓
Salesforce Integration**	✓	✓	✓
ANALYZE			
Marketing Analytics	✓	✓	✓
Blog Analytics	✓	✓	✓
Social Media Analytics	✓	✓	✓
ADMINISTER			
Users	2	5	10
Support	Phone + Success Community	Phone + Success Community	Premium Support
Quick Start Program	$500 + Site Migration	$500	Included In Premium Support
Pricing & Payment Terms	$250/month	$9,000/year	$15,000/year

Figure 7-9. *HubSpot.com, which bundles its online marketing services*

Companies use a variety of tactics when bundling products:

They offer complementary items as a bundle
With this tactic, as a visitor navigates to a product page, items that are complementary to the original item appear on the page. To persuade the customer to increase his order value, these companies will offer a discount when the customer purchases the complementary items bundled with the original product.

They offer higher discounts for purchasing higher quantities of the same item
With this tactic, companies offer customers discounts that increase as the quantity of a particular product being purchased increases. For example, RHDJapan (see Figure 7-10) offers customers the option of purchasing one Tein ID60 200 mm straight type spring for a sale price of $105.94; three at 5% off ($101.20 each), five at 9% off ($96.46 each), and so on.

They offer complementary services as a bundle
With this tactic, companies bundle a variety of complementary services into one main service. For instance, when you bring your car in for an oil change, some companies not only will change the oil and oil filter, but also will inspect your brake fluid level and engine air filtration system, fill your tires, vacuum the interior, and check a number of other components pertaining to your car. Many times customers are unaware of all the other services the company is providing, but they are all bundled into the final price.

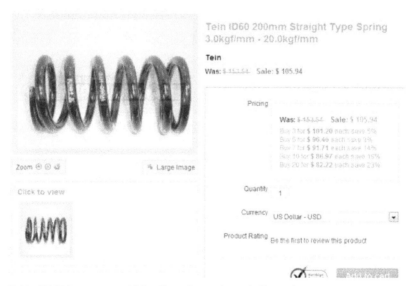

Figure 7-10. *RHDJapan.com, which offers discounts on bulk purchases*

Freebie Marketing

Most people relish the idea of getting a free item. Offering free items is a very useful tactic to get people to "notice" your company. An up-and-coming PR company recently sent our office a bouquet of cookies as a way to market its services—and I definitely took notice. For a cost of only $20, this company stands a chance of drumming up more than $2,000 per month of business from our company, simply because of the memorable way in which it chose to market its services.

Using freebie marketing online to increase conversion

Several companies use freebie marketing online to increase conversion rates. For example, Comcast offers a free DVR to customers who sign on to receive the Comcast DVR service. The average wholesale price of the DVR is around $100, but the lifetime value of the DVR service is worth hundreds of dollars (depending on location); therefore, offering this free DVR quickly pays off for Comcast. Dish Network recently tried to top this by offering free HD for life to new customers. Clearly, for the freebie incentive to work, the company needs to have a monopoly on the freebie it is offering. HD channels, for example, are currently a hot commodity, and they cost a lot to access, so offering HD for free is a strong incentive. However, offering free samples of cologne with every purchase, which cosmetics store Sephora does, is not an example of a strong incentive. You can pick up free samples of cologne in lots of stores, so this incentive does not add any value for the customer.

Ideeli.com, the members-only company mentioned earlier in this chapter, offers many "free giveaway" incentives. To celebrate its third anniversary, the company offered three lucky customers a $1,000 shopping spree. Not only did this help to increase conversions, it also enhanced customer loyalty. And because Ideeli.com is constantly giving "freebies" away, users are logging on to the site regularly to participate in the giveaways and contests.

A recent client of ours, SwissOutpost.com, offered a freebie incentive of a Swiss Army LED Microlight with any purchase on the site (see Figure 7-11). Most visitors considered the incentive a nice free gift that they could enjoy. However, we found that to get their free gift, users had to follow specific steps not outlined on the main web page: they had to add the gift to their cart, and *then* continue shopping for more products on the site. This caused major FUDs. Users would see the incentive and choose items to purchase from the site, but when they viewed their cart before checking out, they would not see the incentive because they hadn't added it to their cart. As a result, they would abandon the site.

Figure 7-11. *A freebie incentive from SwissOutpost.com, which didn't work very well*

Ultimately, the decision of whether to offer freebies on your site depends on what you are trying to achieve. Sometimes spending hundreds of thousands of dollars for merchandise you will be giving away to customers in exchange for a large uplift in revenue makes financial sense. For service companies, sending small gifts or sweets to prospective clients as a way to market their service makes financial sense.

Of course, freebies that are given out with a contingency aren't always as effective as freebies that are given out with no questions asked. Many service companies offer free advice upfront (free estimates, etc.) just for contacting them. These service companies are well aware that every contact they receive results in two or three contracts, which compensates for any time they spend giving customers "free advice." So, for instance, if I want to get my roof shingled, I will likely contact only the companies that will give me free estimates and advice, and not the companies that will charge me for the consultation. Again, incentives are effective only when you fully understand your business processes and what you are trying to achieve as a result.

As a final example of the power of freebies, Gillette developed a razor that required replacement blades. As an incentive to customers who purchased the razor, Gillette offered to give them a set of free removable blades. However, customers would need to purchase more blades to continue using the razor. This long-term strategy paid off, allowing Gillette to gain loyal customers for years. Gillette distributed huge quantities of the blades for free, sending them as promotional gifts to customers and giving them away at stores and tradeshows.

Buy One, Get One Free

Whether you want to consider it a freebie or a bundled marketing strategy, a "buy one, get one free" incentive is popular with users, and it is particularly effective when users are still browsing but not quite invested in the purchase process. The beauty of this type of incentive is that if the user is at a grocery store, for example, and he sees a buy one, get one free incentive, he will often heed the offer and purchase the product, even though he may not need it immediately. For example, I know that if my husband goes shopping, he will return with a lot more than I need. Our refrigerator may be packed with chicken, but if he finds a good buy one, get one free deal, he will not hesitate to take advantage of it, since organic chicken is expensive and rarely goes down in price. Or if he finds a buy one, get one free offer for pop, he'll buy 10 bottles because he knows we will need it eventually, and he may not come across such a good deal in the future.

Behavioral Incentives

There is no way to know exactly how visitors will react to an incentive. You can speculate, or you can analyze market behaviors, trends, and personas to predict visitors' reactions. You can also conduct surveys to estimate visitors' responses, but you can never really know *for sure* what they will be. Therefore, companies have increasingly been creating incentives in response to customer behaviors on their sites. So, whether they insert cookies that track customers' visits and trends in shopping behavior, or they track when and how customers abandoned their site, companies can become far more intrusive online than offline.

Tracking Customer Behaviors

Hotel chains excel at tracking online customer behavior. Understanding customer buying patterns helps them map out when and where an incentive will appear to reel customers in. These incentives are time-sensitive, since customers aren't always ready to reserve a hotel room. They are based on customers' behaviors in terms of checking airfare for flights to a specific city, and when customers generally decide to make their reservations prior to traveling.

The banner ads on websites (see Figure 7-12) often are a result of knowing what you like to see and when you like to see it so that advertisers can better persuade visitors to buy from them. To succeed with this type of marketing, you must be subtle so that customers don't feel like you are being too intrusive.

Figure 7-12. *Banner ads that can appear on sites you visit, or even in your email, and not always coincidentally*

Abandoned Cart Incentives

Imagine you are debating whether to purchase a sweater from your favorite online store, but it's expensive, so you decide to abandon the transaction. Twelve hours later, you receive a phone call from the online store telling you that for the next 24 hours, you are eligible for a 15% discount on any purchase you make. You realize you can now buy your sweater for a discounted rate—and wow, what a company to actually call you so that you can take advantage of this great offer!

Companies employ this strategy when a user abandons a cart or stops the checkout process before completing a purchase. However, there's a catch to doing this—customers can learn behaviors based on the online store's actions as well. In our research, we found that many customers figured out rather quickly that every time they abandoned a site, they received a discount. So, even when they weren't planning to abandon a site, they did so purposely to get the call.

This type of incentive can still be used via email marketing campaigns, reminding users of their carts and possibly offering them a discount—if not for their use, then for making a referral or something similar. There has to be some sort of contingency so that customers don't take advantage of this.

How to Apply Incentives

Incentives are a great way to counter FUDs, reduce anxieties, relieve friction, and instill trust. As mentioned in Chapter 6, though, an overwhelming number of sites require users to enter a discount code rather than giving the customer the discount automatically. You can find this approach in brick-and-mortar stores as well, particularly in grocery stores. You must bring in a coupon, or become an affiliated member of the store, to receive the savings the store has listed.

Whether to offer incentives such as these is a business decision every company ends up making, and it comes down to the goals it is trying to achieve by offering the incentives. If the goal is to increase brand and store loyalty, it might not be such a bad idea to ask customers for a discount code or coupon that only members can receive. However, when it comes to moving merchandise, discount codes will only be an obstacle in the way of accomplishing that goal.

Typically, we've noticed that every time clients place the discount code box somewhere in the checkout process, their users abandon the site at a higher rate than usual. This is due to customer trends and behaviors: if they see the discount code box, they assume the store is offering some sort of sale that they are unaware of, so they begin to search the Internet for the discount code, which many times isn't published (since it's for members only). As a result, they abandon the sale. In this case, although you are trying to offer an incentive, you've instead lowered your sales and created more FUDs and anxieties.

Another issue arises when the discount code is difficult to locate. If you offer a discount code on your site, don't hide it from your customers. Remember, you want the shopping experience to be easy and enjoyable; making a discount code difficult to find and use results in the opposite.

Additional Tips for Using Incentives

You can maximize the effectiveness of incentives by doing the following:

Frame your incentives in a way that will appeal to the persona of your clients
> Remember that everything within your site is designed, created, and deployed with personas in mind. So, when utilizing incentives, you must offer something your clients are interested in.

Place incentives early in the site so that prospective buyers can see them
> Upon entering some sites, you can quickly see incentives they may offer in the form of sales, free shipping, or free subscriptions and downloads. Placing these incentives early on will help relieve some anxieties a visitor may feel upon entering the site.

Place additional incentives before the checkout process
> A great way to capitalize on the ability to generate additional sales is to offer incentives, promotions, and upgrades right before checkout. How you word these incentives is key to maximizing their effectiveness.

DON'T FORGET!

Incentives do not replace the groundwork for your site. Low conversion rates are not due to a lack of incentives offered on your site, but rather a lack of consideration to the other principles within the Conversion Framework.

CHAPTER EIGHT

Engagement

CAN YOU PIQUE YOUR CUSTOMERS' INTEREST IN YOUR SITE OVER YOUR COMPETITORS'?

Some stores change their inventory daily, and thereby keep customers engaged because they're giving them something new to see each time they shop. Other companies run frequent sales to keep their store on customers' radar. With so many options on the Web, however, it becomes difficult to continue to engage users' interest in your offering.

Restaurants face this issue every day because customers have so many dining options to choose from. How will you pique potential customers' interest? You can offer incentives, but incentives are not a long-term strategy, whereas engagement is. For instance, Red Lobster offers seasonal seafood options that customers can enjoy. The restaurant has shrimp, crab, and lobster "fests" throughout the year to engage customers and get them to stop in for a meal.

As you work to engage visitors, it is important to set specific key performance indicators (KPIs) to measure visitors' engagement. Measuring a return on engagement activities can be difficult, especially because some activities will take place outside of your website and in media over which you have little control.

Measuring the Effectiveness of Engagement

Several metrics can measure visitor engagement. Some of these metrics are internal to your website, so they are straightforward to measure; others will require visitors' engagement on outside platforms.

Internal Metrics

Internal metrics measure visitors' interaction on your website. These metrics are reported by your analytics program. Here are some examples:

Average time on site

In general, it is true that the longer visitors stay on your site, the more likely they will buy from you since they are engaged and invested. However, you must review your analytics and conduct usability studies to ensure that time spent on your site is a true reflection of engagement and not visitor confusion. We pointed out some of the issues that surround how analytics programs report the average time a visitor spends on a website, so you must keep in mind that this metric might not be very accurate.

Pages per visit

The number of pages visitors navigate to while on your website could be a good indicator of how engaged they are with your site. This metric will vary greatly based on the type of website you run. We generally find that for ecommerce websites, the average number of pages per visit will increase as the website conversion rate increases. Some of our customers report an average of 9 to 13 pages per visit. Content-based websites will report a greater number of pages per visit since the survival and success of these sites are based largely on the number of page views.

On-site social interaction

If your website uses social tools to engage visitors, such as blogs or forums, you should examine how visitors interact with these tools. Each tool has its own metrics that indicate how engaged visitors are. With forums, for example, you should track:

- The number of overall registrations

- The number of active users on the forum

- The number of active discussions

As you develop other tools to engage visitors, you must think about what metrics you should use to measure engagement.

Tool-specific metrics on the website

In many instances, websites provide mechanisms for visitors to share content on the site with others. Content-based websites such as news websites or blogs allow visitors to email stories or blog entries to others. Figure 8-1 shows two ways an ecommerce website allows visitors to share product information with their friends. Visitors can click the "Tell a friend" button, or share the information on social networks by using the "Share This" functionality. Regardless of the tools you provide to your visitors for sharing your content, it is important to track the use and effectiveness of these tools.

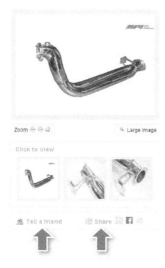

Figure 8-1. *The use of social tools to increase engagement*

External Metrics

The following are some of the external metrics you can use to track engagement:

The number of inbound links to your website

Links are the currency of the Web. The more *quality* links that point to your website, the more authority your website builds. Links are also a good indicator of how much a person was engaged by your website. People will link to content that moves them (in a positive or negative way). Several tools are available for tracking inbound links to a site, including Yahoo! Site Explorer (free), Open Site Explorer (a free version is available), and Majestic SEO.

The number of external mentions

With the advent of social media, a lot of the interaction and discussion regarding your business can occur away from your website. It is important to track these discussions and engage those who are involved.

Social Media

In the past decade, online tools have caused the idea of engagement to grow in popularity. Twitter, Facebook, and other social media outlets are the primary tools used today to engage customers. Although we've seen companies realize the importance of engagement through social media, they do not always put forth an effective strategy that considers their end goal and ROI.

Companies see that retailers are on Twitter, so they are too. Or they see that their competitors have Facebook accounts, so they must have one also. Throw up a blog and get social—it's as easy as one, two, three, right? Wrong. "Copying" your competitors will never yield positive results. Engagement through social media is a long-term strategy, and it requires time and investment in planning, executing, and tracking the engagement campaign. The ROI from these social media strategies won't disappoint—as long as you take the right steps.

Blogs

If you've attended social media-related seminars or conferences, you must have heard at least one person mention how easy it is to create a blog. There is some truth to this, since creating a blog is rather straightforward. However, merely creating a blog will not bring you a return on your investment.

It's great that you have a blog, but how focused is it on the topics that are important to your customers? What value will customers derive from it, and how will it lead to a conversion? Is the blog created to achieve a greater ROI by engaging customers, or does it serve another purpose? Are any visitors even reading your blog? You must answer all of these questions to create an effective strategy for a successful blog that is measurable and gives you a positive ROI.

You may want to achieve a number of goals with your blog. Most companies want to see some sort of ROI as a result. For example, some companies may create a blog simply to get links and increase their online visibility. They are using their blog as a search engine optimization (SEO) strategy. Other companies like to use their blog to engage customers and interest them further in their offerings. For instance, a clothing store may use a blog to feature specific clothing brands or lines to highlight their availability or special offers. It may offer tips on how to dress and the right makeup for specific outfits. This type of blog is used to "create a community" around the company, thus creating more loyalty, which yields more engaged customers.

The more time a user spends on your blog or the more pages he views, the more he is engaged. With blogs, you should track:

- The number of comments visitors leave
- The number of RSS subscribers using RSS readers

- The number of email subscribers to the email feed

- The number of email subscribers to different discussions

The most important issue to consider before creating a blog is the time involved. Time is required to plan a blog (topics, goals, writing) and to execute it.

Forums

Zappos.com recently created a subscription-based forum, Zappos Insights, which gives people advice and information on how to become successful business leaders, based on Zappos' success. Although this type of forum is not designed to gain more customers, it does keep people talking about Zappos and gives the appearance that the company has a leading strategy for business.

Crutchfield.com (see Figure 8-2), an online electronics store, gives members the option of discussing issues regarding specific products right on the site. It's all about bringing the discussion back to the company; users will discuss these things regardless, so the company might as well be in control of the discussion. For instance, if I'm debating which LCD TV to purchase, I can hop on to the Crutchfield.com forums and see what other customers are saying. Crutchfield has a ways to go toward incorporating this activity and relating it directly to its product offerings; however, it has certainly taken a step in that direction.

RHDJapan, the largest high-performance, original, and after-market equipment auto parts provider online, has created a community around its site with its MyRidez competition and discussions. Figure 8-3 displays the RHD MyRidez page. Not only does it recruit users to demonstrate how to install and upgrade vehicles, it has also made the page fun by asking users to submit photos of the finished vehicle and then offering a monthly prize to the winner after all user votes are submitted. This type of forum can yield a lot of activity and engagement. It has also created a means to get useful information to users about specific products and auto parts installations.

Other sites try to use forums to start a discussion about a specific brand. Ideeli.com, shown in Figure 8-4, starts a forum discussion for every "sale" it generates. The sales offered on the site are generally a specific collection for a designer. Users can ask questions and get answers from specialists, as well as other customers, about the designer and the products offered in that particular sale.

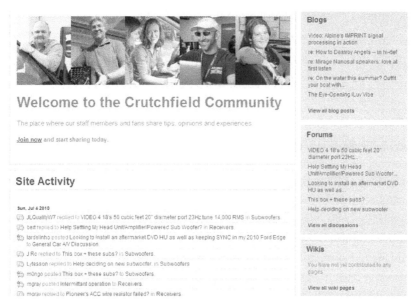

Figure 8-2. *The Crutchfield forum*

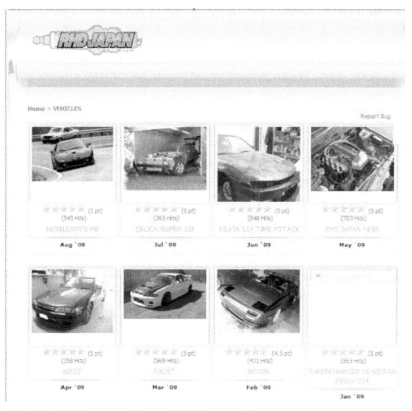

Figure 8-3. *The MyRidez competition and RHD community*

Figure 8-4. *The Ideeli.com forum, which allows users to discuss products in a particular category*

Facebook

It is difficult to ignore the importance of Facebook and its hundreds of millions of users. To measure engagement on Facebook, you should track:

- The number of fans (subscribers) to your Facebook page

- The number of daily or weekly visits to your fan page

- The number of mentions of your business or fan page

Facebook, like any social media website, will broaden your company's reach and access if you use it correctly. It also helps further your interaction with users. Like with any social media activity, Facebook will help keep your company current. It's important, however, to see who in your target market uses Facebook (by looking at Facebook demographics information and trends), which will help you understand how to position your Facebook page. For example, some service companies are well aware that their target market is not on Facebook (or will not use Facebook to search for them), so they use their Facebook page to provide information and to connect people in the industry. On the other hand, a specialty gifts ecommerce store, for example, may find that its target market is present on Facebook and ready to make a purchase, so this store uses its Facebook page to display best-selling items, further engaging and persuading users to make a purchase.

Twitter

Twitter has taken the social media world by storm. Almost every major retailer has a Twitter account. Figure 8-5 shows the Twitter page for Nordstrom. However, much like blogs, merely having an account with thousands upon thousands of followers can be meaningless if you do not have a strategy for how to convert or benefit from this activity.

Twitter allows customers to have an almost direct connection with a company; this helps users' complaints be heard more effectively, and it enables companies to do some immediate damage control in the event of negative chatter. Twitter is also effective for promoting deals and special incentives.

Figure 8-5. *Nordstrom's Twitter page*

To measure engagement on Twitter, you should track:

- The number of Twitter followers

- The number of retweets your account receives

- The number of mentions your business receives

Customer Reviews

The power of selling through the testimony of other customers is unrivaled. Depending on the product, customer reviews can help persuade users to move forward with a purchase. Customer reviews are considered an engagement tool because of their effectiveness in *keeping the customer online*. Amazon.com is known for its use of customer reviews for the majority of products on the site. As visitors come to your site to see what others have to say about your products, they may opt to purchase the product from you. Now, we cannot all become Amazon.com, but you can help engage your users by providing reviews for most of your products so that users don't have to search other sites to read reviews.

Negative Reviews Are Important

Too many companies believe that negative reviews are no good, but they are actually helpful in increasing conversion rates. Although negative reviews highlight what is wrong with a product, they also increase visitors' confidence in how authentic the reviews are. Visitors have more trust in products that have received some negative reviews than they do in products that have received only positive reviews.

Think of the last time you thought about trying a new restaurant. What if, prior to heading out the door, you went online and read reviews for the restaurant. If the restaurant received negative reviews that describe it as a dirty place that serves terrible food, you most likely would not go. However, if the negative reviews describe it as a restaurant with great food but dated décor, they would probably not stop you from eating there.

Negative reviews are also useful for improving whatever product or service you offer. By understanding customers' pain points with your offering, you can continuously improve and evolve it. Figure 8-6 is an example of how Amazon.com displays negative reviews.

Figure 8-6. *Negative reviews on Amazon.com*

Gathering reviews for the different products on your website will take time. You can start gathering reviews by:

- Sending follow-up emails to customers who purchased a given product and asking them to provide feedback

- Offering discounts to encourage customers to write reviews of products they purchased

- Incorporating product reviews from other websites onto your own site by utilizing a service such as ProductWiki.com

Finally, until you have enough reviews on the site, we recommend not taking up prime real estate on the page with an element that indicates there are no reviews yet (see Figure 8-7).

Figure 8-7. *No reviews yet on a product page*

Cross-Sells and Upsells

Increasing the average order value is one way that many retailers have been able to increase their online revenue. By understanding customers' buying intents, retailers can display complementary or similar items as *cross-sells* or *upsells* on the page. Cross-sells are items that are complementary to the product selected, whereas upsells are products that are similar to but more expensive than the product selected.

Three factors contribute to the success of cross-sells and upsells: how they are displayed, how easy they are to access, and where they are located on a page or within a buying process. As we discussed in Chapter 7, some companies bundle multiple items into one package (i.e., purchasing eyeliner, eye shadow, and mascara together is far less expensive than purchasing each product on its own) to encourage customers to purchase the cross-sells. Other companies sell multiple units of the same product (bundles) at discounts that increase as the number of units increase (upsell). An excellent example of this is 1800Contacts.com (see Figure 8-8), which sells one contact lens pack for $29.99 and a 12-pack bundle for $335.88 (equal to $27.99 per pack).

Figure 8-8. *Upsell example from 1800Contacts.com*

Upsells Versus Cross-Sells

As we mentioned before, the main difference between upsells and cross-sells is that cross-sells offer items that complement the product being considered, whereas upsells are the same type of product but at a greater cost.

Whether you should offer cross-sells or upsells or both will depend on what you are selling. Some items lend themselves nicely to cross-sells. For example, clothing stores typically cross-sell; they may show a sweater along with a scarf that complements the sweater, since a shopper looking for a sweater may also be interested in a scarf that goes well with it.

Other items that can be upgraded for an increase in price lend themselves nicely to upsells. Companies that sell gifts and flowers use upsells heavily. For example, Figure 8-9 shows a page from the Harry & David website that highlights a $30 box of chocolate truffles. As an upsell, customers can "Go Deluxe" and purchase the Moose Munch Party Drum, which contains an assortment of goodies, for only $9 more. By upselling in this way, Harry & David increases its average order value.

Anticipating what the user will want to buy is crucial when considering an upsell strategy. That's why companies display best sellers in different categories, or show what other items are usually purchased with a particular item.

Figure 8-9. *Upsell on the Harry & David website*

Placing Cross-Sells and Upsells

We have seen cross-sells and upsells on all the pages throughout a site. Before you do this on your site, it is important that you understand the objective you are trying to achieve without overshadowing other, more important objectives on the site.

Product page

Figure 8-10 shows how Newport-News.com displays a cross-sell on the righthand panel of a product page. Although this tactic shows users some items that complement the main item on the page, it may also impact their decision to buy because it interferes with the main objective of the product page: adding an item to the cart. This point came up recently with a client of ours. We were discussing rearranging elements on a page, which ultimately would push the cross-sell section on the page below the fold. Our main objective was to get users to "add to cart," not to highlight the cross-sells. Remember, although cross-sells are a wonderful tool, they should never supersede the goal of the page.

Figure 8-10. *Cross-sells on the righthand panel of a product page*

Another important aspect of using cross-sells and upsells on a product page is whether users can add the cross-sell or upsell item immediately to their cart. With upsells, users have the option to upgrade directly from the page they are currently on, but with cross-sells, users must navigate from the product page they're on to a new product page. This may result in greater site abandonment. Some sites have mitigated this limitation by offering users the option to add the cross-sell without having to navigate away from the main product page. Figure 8-11 shows how visitors to Gymboree.com can "Complete the Look!" and add cross-sells immediately to their cart.

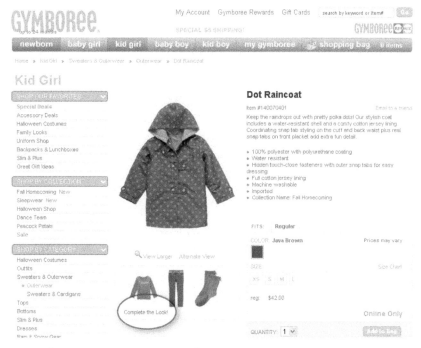

Figure 8-11. *Easy access to cross-sells on Gymboree.com*

Shopping cart page

The process of selling online, much like that of selling offline, must be restrained. So, an online store that employs annoying pop ups that continually try to sell items to site visitors can have a negative impact on those visitors. The same is true of shopping cart cross-sells. Many sites find the shopping cart to be an opportune place to promote their products further, and therefore sell more. Figure 8-12 shows how Newport-News.com uses cross-sells on its cart page. However, we feel this use of cross-sells goes too far. We discourage the use of shopping cart cross-sells for the following reasons:

- Once the user is on the shopping cart page, she is pretty much ready to buy. As we often encourage customers to remove distracting elements such as the lefthand navigation panel from the cart, we also encourage them to remove cross-sells, which compete directly with the user's decision to proceed to checkout.

- Cross-sells on the cart page are not as relevant to cross-sells on a product page. Cross-sells work on a product page because they relate directly to the product in question. Upsells have been successful on the cart page for upgrading purposes.

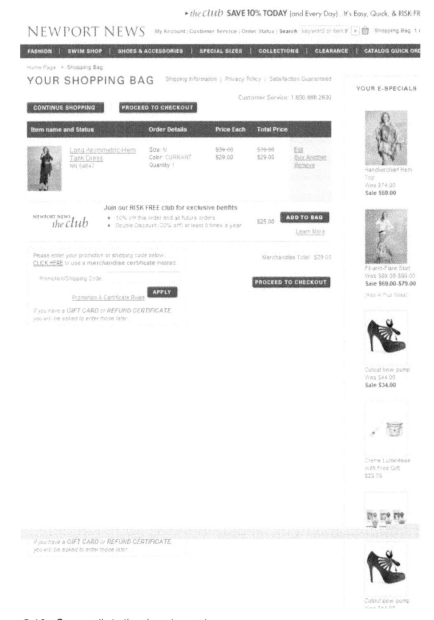

Figure 8-12. *Cross-sells in the shopping cart*

Customer Feedback Tools

The best way to understand your customers' motivations and needs is to get this information directly from them. An added benefit of asking for customer feedback is that doing so engages your customers and lets them know you truly care. With some companies, the customer feedback tool appears when users exit the site without making a purchase so that they can better understand why. With other companies, the tool appears after users have made a purchase so that they can understand what these users enjoyed and what persuaded them to buy. However, most companies make their customer feedback tool accessible via an icon that appears on the lower-left corner of the page, and the user can click on it at any time to give feedback about the site.

Of course, customer feedback is most useful when compiled and analyzed across various customer demographic, geographic, and socioeconomic levels. Insights from feedback analysis can provide a wealth of information regarding ways to enhance the site with specific personas in mind and addressing specific customer pain points.

Informational Videos

YouTube has become the hub for tutorials and informative videos about products and services. But what if you could bring that discussion to your site? Again, engage your customers by understanding what they need. Skis.com, shown in Figure 8-13, realized early on that some customers did not understand the difference between certain types of skis, and had other questions about using their products. So, the company created several videos informing users about its products and addressing some of their main questions. Skis.com realized that a more informed user is a better potential customer. By providing the information users sought, instead of allowing them to navigate away from the site to search for the information, Skis.com engaged its users and increased its business tremendously.

Figure 8-13. *Skis.com's use of video to inform users of its products*

Another engagement tool that is related to videos and has gained some traction in recent years is video spokespeople. As a conversion optimization company, Invesp has never been a fan of this tool, although companies have succeeded in implementing it. A company would use a video spokesperson to explain its product or service in an engaging way and point out areas of interest or facts pertaining to the product or service. However, one of our clients deployed video spokespeople on their brand pages to explain the brand to users, and they were shocked by the results (but we weren't): they experienced a 19.2% decrease in conversion rate after running the test for more than a month. Customers complained that the video spokespeople were annoying, and customers also did not appreciate the information they received. However, it's important to note that with some sites catering to the services industry, such as consulting, video spokespeople have proven to be minimally successful.

Virtual Closets

Most customers want to "try clothes on" before buying, because the last thing they want is to have to return their purchases. This is more of an issue online than offline, because online you can completely miscalculate the way a garment will look on you. Virtual closets give users the flexibility of virtually trying on clothing. The user enters data such as her body type, measurements, weight, and height, and special software provides her with a virtual reflection of her body. Once she chooses an article of clothing she's interested in, the tool mimics how the article would look on her based on the body description she provided, allowing her to gauge whether the piece works for her. Of course, the technology isn't quite there yet, but if it becomes successful, it could address the needs of the many shoppers who refuse to purchase clothes online because they fear the clothing will not look right or fit properly.

Virtual Help

Whether you're shopping online or offline, you want someone to be available if you need help. This is why many online companies are providing virtual help (see Figure 8-14) to answer users' questions, and thus get them engaged and motivated to move forward in the buying funnel. However, virtual help is an engagement tool that must be measured. The extent to which the virtual help pop ups are intrusive, actually provide help to users, and even whether they are placed effectively, all play a role in how successful this engagement tool will be. Who wants a nagging salesperson continually pestering you to see if you need help? Remember, providing a little help for the user, and letting him know you are only a click away, goes a long way.

Figure 8-14. *The use of virtual help as a way to engage visitors*

Ultimately, virtual help is only one type of engagement tool, and it is only as successful as the strategy and measurement that defines it. Indeed, engagement manifests itself in many different ways on a website. Once a company can successfully track each aspect of its users' engagement with its site, it will be able to modify and measure the impact of the engagement tools it uses.

CHAPTER NINE

Testing: The Voice of Visitors

EVERY WEBSITE IS DIFFERENT. What works for one website may or may not work for yours.

Best practices are great in theory, but difficult in practice. Team members often disagree on the best website or landing page design, the best visitor flow, or the best sales. Stakeholders usually have different opinions of what changes you should make to your website.

Resolving these differences is challenging. You should judge the quality of any change that you make to your website or sales process based on its impact to your bottom line in both the short and long terms. We are always looking for designs that persuade more visitors to convert. So, how do you make that determination? How do you measure the impact a particular change to your sales funnel will have on your conversion rate? You must test any modifications you introduce to your website and compare your new conversion rate to your previous conversion rate.

Direct mail marketing companies have been testing the impact of different mailers on conversions for more than 40 years. Before running a large national direct mail campaign, a marketing company usually prepares several versions of the mailer that include variations in design, copy, elements, and so forth. The company then sends the mailers to different target prospects and monitors the results. The mailer that generates the best response is the one it will use in its national campaign.

Testing software allows you to do the same online. By testing variations of a page against one other, you can observe which designs result in higher conversions. Usually you would do this after you've created the page variations, using the software to direct a percentage of visitors to each variation and then comparing different key metrics for each page. For example, testing software allows you to determine which of two main home page designs is better for conversion. If the main home page receives 15,000 visitors per day, the software can direct 7,500 visitors to one design and 7,500 visitors to the other design. The software will then record which of the two designs generated more orders. By monitoring visitors' reactions to each design and reporting the different metrics on each design, you can decide which design to keep and which to toss.

Testing gives your visitors a voice in the design process. It allows you to determine what works for visitors and what does not. When implemented correctly, testing removes the guesswork from conversion optimization. It resolves many of the political battles organizations have when designing a website. Many companies paid little attention to conversion optimization or testing prior to 2005. There has been a large shift in thinking since then. Two main factors changed how marketers perceive the value of conversion optimization:

The release of Google Website Optimizer
> In October 2006, Google announced the release of its website testing tool, Google Website Optimizer. Although the tool is less powerful than some of its commercial counterparts, it allows most websites to introduce testing into their online marketing initiatives.

The recession of 2009
> As the economy tanked in 2009, many online marketers had to find new ways to convert their existing traffic into revenue. So, although visitors still mattered, conversions mattered even more.

Chapters 3 through 8 introduced the principles of the Conversion Framework that guide how a visitor interacts with your website. Each of these elements impacts whether a visitor is persuaded to stay on your website and ultimately convert, or whether he leaves. The seventh element of the Conversion Framework asks you to test any change you make against the original design. By doing so, you can determine the impact these changes have on your bottom line.

The Basics of Testing

You can deploy two types of tests on a website. Each will vary in terms of the investment required for deployment, the complexity, and the type of data required before concluding. When testing, we are always looking for a design that "works best." How a design works best is different from one situation to the next. In some instances, you may be looking for a design that generates more orders. In other instances, you might be looking for a design that keeps visitors more engaged. We will refer to the better design as the one that creates more conversions.

A/B Tests

A/B tests allow you to test a baseline design against one or more variations to determine which one converts more. If you are testing more than two designs, you are conducting an *A/B/N test*.

Figure 9-1 shows how A/B testing software works. In this example, the original page receives 100,000 visitors. When testing a second version of the page, the testing software directs 50,000 visitors to the original design and 50,000 visitors to the new design. The software tracks which design persuades visitors to convert. If one design results in more visitors converting, that is the winning design.

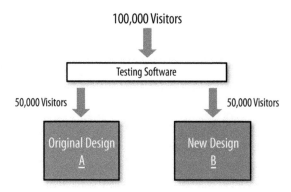

Figure 9-1. *How A/B testing software works*

Figure 9-2 shows the original category page design for one of our clients in an A/B test. Figure 9-3 shows the second version of the category page in the same test. The goal of this test was to increase the click-through rate (CTR) from the category page to the product page. Version B (Figure 9-3) increased the CTR to the product page by 40% compared to Version A.

Figure 9-2. *Original category page design*

Figure 9-3. *New category page design*

Multivariate Tests

Multivariate tests are designed to test multiple elements of a *single* page at the same time. Using testing software, you can test different headlines, images, buttons, or any other elements on a page to measure their impact on your conversion rates.

Figure 9-4 shows how multivariate testing software works. We used the software to test different variations of the page headline, the main image, and the call-to-action button on a page. The software tested:

- The original headline against three other possible headlines, for a total of four possible headlines

- The original image against two other possible images, for a total of three possible images

- The original call-to-action button against three other possible buttons, for a total of four possible call-to-action buttons

This resulted in 48 variations for that one page. The total number of testing scenarios depends on the number of elements you will test on the page (headline, image, buttons, etc.) and the number of variations you will test for each element. You calculate the total number of scenarios by multiplying the number of variations for each element.

The number of scenarios or variations can grow very quickly. Some software allows you to test millions of variations of a single page. We do not like such large-scale experiments for reasons we will address throughout this chapter.

As a visitor arrives at a page, the software displays one of the four headlines, one of the three images, and one of the four call-to-action buttons. Figure 9-5 shows four of the possible 48 designs the software created. Your team does not have to create all 48 designs; the software will swap the different variations and create the designs automatically.

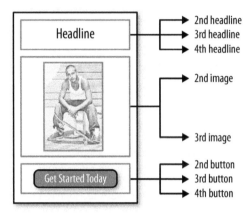

Figure 9-4. *How multivariate testing software works*

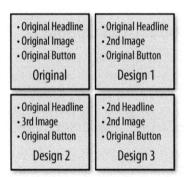

Figure 9-5. *Variations using multivariate testing software*

—— **DON'T FORGET!** ————————————————————————————

- Although it may seem like testing different elements on one page (multivariate test) is less complex than testing one or more pages against one other (A/B test), in most cases the opposite is true. This is especially the case when testing software is used with dynamic websites to insert different variations of elements.
- You can always think of a multivariate test as a specialized form of A/B test.

What Type of Test Should You Conduct?

Should you start with an A/B test or a multivariate test for a particular page? There is no universal answer to this question. A/B tests are good for testing alternative designs of an entire page or process. They are very helpful in determining which high-level changes have the most impact on visitors. Multivariate tests allow for granular testing of a page. They are helpful in determining which elements have the most impact on visitors.

If you have a brand-new page or a limited number of visitors or conversions, we recommend starting with an A/B test. This will let you test major design changes. If you already have an existing page, we recommend starting with a small multivariate test (fewer than 12 different scenarios). The goal of this initial test is to determine which elements (headline, image, benefit list, etc.) resonate most with visitors. Analysis of the first test results will help guide the need for further multivariate or A/B tests.

A successful test starts with a good plan. Consider each of the following elements when creating your first test:

Determine which pages are good candidates for optimization

Most analysis focuses on pages with high bounce and exit rates. This is a simplistic approach to a complex problem and rarely yields significant increases in overall conversion rates.

The number of visitors who will go through the test impacts how quickly the test will conclude

Although your site may have 300,000 visitors per month, a particular test page may receive far fewer visitors during that time. Your goal is to run the tests for fewer than six weeks.

The number of conversions impacts how quickly the test will conclude

With most testing software, you will need a minimum of 200 conversions per month for the test to conclude within the same period.

Pick the right conversion page

Not every test should have the goal of increasing the macro conversion rate. Many successful tests help to increase micro conversion rates. This is particularly important if your website or landing page does not receive enough conversions. Starting out with micro conversion tests allows you to still conduct tests on a smaller scale.

Examine what elements you should test

Not all elements on a page will have the same impact on your conversion rate. Determine which elements will have the most impact on your bottom line based on marketing data, personas, and analytics.

Creating a Successful Test

Tools are useless without people who can properly run them. Most testing software allows marketers to create and start simple tests in a few hours. But that is the easy part. Designing successful test scenarios, assessing results, and creating meaningful follow-up tests are ultimately where many companies fail.

Poorly designed experiments can take years to complete. Even worse, they might not provide concrete insights to which elements will convert more visitors into customers. Imagine a case where you plan to test different headlines on a page. You start by coming up with 10 possible headline variations. What criteria are you going to use to determine which headlines you should test? Why not test all 10? You will most likely find yourself relying on guesswork to determine which versions to include in the test. The same logic, of course, applies to all the elements you want to test on the page. Without being judicious with test scenarios, we have seen clients attempt to test millions of combinations.

Testing is only one important component of any optimization project. It should take place after you have completed other, equally important stages of optimization work, such as persona development, site analysis, and design and copy creation. Each of these elements provides a building block toward a highly optimized website that converts visitors into clients.

Test Hypotheses

Successful testing starts by creating different hypotheses to explain why visitors react to certain elements on a page. You then use your tests to validate the hypotheses. So, how do you come up with the different hypotheses to test? In our practice, we use the elements of the Conversion Framework (trust, FUDs, incentives, etc.) to create the different hypotheses. This approach guides our testing work with every client and removes the guesswork from the process.

Figure 9-6 shows the original design of a shopping cart for one of our clients that sold nursing uniforms. When our team examined the analytics data for the client, we noticed the high checkout abandonment rates. Abandonment rates for unoptimized checkout are usually anywhere from 45% to 80%. This client reported checkout abandonment rates close to 82%. Nothing in the checkout explained this above-average abandonment rate. The team then conducted a usability test. Nurses were invited to place an order with the site while the optimization team observed and conducted exit interviews to gather information from participants. The nurses revealed that the biggest problem that caused them to abandon the site was their fear of paying too much for an item. Nurses are price-conscious, and they can buy the same item from other competing websites or brick-and-mortar stores. So, price was a big factor in deciding where to buy a uniform. Our client was aware of nurses' price sensitivity. The client offered a money-back guarantee and a 100% price-match guarantee. The problem was that most of the site visitors landed on category and product pages first, and the company's price assurances were only displayed on the home page. Therefore, most visitors knew nothing about these assurances.

The hypothesis for this test was as follows: online visitors are sensitive to price, so adding assurances can counter the FUDs the visitors have due to price concerns. Figure 9-7 shows the new design for the shopping cart. The team added an "assurance center" on the cart page's righthand navigation panel reminding visitors of the 100% price match and the money-back guarantee. The new version of the page resulted in a 30% reduction in shopping cart abandonment.

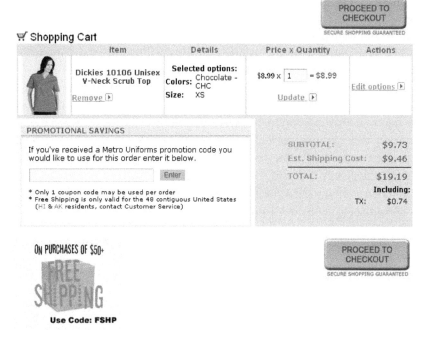

Figure 9-6. *Original shopping cart design for site selling nurses' uniforms, without assurance center*

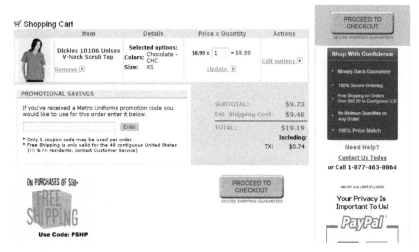

Figure 9-7. *Shopping cart redesign for site shown in Figure 9-6, with assurance center*

It's important to note that a hypothesis that works for one website may not succeed, or even worse, may deliver negative results for another site. After the results of the aforementioned client were published in the Internet Retailer online magazine, another client approached us to test an assurance center on their site. This client was also looking for a way to reduce their cart abandonment rate. Figure 9-8 shows the original design of their shopping cart. Figure 9-9 shows the new design with the assurance center added to the righthand navigation panel. Again, this test had the same hypothesis as the previous one, that most online visitors did not convert on the site due to the price FUD and that adding assurances to the cart page will ease shoppers' concerns. When we tested the new version with the assurance center against the old version, however, we received completely different results. The new assurance center caused the website conversion rate to drop by 4%. So, although the assurance center helped the first client, it produced a negative impact for the second client.

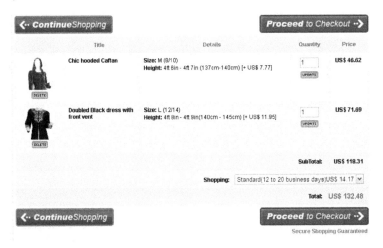

Figure 9-8. *Original shopping cart design, without assurance center*

Figure 9-9. *Shopping cart redesign for site shown in Figure 9-8, with assurance center—but resulting in a 4% conversion rate drop*

Can we say with absolute certainty that adding an assurance center for this client will always produce negative results? No. Several elements could have influenced this particular design and caused the drop in conversion rate. For instance, the assurance center design, copy, or location could have caused the drop. Analyzing how a hypothesis is validated through testing data and creating a follow-up hypothesis is at the heart of conversion optimization. In this case, we needed to test many different elements around the assurance center before we could determine its impact on conversions.

Tests that produce increases in conversion rates are excellent in terms of validating initial assumptions and hypotheses. We do not mind tests that result in reduced conversion rates because we can learn something about our hypotheses from these tests. It is tests that do not produce any increases or decreases in conversion rates that we worry about.

Length of Time to Complete an Experiment

Two factors can impact your conversion rate. These are:

- Internal factors that you can control, such as your design, messaging, copy, and so on.

- External factors over which you have little control. For example, when a competitor runs a large sale, your conversion rates can suffer. If the economy gets worse, you can expect your conversion rates to suffer as well.

Successful testing requires that you pay close attention to external factors. And although you have no real way to control these factors, you should attempt to minimize the time it takes to run your experiments. The less time it takes to run tests, the fewer chances external factors have to influence your test results.

─── **DON'T FORGET!** ─────────────────────────────

When conducting online tests, your goal is to arrive at statistically valid results in the shortest possible time. If you are not careful when designing your test experiments, you will have to run test scenarios for years to come. Pay close attention to create tests that conclude within six weeks.

───

Forty-Nine Things You Can Test on Your Website

As mentioned, you can test a number of elements on your website. In the subsections that follow we discuss the 49 things you should test across your website. We have discussed some of these elements in different sections in the book, but we are including them all here for easy reference.

The Basic Website Elements

1. The header

Too many companies slap too much information into the header. Is your header crowded with information? How much information are you presenting to the user? We consistently find that clean and well-organized headers work best. Figure 9-10 shows the Frys.com header. The header is crowded with information that can overwhelm visitors. Compare this to Figure 9-11, the header for NewEgg.com, which carefully uses white space.

Figure 9-10. *Crowded header on Frys.com*

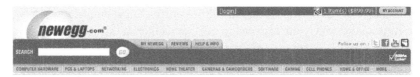

Figure 9-11. *Header with breathing space on NewEgg.com*

2. The tagline

A good tagline that communicates your value proposition will have an impact on your conversion rate. Test different taglines to see which resonates best with your visitors. A word about taglines: think of something unique about your business. It is rare for excellent customer service or lower price to make a good tagline.

3. The search box

With most ecommerce stores, you can expect 15% to 25% of visitors to rely on the search box for navigation. Some online stores, such as auto parts websites, report higher percentages of visitors using the search functionality (close to 40%). Placing the search box in a prominent location will encourage visitors to use the search tool. We recommend testing different placements and sizes of search box. Figure 9-12 shows search boxes on BestBuy.com, CompUSA.com, and Buy.com.

Figure 9-12. *Search boxes on BestBuy.com, CompUSA.com, and Buy.com*

4. Site navigation

Many ecommerce stores fail to pay attention to navigation. Even worse, many stores let their technical teams and engineers determine the site navigation. Site navigation is designed to help users find what they are looking for quickly, so a good scheme should be focused on visitors and the tasks they complete on your website. We recommend investing the time to test different categorization schemes and their impact on conversion rates.

Start by testing multiple navigations for your website with the product page as the conversion page (micro tests). This will allow you to determine which of these navigations helps visitors find their way to the product page more effectively.

5. Hero images

Visitors will most often look at the image first when scanning a landing page. This image can make the difference between whether visitors stay on your site or leave. The most important criterion for choosing an image is its relevance to the product or service being promoted. If you are selling widgets, a great shot of the widget will show your customers precisely what they will get. If a product shot is not appropriate, your image should tie in with any creative or graphic design elements that were used in the advertising that got the visitors to your page.

Images must connect with a value proposition. They also need to be considered from the perspective of personas. A client that sold communication devices displayed an image of nature scenes on their landing page to communicate that their product can be used anywhere and at any time. This did not work for visitors, since they all happened to be busy businesspeople who needed a better reason to purchase the product. We tested an image of a person in an airport using the device against the original image of nature scenes. The new image improved the conversion rate by 34%.

6. Supporting images

You can use other graphic elements, besides the main image, to help convey your message. If your site offers technical information, perhaps a chart or graph can get your point across easily. These supporting images should not overpower the other elements on the page or distract visitors from the path to conversion. With supporting images, you should test:

- Different variations of the images
- Different locations for the images

7. Testimonials

Testimonials are a great asset to help you "seal the deal." Caring and competitive personalities are impacted by the number of people praising your company for exceptional service, great customer care, or wonderful products. It's in our nature to be impacted by words of praise, especially when they come from well-known people. Celebrity testimonials about the acne treatment cream Proactiv have created buzz and excitement, but most importantly, have increased conversions for the product. If a well-known authority has praised your product or service, make sure you flaunt it. For other testimonials or reviews, include a picture of the reviewer, his full name, and possibly his state of residence for authenticity purposes. User testimonials should speak of the benefits of your services and be relevant to your target audience. Visitors will regard testimonials that lack identification with a bit of skepticism. Therefore, it is vital that testimonials are genuine, descriptive, brief, and convincing. With testimonials, you should test the following:

- Placing the testimonials on different pages of the site (home page, landing pages, checkout process)
- Different locations for the testimonial on a particular page
- Different designs for the testimonial (different layouts)
- Information provided in the testimonial (name of person, location, company)

8. Video spokesperson

More websites are now displaying a video spokesperson when visitors land on the site. This spokesperson introduces the website and its services to visitors. Our testing of this feature showed different results for different clients. The majority of our clients did not see any significant improvement as a result of using this feature. In contrast, in a study conducted by Coremetrics and cited on the MarketingVOX blog, experts found "a 35% increase in sales conversions." The videos kept the visitors engaged so much that they spent an average of "2.5 minutes on a particular product." If you plan to introduce this feature, you should test the following three variations:

- Landing page with no video

- Landing page with video playing immediately when the visitor lands on the page

- Landing page with video available to the visitor, but not playing immediately

9. Lead generation forms

Lead generation websites rely on online forms to capture visitor information. Asking visitors to fill out these forms with information that could be captured later will lower your conversion rate. These forms should be as quick and as easy as possible for visitors to fill out. The less time users must spend on your conversion activity, the less time they have to change their mind. Also, never put a "clear form" button next to a "submit" button. You should focus on capturing only the information that is absolutely essential. Test the following with lead generation forms:

- Have the input cursor jump to the next field in the form on its own.

- Pre-populate some of the form fields if possible.

- Reduce the number of fields that need to be filled out (use one field for the visitor's name instead of one each for first and last names).

- Do not ask for a user's city and state if she already entered her zip code.

- Don't ask for fax numbers, as they are generally obsolete for public facing promotions.

10. Distraction test

Too often, marketing staff try to get extra mileage from landing pages. The thinking is, "We got them to the landing page for this promotion, so why not give them a link to our other products too?" The focus of your design is conversion, so anything that diverts your visitor from this is detrimental to your goal. If visitors to your landing page are distracted, they may lose focus and not take the desired action. Landing pages should be specific. There is one and only one topic of interest on your landing page, and anything else should be removed. Identify the top three distraction elements on your page (information, pictures, or items that may sidetrack your visitors), and test the page without these elements.

FUD Tests

Chapter 6 outlined the principles you should pay attention to when designing your website or campaign. Visitors fear giving out personal information because they do not know you. How can you get potential customers to trust you without ever meeting them?

11. Privacy

Assure your customers that their privacy is important to you and will be well protected. Make sure your privacy policy is clear, and easy to understand and locate. Let visitors know that you have taken the time to create safeguards that protect their information. Try placing a link to your privacy policy, an icon that shows precautions have been taken, or a simple statement, such as "Your privacy is important to us," close to the fields where you want customers to enter personal information.

12. Satisfaction guaranteed

Consider testing different types of warranties for products or trial periods for services. For example, you can give visitors 30 days to try your product risk-free; after that period, if they are not satisfied, they can get a full refund. You may also test free consultations so new clients can get a feel for your services without spending any money. This will encourage visitors to convert because their risks are reduced. Make sure visitors to your site can easily see and understand your warranty or satisfaction policy.

13. Social proof

Positive media coverage, industry certifications, awards, Better Business Bureau membership, and compliance with standards are all great elements that can impact conversion. So, include anything a prospect would recognize as being characteristic of a reliable organization.

General Layout Tests

The *fold* is the point on a web page where scrolling is required to view additional content. If visitors have to scroll down to get all the information from your landing page, especially the call to action, you may lose them. Therefore, it is important to know where the fold will fall. Unfortunately, this is an inexact science, as different browsers and different screen resolutions will place the fold at different points on your page.

14. Above the fold

Design your page for the lowest common denominator, which is generally accepted by web designers to be a screen resolution of 1024×768. Designing your page for this format will mean that only a handful of visitors (those still using monitors with a resolution of 800×600—fewer than 3% of PC owners, and shrinking) will need to scroll. Remember, although the screen may be 1024×768, your page design needs to be a little smaller to account for the title, menu bars, and frames of common browsers. This means the size of your page should be no more than 950×750. Many of your visitors will not scroll, regardless of how important or pertinent the information is below the fold. It is imperative that you place a call to action above the fold to capture the nonscrollers.

15. Below the fold

Sometimes, due to the nature of your message, it is necessary to place content below the fold. If this will improve conversion rates, don't hesitate to do it. Indeed, visitors will scroll before they click on a link to another page. If you have too much information to fit comfortably on a single page, allow users to scroll rather than click to it. Depending on the length of your page, you may need to place your call to action in more than one position. A rule of thumb is to have a call to action for every "screen," or about every 400 to 500 lines of vertical resolution.

16. The visitor's view of your page

Keep the most important items (graphics, text, etc.) in the center of the viewer's line of sight. This should be the focal point of the page. Do not allow items on the sidebars to take attention away from this focus. Your message should be conspicuous so that readers who scan the web page will get it. A quick glance at your landing page should be enough for someone to know what you are offering.

17. The call to action

Regardless of its purpose, the call to action needs to be clear on your page. Along with the headline, images, and body copy, the call to action should be distinct and easily identifiable. Using a quick tagline within your call to action, succinctly indicating what action is expected, will help it stand out. Examples include "Buy Now," "Email to a Friend," and "Register Here."

We recommend that our clients at least test the following elements for call-to-action buttons:

Color

> If you have multiple buttons on the page, make sure the call-to-action button for the primary purpose of the page stands out from the rest of the buttons.

Placement

> The rule of thumb here is to place the call-to-action button above the fold. In terms of a long copy page, make sure your call-to-action button is visible with every page down scroll. This usually translates to every 400 to 500 lines, as stated earlier.

Wording

> The standard wording of "Submit" on a call-to-action button will generally have a negative impact on your conversion rates. We recommend experimenting with different wording to see which works better for your visitors.

In the absence of hard-and-fast rules for placement of the call-to-action button, it may be best to discuss where it should *not* be placed:

- Do not place the call-to-action button below the fold!

- Do not overwhelm visitors with too many call-to-action buttons on the page.

- Do not place the call-to-action button too close to one of your other major elements. Placing it immediately below the headline, right next to your main image, or in the middle of your body copy will reduce its visibility and the effectiveness of the other elements. The call to action is the ultimate point of any landing page; it deserves its own space, as do all the other elements.

The Copy

Although 80% of visitors to your landing page will *not* read all your copy, it still needs to be well written—different visitors will read different parts of your copy.

18. Effective copy

Copy is important to communicate your message to visitors. The copy should repeat the title and content of your other creative, but also provide additional information that is both useful and convincing. There is no single right way to write copy; each product, circumstance, and customer (persona) is unique and should be approached differently.

Short Copy Versus Long Copy

There is an ongoing debate among conversion experts and copywriters regarding the merits of different lengths of copy. Some say that the more copy you use, the better you can explain the product or service. Others believe that short copy is better since it reduces the risk of losing your visitor. The reality is that there is no single right answer. Sometimes long copy works more successfully than short copy, and vice versa. The copy length that works best for you will depend on your situation, product, industry, audience, and the call to action.

There are a couple of general guidelines to follow when determining appropriate copy length. Short copy is usually better for giveaways or free offers. If visitors want what you are offering, they don't want to read too much—they just want the freebie. Long copy works better if you are selling big-ticket items. Visitors want to know as much as they can about something before they part with their hard-earned dollars. So, to summarize, the greater the investment required in a product or service, the more copy you will need to provide.

MarketingSherpa and Marketing Experiments conducted tests to determine which had higher success rates: long copy or short copy. They found that on average, websites with longer copy outperformed websites with short copy. However, although this may be true for some sites, it certainly is not true for all of them.

The more important question to consider is, how do I decide, based on my target market/personas and product, when to use long copy and when to use short copy?

—continued—

Step 1: Know Your Target

The best way to create copy is to start by developing personas for your website. Once you know your site visitors, you can implement changes to your current copy or create new copy to appeal to that persona. For instance, a more logical person would like to know details about the product or services you offer. For this person, long copy would do, but someone who is more impulsive wants to get in and out as quickly as possible. So, how can you balance the two? You need to design your copy so that the impulsive person can see the information he is looking for instantly, yet still maintain the long copy format for the more logical person to continue investigating the product or service.

Step 2: Categorize Your Product

Are you in the business of selling paper or providing information on complex medical procedures? A customer looking to buy paper will not be interested in scrolling through pages of copy to determine what type of paper she should buy. Categorizing your products is not always straightforward, so spend some time thinking about what your product or service is, and how much information is really needed.

What does this mean for you? It could mean that having long copy will attract a smaller percentage of your traffic. However, that small percentage is more likely to convert if they read through the copy you provide.

Step 3: Test

It might still be tricky to see which copy would be more suitable for your site, so invest some time and resources in creating trial pages of both long and short copy.

Step 4: Revisit Your Copy

Regardless of whether your copy is long or short, as your product develops and your business grows, make sure you revisit the copy and update it accordingly. You can always tweak your writing in one way or another. A work of writing is never perfect and can always use some type of revision. So, it is crucial to always review your copy and see what can spice it up to attract your personas.

The Headline

Your headline should be clear and easy to comprehend. Make sure the headline stands out as a distinct element of the page by using a larger font, different colors, or a combination of both. The headline should clearly state the product or service you are offering, as well as emphasize the *need* for it. Simply by reading the headline, your visitors should be assured that they stand to benefit from your product or service. The following are five recipes for creating the perfect headline.

19. Pleasing versus painful headlines

A headline should include a benefit that will appeal to your readers, regardless of whether that benefit alludes to something positive or negative. Positive headlines can allude to:

- Saving

- Profiting

- Gaining

- Winning

- Rewarding

Positive headlines focus on the "goodies" your visitors will gain if they continue to read your copy. Here are some examples of positive headlines:

- "Win Your Boyfriend Back"

- "Reward Yourself with a 20% Savings"

- "Gain an Edge Over the Competition"

Negative headlines can allude to:

- Loss

- Embarrassment

- Mistakes

- Uneasiness

- Pain

Negative headlines can help readers avoid making unnecessary blunders that will make their lives miserable. Here are some examples of negative headlines:

- "Have You Even Been Embarrassed at an Expensive Restaurant?"

- "Avoid the Pain of Foreclosure"

- "Do You Ache at the End of the Day?"

20. Appealing headlines

Everyone loves to be part of the "in" crowd. Headlines that can hook the "in" crowd include words such as *secret* and *little-known ways*. Some examples are:

- "The Secrets of Beauty Supply Management"

- "Little-Known Ways to Improve Your Bottom Line"

On the flip side of the coin, no one wants to be left out. "What Everyone Should Know About Growing Azaleas" screams at readers that they may not have the complete story and really need to check the content to make sure they "know it all."

21. Easy and timesaving headlines

Most people hate to waste time, particularly on solving problems. Many men and women would sincerely like to ignore their problems or hope the problems just go away. Consequently, headlines that emphasize speed in solving a problem can be real winners. Examples include:

- "Five Quick Ways to Fix a Drain"
- "A Quick Way to Train Your Dog"

Similarly, no one likes to do "hard" things. Therefore, *easy* is another great hook word. Examples include:

- "Five Easy Ways to Study More Effectively"
- "One Easy Way to Pick Up Incremental Sales"

You can combine *easy* with *quick* for a "double whammy" headline:

- "Five Quick and Easy Steps to Program Your CD"
- "Quick and Easy Recipes for People on the Go"

If your target market includes people who are challenged by issues such as technology or home repair, *easy* is a nice word to have in your arsenal. A variation of *easy* is *lazy*:

- "The Lazy Bachelor's Guide to Doing Laundry"
- "The Lazy Gardener's Path to a Beautiful Yard"

In each case, *lazy* implies that the content will provide information on how to perform the task at hand quickly and easily.

22. Curiosity headlines

Curiosity may have killed the cat, but it won't kill a website visitor. In fact, curiosity is a strong motivation to learn more. Here are some headlines that appeal to those who are curious:

- "Ways to Entice Your Wife or Girlfriend"
- "Interested in Getting the Goods?"
- "The Alluring World of Insects"

23. "Just the facts" headlines

Sometimes simply stating the facts is a good way to go:

- "Learn How Mid-Size Companies Use SAP to Manage Their Business"

- "Ten Time-Management Techniques"

- "Buy a $500 Vacuum Cleaner with a Money-Back Guarantee"

The Lead Sentence

Although your headline is an important tool for getting visitors to stay on your page, an engaging lead sentence will get visitors to read more.

24. An engaging lead

A number of standard types of leads can persuade visitors to read your copy. Here are a few of them:

The question lead
> You can use this to create a sense of need in the reader. The question lead makes the reader want to search for a solution to the problem highlighted by the question. Example: "Leaky basement?"

The teaser lead
> The teaser lead can create intrigue about the information to follow. Example: "You're probably wealthier than you think."

The summary lead
> When your copy is long, you can use a summary lead to make the information that follows easier to digest. Using a summary lead will allow you to get more of your important information out in the first sentence and above the fold. Example: "With more than 10,000 subscribers, the XYZ newsletter is the most read industry resource available online."

The direct address lead
> Readers are more likely to relate your message to their needs if you specifically identify them in your copy. Even if they clicked the link to your landing page, they do not necessarily want to know about your company or what it can do for them. All they want to know is that you understand their problem or need and can provide a solution for it. Example: "You deserve a vacation today."

Again, you don't have a lot of time to hook your visitors, and an engaging lead sentence will make the job easier. Maintain continuity and congruency by keeping your headlines, leads, and link copy consistent to avoid confusing your visitors.

Product Pages

25. Micro and macro conversions

We like to test product pages twice with different conversion goals:

Micro conversion goal
> When a visitor adds an item to the cart, we get a conversion.

Macro conversion goal
> When a visitor completes an order, we get a conversion.

26. Product page images

The right format and presentation of product images can mean significant increases in conversion rates. However, these types of tests are expensive due to the investment required to produce different product images. Of course, the cost will also grow as you add more products. Here are some general guidelines to consider:

Showing the product in use
> Test the page with an image that shows the product in use, and then again with an image that shows the product against a plain background. Although in many cases showing the product in use helps visitors envision themselves using the product, this is not the case for all products. For example, apparel websites seem to benefit from this feature, but electronics or book websites do not see large increases in conversions.

Choosing the right location
> Where should you place the hero image? Common wisdom is to place product images on the right side of product pages. But common wisdom fails to predict how visitors will act on your website. So, test image placement on the left and right to see which converts better.

Zooming in on the product

If you have the software capability, allowing visitors to zoom in and examine a product closely is an excellent feature to test.

Using multiple product images

Consider including multiple images of the product. We usually recommend using three or four high-quality images per product to start. When given the option, we will go with a single high-quality image over multiple low-quality images.

27. Product descriptions

Most ecommerce stores use product descriptions provided by the manufacturer. As a result, you will find the same description on competing ecommerce stores. With your best-selling products:

- Test the impact of having standard manufacturer descriptions versus custom copy your team creates. What impact will that have on the micro conversion (visitors adding items to their cart)?

- Test different versions of the custom copy you create. Not all copy is created equal. You might want to test technical copy versus nontechnical copy. Consider the different personas for your site and what words will have the most impact on them.

28. Product reviews

Reviews are great for increasing conversions. Many studies have shown that product reviews are responsible for up to 30% uplift in conversions. However, if you are just starting out, reviews are difficult to get. So, begin by allowing customers to add reviews to your site, but do not display them on the site immediately. When a product collects enough reviews, share the reviews with your visitors.

29. Add-to-cart buttons

You can test many scenarios with the "add-to-cart" button:

- The location of the button

- Different designs for the button

- The wording on the button

30. Cross-sells and upsells

Cross-sells and upsells can help you sell more to customers by providing them with items that complement the products they already selected. But cross-sells and upsells can also distract visitors. So, test the placement of cross-sells and upsells on your product pages as well as other pages of the site.

31. Pricing

Most website visitors will do some sort of comparison shopping. Testing different prices will determine their impact on conversion rates. In 2007, one of our clients reported a 135% increase in conversion rate by lowering product prices by 10%. Price testing is more complex compared to other forms of testing. Yet during a recession, when visitors are price-sensitive, price testing can produce the most impact on conversion rates.

32. Product availability

Customers do not like to add an item to their cart only to discover when they're ready to pay that the item is out of stock. Linking ecommerce stores with an inventory system will help you avoid such hassles. Here are some general rules of thumb to follow:

Bad
> There is no mention of product availability on your site.

Good
> You always display product availability on your site.

Excellent
> You display messages to encourage customers to buy a product if you have limited stock available. Example: "Only 5 left in stock—order soon!"

Figure 9-13 shows the product page from Ecost.com. Although the page design is crowded with information and is not well designed, the site displays product availability information and shows a message to encourage visitors to place an order within a certain time frame.

Figure 9-13. *Ecost.com's use of product availability information*

33. When can I have it?

Tell visitors when the product will be in their hands. Being vague and telling them their order will arrive sometime in the next few weeks will simply kill your conversion rate, or at least irritate customers.

34. Bundled shipping costs

Consider bundling shipping costs with products so that visitors will not have to worry about paying for shipping. We highly recommend bundling shipping costs if they are too complicated to understand, or if they are expensive.

35. Navigation after clicking the add-to-cart button

Where do you direct visitors after they click on the add-to-cart button? Are you forcing them to view the cart page? If this is the case, you are polluting the cart page analytics with the number of visitors who are forced to be there. Test different locations to redirect visitors after they add an item to their cart:

- Direct visitors to the standard cart page.

- Direct visitors to a special upsell and cross-sell cart page. This is a custom cart page that will contain a summary of the items in the cart with a focus on upselling additional products to the visitor.

- Keep visitors on the same product page, but display a small pop up with a mini-cart.

- Keep visitors on the same product page, but display a small pop up indicating the item was added to the cart page.

The Cart Page and the Checkout Process

A well-designed checkout process moves visitors in a single direction: toward a conversion. Take a close look at your checkout funnel and examine how visitors move through it. Are a percentage of your visitors going back and forth between different steps of the checkout process? We refer to this phenomenon as the *checkout bounce-around effect*. If your site suffers from this, you should tweak the design of some of the checkout pages. The following is a list of items you should test on your cart page.

36. Shipping options and pricing

If you charge customers for shipping and allow customers to choose different delivery speeds (regular, two-day delivery, next-day delivery), make sure these options are displayed on the cart page prior to visitors starting the checkout process. Doing so will ensure that visitors will *not* start the checkout process when they really are merely trying to find how much it will cost to ship their order.

37. Assurance center

What FUDs do your visitors have? What would stop them from buying from your site? An assurance center is a great way to combat these fears and concerns. Here are the steps for creating an assurance center for your site:

1. Start by listing the FUDs your visitors might have. This usually happens during the persona creation process of any conversion optimization project.

2. Prioritize these fears in terms of importance to your visitors.

3. Create the different elements of the assurance center to deal with each FUD.

Remember that not every website needs an assurance center. Test the following on your assurance center:

- The placement of the assurance center on different pages of the site (cart page, product pages, different steps of the checkout)

- The elements you include in the assurance center

- The order of the elements you include in the assurance center

- The design of the assurance center

38. Cart page layout

The goal of the cart page is to provide visitors with a simple and quick way to review the items they have selected. Test your current cart page with a design that shows product thumbnails as well as a clear product description for the items in the cart.

39. Update and delete buttons on the cart page

Some visitors will want to remove items from their cart, update quantities and options, and so forth. Many designers do not pay attention to the delete and update buttons. Figure 9-14 shows the different buttons for each item BestBuy.com has on its cart page. Test having a single update or delete button on the cart page versus having these buttons for each item.

Figure 9-14. *Different buttons on the BestBuy.com cart page*

40. Side navigation

We do not like side navigation on the cart page because it allows visitors to navigate away from the page. If the cart page already has a top navigation panel, in most cases there is no need to add side navigation as well. We recommend testing the impact of removing the side navigation panel on both the conversion rate and the average order value.

41. Payment options

Offering users multiple ways to pay for their orders is an excellent method for increasing conversion rates. But keep a few things in mind:

- Too many payment options can confuse visitors.

- Offer visitors a way to complete their transaction offline either by calling their order in or by sending a check via mail.

42. Cart page and multiple checkout paths

Many ecommerce stores offer visitors multiple ways to complete the checkout process through external websites. Although this can be a great way to increase conversion, how these options are presented to visitors can have an impact on conversion rate:

- If you allow visitors to complete payment on an external site such as PayPal, Google Checkout, or 2CO, let these visitors know they will be navigated to an external site where they will complete the checkout.

- Remember that external websites have their own holes in the checkout process and some of your visitors will drop off as a result. Our testing of PayPal and Google Checkout shows that these sites suffer from close to 40% drop-off rates.

- At a minimum, you should know how many visitors you are sending to external payment sites, and how many of these visitors are actually converting.

43. Presenting different payment options

Throwing a bunch of buttons on a screen and hoping your conversion rate will not be impacted rarely works. Figure 9-15 shows how different payment options are represented on two competing websites.

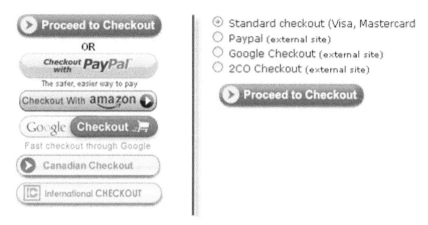

Figure 9-15. *Different presentations of payment options*

44. Continue shopping button

The cart page design will impact your ability to persuade visitors to proceed to the checkout process or continue their shopping, or may cause them to abandon the site altogether. Small changes to the cart design can make a 10% to 20% difference in ecommerce conversion rates. Figure 9-16 shows different designs for a "Continue Shopping" button.

Figure 9-16. *Different designs for a "Continue Shopping" button*

You can test several things with a "Continue Shopping" button:

- The location of the button

- The text on the button

- The design of the button

We do not like copying other websites because what increases conversion with one website can kill your conversion rate. Figure 9-17 shows the cart page from Amazon.com. The page does not have a "Continue Shopping" button. The site compensates for the missing button by allowing visitors to navigate back through the header and the cross-sells and upsells.

Figure 9-17. *Amazon.com cart page with no "Continue Shopping" button*

45. Proceed to checkout button

This might be one of the most obvious things to test on a cart page. Designers sometimes think that using a particular color for the "proceed to checkout" button, such as red, is bad. That is not necessarily the case. What doesn't work for one website might work for another. So, test different designs to find the one that increases your conversion rates. Different designs of the "proceed to checkout" button will impact your conversion rates; however, it is rare that these designs will result in huge uplifts in conversion.

46. Steps in the checkout process

Conventional wisdom is that the fewer steps you have in the checkout process, the fewer chances your visitors have to exit. As a result, there is a growing trend toward using a single page for the checkout process. That is not always a good option. Yahoo! offers its ecommerce customers a single-page checkout. Checkout abandonment rates for these stores is comparable to industry rates (45% to 80%), and the single-page checkout does not show any considerable improvement. There is no magic number for how many steps you should have in the checkout process. A good rule of thumb is to limit checkout steps to fewer than five. Combine different steps in the checkout and examine how they impact your conversion rate.

47. Allowing visitors to check out as guests

If visitors place orders on an infrequent basis, allowing them to check out without creating an account can help increase conversions. You should still capture visitors' email addresses to notify them of their order status and to conduct any future marketing; you just do not need to require them to store all their information on your website. Figure 9-18 shows how BestBuy.com allows visitors to check out as guests without creating an account on the site. Although the functionality of the page is excellent, the design could use significant improvements based on some of the concepts we discussed earlier in this chapter.

Select Checkout Method

Returning Customers	New Customers
Sign in for faster checkout and to earn points on your purchases if you are a Reward Zone® program member.	**You do not need to create an account** to place an order. Just click Checkout As Guest to continue.
E-Mail Address Update e-mail address.	Reward Zone® program members: Create an account to earn points on your order.
Password Forgot your password?	CREATE ACCOUNT NOW >
SIGN IN >	CHECKOUT AS GUEST >

Figure 9-18. *BestBuy.com's checkout options*

48. The bounce-around effect

A well-designed checkout process moves visitors in a single direction. Take a close look at your checkout funnel and examine how visitors move through it. Do you notice that a percentage of visitors are going back and forth between different steps of the process? We call this the checkout bounce-around effect. Checkout bounce requires that you tweak the design of some of your checkout pages. For example, if you notice that a high percentage of visitors keep going back from the last step of the checkout to a previous step, this indicates that you need to move some information or design elements from the previous step to the last step.

A Case Against Multivariate Testing

Conversion optimization approaches let you get instant feedback on a marketing initiative, adjust it accordingly, and receive even more accurate feedback. The more companies we talk to, the more we are reminded that multivariate testing is one of the main factors that reduces the quality of optimization work.

When I (Khalid) was at the University of Texas at Austin, I attended lectures by some of the great modern-day minds in computer science. Among the intellects I had the pleasure of meeting was Dr. Edsger Dijkstra, who had contributed some of the most influential algorithms in modern computing. He was also known for his low opinion of the GO TO statement in computer programming. This led to his writing an important paper in 1965, which was culminated in the 1968 article "A Case against the GO TO Statements."

Dijkstra argued that programmers relied heavily on compilers to discover bugs in their code rather than investing time upfront to verify the accuracy of their programs and ensure the preciseness of their algorithms. This reliance of software on compilers is one of the main reasons we have ended up with lower-quality programs. The compiler should play a supporting role. It is not meant to replace the intellectual activities of humans ensuring the quality of software.

—continued—

This brings me to the topic at hand: multivariate testing plays a major role in conversion optimization, and no one can argue the benefits of using this method in testing. Our average client who uses any form of testing reports a 65% increase in conversion rates. When multivariate testing becomes the main activity of optimization, though, it does a disservice to conversion optimization efforts. Too many clients rely on multivariate testing software to tell them which combination of elements on a page converts better. To do so, many elements on a page must be tested with different combinations.

Let's do some simple math. Say you want to test six different elements on a page (headers, benefit list, hero shots, etc.). For each element, you will choose four different options. This means you will have a total of $4^6 = 4{,}096$ possible scenarios that you will have to test. Google's Website Optimizer allows a maximum of 10,000 combinations.

As a general rule of thumb, you will need around 100 conversions per scenario to make sure the data you are collecting is statistically significant. This translates into $4{,}096 * 100 = 409{,}600$ conversions. If your website converts around 1%, you will need $409{,}600 * 100 = 40{,}960{,}000$ visitors before you start gaining some confidence in your testing results. If testing 4,096 variations sounds difficult, imagine how complicated matters will get by adding variation in campaigns, offers, products, and keywords.

Running this many test scenarios is not unheard of for many larger websites. But why deal with this headache in the first place? Why spend hundreds of thousands of dollars on pay-per-click (PPC) because you need to test whether the variation works? And there is no guarantee you'll get the accurate results you are looking for. This only happens because an activity designed to take place at the very end of the optimization effort becomes the centerpiece of that effort. Optimization that relies heavily on testing assumes that websites have an endless number of resources to test all possible combinations. This is simply not the case.

The science of marketing is about studying human behavior and how to influence it. When relying heavily on multivariate testing software, I find that marketers are not doing what marketers traditionally do; instead, they are taking a back seat to software programs. Yes, software is important, but human power and intellect should be what guides that software.

Optimization done correctly starts with a full analysis of the target client and gaining a deeper understanding of their business goals. This should lead to developing site personas as a first real step in conversion optimization efforts. These personas guide how pages are designed, how copy is created, and how site navigations are laid out. Only after you have employed all of these methods should you use multivariate testing software.

49. Usability testing

Our discussion has focused on quantitative testing with measurable results. Though it goes beyond the scope of conversion optimization, you should *not* ignore the value of usability testing to see how visitors interact with your website. Designing a good usability test can be tricky. Consider the following when designing your usability tests:

- Create a list of different tasks you want your visitors to complete on your website. These tasks should vary in complexity and test different functions of the website.

- Record users' interaction with your website during usability tests. You can always go back and review how people reacted to the site.

- Interview users after a test is completed and ask them about the different tasks they had to perform.

—— DON'T FORGET! ——

- The length of time it takes to implement a test will vary based on your website. Incorporating testing software with dynamic ecommerce websites might take a few hours to a few days.

- The notion that you should pick something, anything, and just start testing is *wrong*. If you pick the wrong page to test, you will end up with no conclusions. Your aim with the first test is to pick the area where you can have some level of impact.

CASE STUDY

Increasing Account Sign-Ups at YouTube

YouTube is the global leader in online video sharing and is the third most trafficked site in the world (Alexa, August 2010), attracting approximately 102 million unique visitors per month (Compete.com).

YouTube needed to increase account sign-ups from its home page because:

- YouTube relies on fresh video content being constantly uploaded by users. A user must have an account to upload a video.

- Once a user signs up for an account, YouTube is able to provide the user with added site functionality, such as video playlists, favorites, and so on. This additional functionality helps to increase both user engagement and user retention.

- Crucially, YouTube is able to gather information about account holders during the sign-up process. In addition to this, as members interact with the site over time, their behavior and interests provide further information. This insight into its members is critical in enabling YouTube to fully leverage and target its on-site advertising.

- Finally, YouTube intends to increase the amount of premium content that can be purchased on the site. User accounts are required for premium content.

While devising a plan to increase the conversion rate, the optimization team that worked on this went through the following steps.

—continued—

Step 1: Researching

The team started by researching the types of visitors using the test page (home page) and what they were looking for. The goal was to understand the gap between user intent and page purpose. For example, if a user lands on the home page and is looking for a video, what benefits should the page offer to get the user to change course and sign up for an account instead? If visitors land on the home page and want to create an account, how could the page help them achieve this goal?

Step 2: Developing Hypotheses

For the home page, the team had three main hypotheses:

- They could persuade visitors to sign up by clearly spelling out the relevant account sign-up benefits.
- The most compelling sign-up benefits for YouTube's users were related to participation in community, creation of playlists, and rating and uploading videos.
- Increasing the prominence of the sign-up button would enable more visitors to find and use the sign-up feature.

Step 3: Testing the Plan

The optimization team used the test hypotheses as the basis for the test plan. The test plan outlines the test structure, test goal, test hypotheses, and test elements to compete against the original page and validate the test hypotheses.

Figure 9-19 shows the three elements on the YouTube home page that related to account sign-ups. Two of these elements were in the header banner, and one was located in the righthand column.

The large volume of traffic that YouTube receives enabled the team to devise an unusually massive multivariate test with 1,024 variations:

Section 1: 2 variations
Section 2: 16 variations
Section 3: 32 variations
Total: 2 * 16 * 32 = 1,024 combinations

This was a very large test—not typically recommended for most sites. But given the massive traffic levels YouTube generates, the sample size was sufficiently large to reach statistical significance quickly. This was the largest Google Website Optimizer test run to date (in terms of traffic volume), and statistical significance was attained within a day or two.

Figure 9-20 shows the test results from Google Website Optimizer.

Figure 9-21 shows the original (control) page.

Figure 9-22 shows combination 28, which came out on top, with a 15.7% increase over the control.

Figure 9-19. *Three elements on the YouTube home page relating to account sign-ups*

	Combination	Status ?	Est. conv. rate ?	Chance to Beat Orig. ?	Observed Improvement ?
	Original	Enabled	–┣━━━━━━━━┫+	—	—
☆ Top high-confidence winners. **Run a follow-up experiment »**					
☐	**Combination 28**	Enabled	–┣━━━━━━━┫+	99.9%	15.7%
☐	**Combination 52**	Enabled	–┣━━━━━━━┫+	99.9%	15.3%
☐	**Combination 20**	Enabled	–┣━━━━━━━┫+	99.9%	15.2%
☐	**Combination 68**	Enabled	–┣━━━━━━━┫+	99.9%	15.0%
☐	Combination 76	Enabled	–┣━━━━━━━┫+	99.9%	14.9%
☐	Combination 4	Enabled	–┣━━━━━━━┫+	99.9%	14.5%
☐	Combination 12	Enabled	–┣━━━━━━┫+	99.9%	13.8%
☐	Combination 36	Enabled	–┣━━━━━━┫+	99.9%	13.0%
☐	Combination 17	Enabled	–┣━━━━━━┫+	99.9%	12.9%
☐	Combination 53	Enabled	–┣━━━━━━┫+	99.9%	12.8%

Figure 9-20. *Test results from Google Website Optimizer*

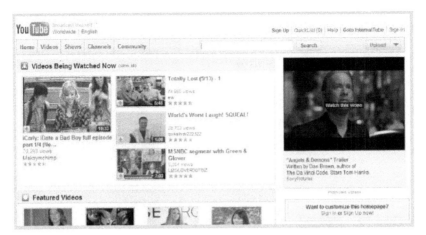

Figure 9-21. *Original (control) page*

Figure 9-22. *The winning combination*

CHAPTER TEN

Be Iterative

THIS BOOK INTRODUCED YOU TO A FRAMEWORK that should apply to any marketing or sales effort you run online or offline. The principles of the Conversion Framework guide how you should interact with prospects, how they view your product or service, and whether they are persuaded by your offer. At the heart of the Conversion Framework is the belief that customers are the focal point of any successful marketing effort.

The first three elements of this deal with the initial part of the conversion process. These are:

- Understanding your website visitors through personas

- Gaining visitors' trust and confidence

- Designing your website for the different buying stages

These elements demonstrated how to translate marketing information into personas that have needs, wants, and fears. You no longer talk about a generic marketing segment, but rather about a specific persona that guides the creation of every element on your website. As visitors land on your website, your first task is to convince them to stay by gaining their trust. Visitors decide whether they trust your website in less than one second. And confidence is built through a long-term relationship with your customers. Of course, not every website visitor is ready to buy. Visitors come at different buying stages. Each stage requires you to present customers with various designs and information to persuade them eventually to convert. Designing for different types of personas at different buying stages is one of the most complex elements of conversion optimization.

The next three elements of the Conversion Framework deal with the latter part of the conversion process. These are:

- Understanding the impact of FUDs that cause visitors to exit the conversion funnel

- Motivating visitors to convert by utilizing offers and incentives

- Creating a website that engages visitors and persuades them to convert

In a time where many ecommerce websites look like copies of each other, engaging visitors can set you apart from your competition. The longer customers stay on your website, and the more they are motivated to visit your website and refer friends to it, the higher the chances of a conversion. But this conversion does not happen without removing many of the FUDs visitors face when attempting to place an order. Even highly motivated prospects can lose interest if they start doubting your company. A good way to combat some of the FUDs is to use incentives at the right place.

The seventh element asks you to test every change you make against the original design. By testing, you judge the effectiveness of the principles of the Conversion Framework. In many instances, our clients have tried to skip the testing phase. They've told us they are looking for best practices to implement quickly on their sites, which is a shortsighted approach. Although best practices are an important consideration, it's also important to remember that what works for one website may not work for another.

The last element of the Conversion Framework focuses on how you should run a conversion optimization project: in an iterative manner. Conversion optimization is a long-term commitment. You will see incremental improvements in your conversion rate as you start deploying the methods outlined in this book. However, you should focus on a holistic approach to conversion. Large increases in conversion rates are always welcome, but realistically, the goal is to deliver small and consistent improvements in conversion rates from month to month.

When Conversion Optimization Succeeds

Conversion optimization is successful when:

The correct target pages are selected for optimization
There are typically hundreds of possible areas of optimization in any website. It's important to data-mine the pages and select key areas that will have an impact on your bottom line. This is best done through software.

The conversion framework is utilized
Use the first six elements of the Conversion Framework (personas, trust, buying stages, FUDs, incentives, and engagement) to examine pages you want to optimize. Create different hypotheses for which changes should be made on each page.

Changes are tested
> Testing will let you know whether the changes you made work for your visitors. We are looking for small, consistent wins when we conduct tests.

Test results are assessed
> Analyze the results of each test. Hypotheses that generate increases or decreases in conversion rates are great. Hypotheses that do not move the needle in any direction are the enemy of conversion optimization.

Analysis is applied to the process
> Conversion optimization is a long-term commitment. If you plan to conduct conversion optimization for a couple of months, it might not be worth the investment. You should plan on a minimum of four to six months of conversion optimization.

When Conversion Optimization Fails

An Invesp informal survey of nearly 200 ecommerce companies that tried conversion optimization in 2009 reveals that more than 60% of them did not see significant improvement from their conversion optimization projects. This data should concern anyone who is considering conversion rate optimization, as well as companies considering offering it to their clients. The following are some of the reasons conversion optimization projects do not succeed.

Poor Resource Planning

A critical component to the success of conversion optimization projects is the ability by technical staff and designers to make required changes on the website. Some clients do not have the technical staff to implement the required modifications. In some instances, the technical staff has a large list of responsibilities already, and conversion optimization projects are added to the end of the list and are given a lower priority. Both of these issues can kill any conversion optimization effort. We handle this in our practice by doing the following:

- Working closely with clients to ensure that they have the staffing levels ready to implement our recommendations

- Asking client teams how much they can dedicate to implementing our conversion recommendations

- Keeping the amount of time required to implement recommendations to fewer than 60 hours per month

Platform Limitations

The technology used in particular websites can complicate your ability to make changes to the site. Conversion optimization requires some integration between the website technologies and the testing software used to determine which design converts better. There are also certain platforms where making any changes is either too expensive or simply not possible. We have worked with an ecommerce client in the past that used hosted ecommerce solutions. The hosted solutions, although fast to deploy, offered very little flexibility in terms of making any changes to the site. As a result, our client was not able to implement most of our recommendations. Examining the technology used in the site will minimize any issues that can come up later during testing deployment.

Poor Expectations

Some clients expect large improvements in conversion rates every time they run a test. This is not sustainable. Achieving small, consistent improvements month to month is a better approach. Although our teams delivered an average of 65% uplifts in conversion rates in 2009, we did this by delivering 4% to 8% uplift in sales month to month. Since the increases in conversion rates are cumulative, 5% uplift in monthly conversion rates translates to 80% uplift on an annual basis.

The Guessing Game

Starting conversion optimization on the right page will have a direct impact on the ROI you see from your efforts. There is a trend among industry consultants to emphasize the need to start testing, yet little focus on where you should start. As a result, clients pay for the consultant's time, they pay for technical resources to implement the modifications to their site, and they do not see any significant improvements in conversions. Picking the right place to start conversion optimization requires:

- Quantitative analysis to examine the data analytics provides
- Qualitative analysis through usability and persona analysis to understand what areas of the website can stand the most improvements

Brute Force Testing

A conversion or usability consultant can suggest hundreds of changes to a single screen. Testing will let you know which of these changes will work. Testing a few changes on a page is a good starting point; testing thousands of changes can be overwhelming. In most of our projects, we limit the number of scenarios we test to fewer than 100. Of course, in some instances we've tested more variations of a single page, but these are the exception. You should also consider the limitations of the testing software you use, and how many conversions it requires for the test to conclude in a four-week period. As a rough estimate, Google Website Optimizer requires 100 conversions for each scenario you test.

Follow-up Experiments

Follow-up experiments are at the heart of the last element of the Conversion Framework. In early 2008, we worked with a client who started with a conversion rate of around 3%. After we did the initial redesign and testing, we were able to increase their conversion rate to 9.8%. The client was so pleased with the results they decided to suspend the campaign they already paid for. Two months later, our team convinced the client that they should continue testing and that they had the potential to increase their conversion rate further. By learning from the lessons of the first test and designing follow-up experiments, we increased their conversion rate to 14.9% with just two more months of testing.

The Upward Spiral

Ultimately, everything about your sales and marketing efforts begins and ends with research. We begin the process by understanding your visitors and learning what they like and dislike about your website. We look at your analytics to understand how your website is performing and what areas can generate the highest impact on your bottom line. We then move to testing and modifications. The testing completed for one page will be the basis for the research for the next one. However, there really is not an end to the process; it is a cyclical, agile approach that is built on the premise of constant and consistent improvement. What is learned from one page becomes the basis for the next; and so it goes, in an upward spiral of ever-increasing results.

This book outlined guidelines and elements that will help you create a successful website, but there is no set formula that anyone can say will absolutely maximize your results. Some of the elements on your page might be performing at their best prior to starting any optimization effort. Other elements can stand to improve greatly from optimization.

People always ask what conversion rate they should be targeting. There is no magic number. The real answer is that you should always be improving your conversion rate.

Index

Symbols

404 errors, 149

1800Contacts.com, upsell example, 184

A

abandoned cart incentives, 172

A/B tests, 195

   deciding between multivariate tests and, 198

active paid membership base, 26

ad copy

   measuring effectiveness of, 55

   personas and, 81

add-to-cart buttons, 216

   clicking, as micro conversion, 27

   location on ecommerce websites page, 154

   navigation after clicking, 218

   on product pages, 12

advertising

   continuity in online advertising, 97

continuity problems from poorly constructed campaigns, 104

online, 8

online advertising budgets versus consumer spending, 9

online versus offline media, 5

relevance to target personas, 102

aggressive persona (rational), 77

AIDA, 141

Amazon.com

   cart page without Continue Shopping button, 221

   community feedback and reviews, 87

   email preferences on, 124

   landing pages for search term Dora Dolls, 100

   negative reviews on, 183

   PPC ad appearing for search on Dora Dolls, 98

   user profile preferences, 123

anonymous checkout, 222

AOV. *See* average order value

Aristotle, 73

artisans, 74
    impulsive persona, 76
assurance centers
    adding to shopping cart page, 200–203
    creating for your site, 218
average order value (AOV), 24
    increasing with cross-sells and upsells,
        184
    use in budgeting conversion
        optimization on ecommerce sites,
        28
average subscription length, 27
average time on site, 176
awareness stage (in building trust), 86

B

B2B markets. *See* business-to-business
    markets
B2C markets. *See* business-to-consumer
    markets
banner advertising, 5
    stimulating consumers to recognize a
        need, 122
    traffic from, 51
behavioral incentives, 171
behavioral market segmentation
    B2B market, 67
    B2C market, 66
behavioral profiles of customers, 72
behavioral trends (online), mapping to
    demographic trends, 78
Best Buy, 63, 160
    buttons on cart page, 219
    customer persona, 69
    landing page for search term laptops,
        127
    search box placement on, 204
Bing search engine, 47. *See also* search
    engines; SERPs
    results for search term laptops, 121
blogs, 176
    creation and uses of, 178

Bluefly.com, 88
Bookpool.com, 89, 135
bounce-around effect, 152
    case of the confused customer, 153
    testing checkout process for, 223
bounce rate, 38
    calculating, 41
    definitions of, 38
    determining your real bounce rate, 40
    for direct and referring websites, 49
    examining for keywords, 53
    exit rate versus, 43
    in offline sales, 43
    traffic from social media sites, 50
    using to evaluate performance of web
        page, 39
brand name, customers defaulting to
    more well-known brand, 146
brand websites, 11
breakeven conversion rate, 32–34
    lifetime value (LTV) in calculations, 33
browser issues, contributing to FUDs, 151
brute force testing, 232
bulk purchases, discounts on, 168
bundled prices, 166–169
    encouraging cross-sells, 184
    shipping costs, 218
    tactics for product bundling, 168
business-to-business (B2B) markets
    bases for segmenting, 66
    complexity of product and buying
        funnel, 140
business-to-consumer (B2C) markets
    bases for segmenting, 65
    using product videos, 137
business value for KPIs, 24
business websites, categories of, 10
Buy.com, search box placement, 204
buyer's remorse, 137
buying decisions and FUDs, 145. *See
    also* FUDs
    risks perceived by customers in
        ecommerce, 145

buying funnel. *See also* buying stages
    different terminology for, 141
    product complexity and, 140
buying guides and wizards, 126–130
    CNET.com TV buying guide, 129
    designing wizards, 128
    Massage-Tools.com buying guide, 128
    Massage-Tools.com wizard, 128
    steips in implementing buying guides, 129
buying process, 1
buying stages, 119–142
    analyzing visitors' motivation for landing on website, 120–122
    complexity of product and buying funnel, 140
    different terminology for, 141
    evaluation of alternatives stage, 131–136
    information search stage, 125–131
    need recognition stage, 122–125
    post-purchase evaluation stage, 137–139
    purchase stage, 137
buy one get one free, 170

C

call-to-action buttons
    difficulty in locating, 153–155
    distinct and easily identifiable, 209
    placement of, 209
caring persona (idealist), 76
Carters.com, discount codes, 156
cart pages. *See* shopping carts
category pages, CTR to product page, 195
celebrity endorsements, using for social proof, 110, 206
    misuse of, 111
checkout process, 218
    abandoned cart incentives for, 172
    abandonment rate, 25
    anonymous checkout, 222

bounce-around effect, 223
    cart page and multiple checkout paths, 220
    giving customers sense of security in, 151
    optimizations (case study), 19
    payment options, 220
    placing additional incentives just before, 173
    proceed to checkout button, 222
    steps in, 222
choleric temperament, 74
click-through rate. *See* CTR
CNET, TV buying guide, 129
colors
    flashy colors that distract site visitors, 116
    testing for call-to-action buttons, 209
community, establishing around your site, 135
    using blogs, 178
    using forums, 179
company, customers' anxiety about, 145
company type (B2B maket), 66
competition
    analyzing, 71
    differentiating your site from, 134–137
complementary services, bundled, 168
complexity of product and buying funnel, 140
CompUSA.com, search box placement, 204
confidence, building with customers, 85. *See also* trust, establishing with customers
    case study, increasing conversion rate by 400%, 117
    factor in overcoming FUDs, 145
confidence level in test results, 198
congruency, 105–110
    how site elements support it, 105
    lack of, on landing pages, 106
    on product or service pages, 107

content-based websites, 11
    common KPIs for, 26
    tools for sharing content, 177
continue shopping button, 221
continuity, 96–104
    addressing issues relevant to personas, 102
    ensuring through website design, 115
    maintaining in online advertising, 97
    problems in maintaining, 104
conversion data, difficulty of tracking, 16
conversion framework
    principles, xi
    summary of steps and processes, 229
conversion goals
    advancement of, evaluating on pages, 105
    testing on product pages, 215
    and value proposition, congurency in support for, 107
conversion optimization, xi
    blend of science and art, 17
    case against multivariate testing, 223
    conversion bottlenecks, 19
    expectations for results and work required to achieve, 17
    failure of, 231
    increased investment in, 10
    key elements, 21
    main approaches of, 18
    potential accomplishments, 16
    right place to start, 232
    successful, elements in, 230
conversion rates, 10
    averages, 14
        top converting websites compared to, 15
    basic equation for, 29
    breakdown based on traffic sources, 48
    breakeven, calculating, 32–34
    calculating, 11
    calculating for lead generation sites, 34
    constant and consistent improvement in, 233
    double-digit, possibility of achieving, 17
    impact of quality of traffic, 47
    impact on profitability of ecommerce PPC campaign, 31
    low, reasons site operators tolerate them, 16
    measuring effectiveness of ad copy, 55
    monetization models and, 36–38
    for PPC campaign on different search engines, 52
    in purchase stage, 137
    unrealistinc expectations for improvements in, 232
    using to budget campaigns on ecommerce sites, 28–34
conversion ratios, free to paid accounts, 26
conversions
    KPI for ecommerce websites, 24
    KPI for lead generation websites, 25
    macro, 22–24
    micro, 27
    relationships among, and with website KPIs, 28
Cooper, Alan, 61
copy, 210–215
    adapting to personas, 81
    categorizing your product, 211
    effective, 210
    headlines, 211–213
    knowing target for, 211
    lead sentences, 214
    short versus long, 210
Coremetrics, test on use of video spokesperson, 206
creative supporting services, 136
cross-sells, 184–188
    placement of, 186
    placing on product pages, 186

placing on shopping cart page, 187

testing placement on product pages, 216

upsells versus, 185

Crutchfield.com, forum, 179

CTR (click-through rate)

measuring effectiveness of ad copy, 55

testing for increase in, 195

curiosity, headlines appealing to, 213

customer acquisition costs (high), offsetting by product bundling, 166

customer feedback

tools for, 189

tracking, 71

customer life cycle, 141

customer profiles

creating, 70–72

using in persona creation, 78

customer reviews, 182

gathering, techniques for, 183

importance of negative reviews, 182

customers

getting to know, 59–61. *See also* personas

implicit preferences, 123

lifetime value (LTV) of, 32

number of, using as social proof, 109

preferences expressed by, 123

purchase history, 123

well-known, using for social proof, 110

D

Dell, landing page for search term laptops, 127

demographic factors in B2C market segmentation, 65

demographic profile of target customers, 71

design, 114–117

functionality and usability, 115

guidelines for enhancing trust, 114

other factors, 116

testing. *See* testing

using to learn about your market, 71

desirability in value propositions, 95

differentiation, 134–137

basic principles in defining positioning, 134

focusing on product benefits, 136

how to stand out from competition, 135

selling more than products on your site, 135

Digg

banner advertisement for Omniture, 122

website traffic from, 50

Dijkstra, Edsger, 223

direct traffic, value of, 48–50

discount codes, 156

problems with, 172

discounts on bulk purchases, 168

dissatisfaction with product, 138

distraction tests, 207

DollarDays.com, 164

doubts (of customers), 145, 156. *See also* FUDs

raised by discount codes, 156

E

Ebay.com, 88

ecommerce

brief history of, 7

using personas in, 68

ecommerce websites, 10

budgeting campaigns on, using conversion rates, 28–34

common KPIs for, 24

conversion goals, 22

order funnel, 13

selling more than products, 135

usability studies for, 73

Ecost.com, product availability information, 217

email addresses, capturing for visitors, 22

email advertising, 51
    use of customer data, 123

email marketing, 4

emails to customers, post-purchase, 139

Endless.com, 90–93
    main home page, 92

engagement, 175–192
    cross-sells and upsells, 184–188
    through customer reviews, 182
    customer feedback tools, 189
    through informational videos, 189
    measuring effectiveness of, 176
    measuring with external metrics, 177
    measuring with internal metrics, 176
    through social media, 178–182
    using virtual help, 190
    using virual closets, 190

evaluation of alternatives stage, 119, 131–136
    differentiate or die, 134
    focusing on product benefits, 136
    search for a VoIP system, 132

exit rate, 41
    bounce rate versus, 43
    calculating, 41
    determining acceptable rate for a page, 42
    in offline sales, 43
    reporting of time spent on page and, 44
    using to determine starting point in optimization process, 42

expectations about conversion rate improvements, 232

expectations of customers who place orders, 138

experiments, follow-up, 233

expert status, using as social proof, 110

external metrics, measuring engagement, 177

external stimuli for consumer need recognition, 122

extroversion, 74

F

Facebook, 113
    company page, 112
    measuring engagement on, 181

fast food companies, product bundling, 166

fears (of customers), 144, 148–152. See also FUDs
    caused by browser compatibility problems, 151
    caused by long forms with unnecessary fields, 149
    caused by site errors and 404 errors, 149

fears, uncertainties, and doubts. See FUDs

feedback from customers. See customer feedback; customer reviews

field studies, 72

Fireclick Index
    average conversion rate by industry, 14
    average ecommerce conversion rate, 10

Firefox, 151

flashing colors that distract site visitors, 116

fold on web pages, 208
    above the fold, 208
    below the fold, 209

Ford Motor Company, use of social media, 112

forms, lengthy, with unnecessary fields, 149

forums, 176, 179
    use to start discussion about specific brand, 179

404 errors, 149

freebie marketing, 169

free to paid account conversion ratio, 26

Frys.com, crowded header, 204
FUDs (fears, uncertainties, and doubts),
    143–158
  addressing, using personas, 146
  buying decision and, 145
  combatting with assurance center, 218
  concerns of online customers about
    risks, 144
  countering by adding price assurances,
    200
  decreasing with incentives, 160
  defined, 144
  doubts, 156
  fears, 148–152
  increased, in freebie marketing, 169
  membership requirements as FUDs,
    165
  testing website elements for, 207
  uncertainties, 152–157
  using to increase conversions, 158
functionality and usability (in site
    design), 115

G

Galen, 73
Geiko.com, emergency car service, 153
geographic factors in B2C market
    segmentation, 65
geotargeting of ads, 101
Gillette, freebie incentive, 170
Google Analytics
  bounce visitors in time spent on site,
    45
  definition of bounce rate, 38
  formula for calculating exit rate, 41
  list of customers used as social proof,
    110
  metrics reported at page level, 39
  top exit pages report, 42
Google Chrome, 151

Google search engine, 47. *See also* search
    engines; SERPs
  conversion rates for PPC campaign on,
    52
  results for search term laptops, 121
  traffic from, organic and paid, 51
Google Website Optimizer, 194, 224
  test results on YouTube home page,
    227
guardians, 74
  logical persona, 75
guests, visitors checking out as, 222
guided selling tools. *See* wizards
Gymboree.com, cross-sells on, 187

H

Harry & David website, upsell on, 185
Hasbro.com, use of flashy neon colors,
    116
headers, testing, 204
headlines, 211–213
  appealing, 212
  appealing to curiosity, 213
  easy and timesaving, 213
  pleasing versus painful, 212
  simply stating the facts, 214
help, virtual, 190
hero images, 205
HomeGalleryStores.com, 102
hosted ecommerce solutions, 232
HubSpot.com, 167
Hyundai, countering FUDs in down
    economy, 148

I

IBM
  use of FUDs in marketing campaign,
    158
  use of self-actualization on its home
    page, 130
idealists, 74
  caring persona, 76

Ideeli.com, 164
    forums, 179
    free giveaway incentives, 169
images
    main image, appropriateness of, 205
    on product pages, 215
    product, 116, 136
    supporting, 206
impulsive persona (artisan), 76
inbound links to your website, 177
incentives, 159–174
    abandoned cart, 172
    behavioral, 171
    bundled prices, 166–169
    buy one get one free, 170
    definition and descriptions of, 161
    engagement versus, 175
    freebie marketing, 169
    maximizing effectiveness of, 173
    membership-only stores, 164
    positioning, 164
    types and goals of, 162
    value proposition versus, 163
informational videos, 189
information gathering, providing to
        reduce customers' FUDs, 145
information search stage, 119, 125–131
    buying guides and wizards, 126–130
    need identification, 130
    self-actualization, 130
Inmates Are Running the Asylum, The,
        61
internal metrics, measuring engagement,
        176
internal stimuli for consumer need
        recognition, 122
Internet Explorer, 151
interviews with top customers, 71
introversion, 74
IRS, use of need identification on its
        website, 130
item rating email, 139
items per order, number of, 25

iterative conversion optimization,
        229–234
    factors in successful conversion
        optimization, 230
    reasons for failure in conversion
        optimization, 231
    summary of steps in conversion
        framework, 229
    upward spiral, 233

J

Jung, Carl, 74

K

Keirsey, David, 74
key performance indicators. *See* KPIs
keywords, 53–56
    analysis of visitor intent based on, 120
    analyzing keywords that drive visitors
        to site, 121
    bounce rates for, 53
    motivating customers, 96
    reasons for too high bounce rate, 54
Kmart, countering FUDs in down
        economy, 148
knowledge stage (in building trust), 86,
        105
KPIs (key performance indicators), 24
    for content websites, 26
    for ecommerce websites, 24
    for lead generation websites, 25
    measuring visitors' engagement, 175
    relationships with macro and micro
        conversions, 28
    for subscription websites, 26

L

landing pages, 4–6
    continuity elements, 98–103
    costs for designing and optimizing, 30
    distractions on, testing, 207
    key role of personas in creation of, 102

maintaining continuity in PPC advertising, 104

options for increasing profitability of, 36

relevance to keywords and customer motivations, 96

layout

cart page, 219

general layout tests, 208–210

placing elements in right place, 115

lead generation websites, 10

budgeting advertising campaign, 34–36

campaign profitability, 36

factors controlling success of campiagns, 35

common KPIs for, 25

conversion goals, 22

testing lead generation forms, 207

lead sentences, 214

Lewis, Elmo, 141

lifetime value of a customer. *See* LTV of a customer

liking stage (in building trust), 86

links to website, inbound, 177

logical persona (guardian), 75

LTV (lifetime value) of a customer, 32–34

issues with calculation of, 34

M

macro conversions, 22–24

relationships with micro conversions and website KPIs, 28

testing for product pages, 215

market segmentation, persona development versus, 65–67

Mashable.com, 50

Massage-Tools.com

buying guide for methodical persona, 128

wizard for selecting products, 128

melancholic temperament, 74

membership-only stores, 164

memberships/affiliations with professional organizations, 111

mentions of your business, external, 177

micro conversions, 22, 27

relationships with macro conversions and website KPIs, 28

testing for product pages, 215

Microsoft

"I am a PC" ads, 112

product bundling, 166

monetization models, conversion rates and, 36–38

monthly page views (content websites), 26

monthly visitors (content websites), 26

motivations for visiting websites, 93

Motorola.com, site errors causing FUDs, 149

Motrin, adverse reactions from social media campaign, 113

multivariate tests, 196

case against, 223

deciding between A/B tests and, 198

MySpace, 113

MyToyBox.com, landing page for search term Dora Dolls, 99

N

navigation (websites), 115

bounce-around effect, 152, 223

case of the confused customer, 153

directing visitors after clicking add-to-cart button, 218

errors in, causing FUDs, 149

linear and non-linearr ecommerce paths, 152

side navigation on cart page, 220

testing, 205

need identification, 130

need recognition stage, 119, 122–125

case study, stimulating customer needs, 124

negative buzz about your company, clearing up, 112

negative reviews, importance of, 182
neutral opinion of product, 138
NewEgg.com
    call-to-action buttons, 154
    header design, 204
Newport-News.com, 165
    cross-sell on product page, 186
    cross-sells on shopping cart page, 187
newspaper and PR mentions, using as
    social proof, 110
Nielsen, Jacob, 50
Nielsen's MegaView Online Retail report,
    14
Nike Shox product page, congruency in,
    108
Nordstrom, Twitter page, 181
number of clients, using as social proof,
    109
numbers game, sales as, 18

O

offline close ratio (lead generation
    websites), 25
offline conversion rates, 34
offline sales, bounce and exit rates in, 43
Omniture, banner advertisement on Digg,
    122
1800Contacts.com, upsell example, 184
optimization questions based on
    personas, 79
order funnel on ecommerce websites, 13
order status emails, 139
organic search results, 4
    traffic from, 51
    value of ranking first in, 104
OrientalTrading.com, 167
OvernightPrints.com, apology email from,
    139

P

package deals, 166
pages per visit, 176

paid memberships (active), on
    subscription websites, 26
paid search results, 4
    traffic from, 52
path scenarios, 115
Payment Card Industry (PCI) standards,
    111
payment options, 220
    presenting different options, 220
pay-per-click advertising. *See* PPC
    advertising
personality types. *See* temperaments
personas, 61–84
    adjusting selling process through, 83
    aggressive persona (rational), 77
    appealing to with testimonials, 206
    benefits of, 63
    caring persona (idealist), 76
    case against, 68
    copy that appeals to, 211
    creating buying guides for, 126
    creating using customer profiles and
        temperaments, 78
    definition and description of, 61
    evaluating value proposition through,
        96
    framing incentives to appeal to, 173
    history of four temperaments, 73
    impact on copy, 81
    impulsive persona (artisan), 76
    key role in creating ad campaigns,
        landing pages, and entire sites, 102
    logical persona (guardian), 75
    market segmentation versus, 65–67
    using in ecommerce, 68
    using to address FUDs, 147
    using to optimize website, 79–81
phlegmatic temperament, 74
physical-store conversion rates, 16
platform limitations, causing conversion
    optimization failure, 232
positioning, 134
    essential principles in defining, 134

post-purchase evaluation stage, 119, 137–139
  customer expectations and comparison with benefits of products, 138
  emails to customer to follow up transactions, 138
Powell's Books, 89
PPC (pay-per-click) advertising, 51
  ads appearing for search term Dora Dolls, 98
  budgeting for ecommerce site, 29–34
    breakdown of campaign profitability, 31
    calculating maximum PPC, 31
    conversion rate impact on profitability, 31
    determining breakeven conversion rate, 32
    determining how much to spend per click, 30
    lifetime value (LTV) of a customer, 32–34
  budgeting for lead generation site, 35
  campaign profitability, 36
  conversion rates for campaign on search engines, 52
  keyword quality and, 96
  maintaining continuity with, 104
  results on search for Cisco 7960 phone on Google, 133
  for VoIP systems, 132
PR and newspaper mentions, using as social proof, 110
price
  adding assurances about, to counter user FUDs, 200–203
  anxieties or FUDs about, 145
  bundling shipping costs with products, 218
  as differentiation strategy, 136
  testing different pricing, 217

privacy concerns, 144, 208. *See also* fears; security and privacy concerns
  personas and FUDs, 147
proceed to checkout button, 222
product benefits, focus on, 136
product descriptions, 136
  testing, 216
product expectations, 138
product images, 116, 136
product pages, 215–218
  cross-sells and upsells on, 186, 216
  CTR from category page, 195
  on an ecommerce websites, 12
  images on, 215
  telling visitors when order will arrive, 217
  testing micro and macro conversions, 215
product presentation, 116
product promotional incentives, 162
products
  anxiety about, 145
  availability, 217
  bundling, 166–169, 184
  categorizing, 211
  customer reviews on, 182
  doubts of customers about, 145
  reviews of, 216
product videos, 137, 189
ProductWiki.com, 183
product wizards. *See* wizards
professional organizations, memberships/affiliations with, 111
profitability
  calculating for lead generation campaign, 36
  conversion rate impact on, in ecommerce PPC campaign, 31
profit from advertising campaigns, use in determining marketing budgets, 29
psychographic factors in B2C market segmentation, 66
Psychological Types, 74

purchase history of customers, 123
purchase stage, 119, 137

Q

quality of leads, 47
quality of traffic, 47–58
    controlling with keywords, 53–56
    effects of ad copy on, 56
    from social media websites, 50
    sources of traffic, 47
    traffic media in ad campaigns, 51
    value of direct traffic, 48–50

R

rationals, 74
    aggressive persona, 77
recession of 2009, 194
Red Lobster, customer engagement, 175
referral websites, 48
regret and remorse after purchases, 137
relevance and scent, 97. *See
    also* continuity
reputation management, 112
    avoiding social media mistakes, 113
    monitoring social media, 112
    notifications about negative
        comments, 112
    responding to negative buzz, 112
resource planning (poor), for conversion
    optimization, 231
reviews
    customer reviews, 182
    negative reviews, importance of, 182
    product, 216
reviews of this book, xiii
RHDJapan, 68
    community building with forum, 179
    customer motivations and value
        proposition, 94
    discounts on bulk purchases, 168
    social proof for, 109

risks of buying a product or doing
        business with a company, 145
ROI (return on investment) from blogs,
    178

S

sales funnel
    ecommerce order funnel versus, 13
    offline sales, 43
Sam's Club, 165
sanguine temperament, 74
satisfaction
    guarantees for, 208
    increasing for customers with product
        bundling, 166
    with product, 138
scent and relevance, 97. *See
        also* continuity
screen resolutions, 208
    designing for lowest common
        denominator, 208
    placement of calls to action and, 209
scrolling, visitors' reluctance at, 208
search boxes, placement of, 204
search engine optimization. *See* SEO
search engine results pages. *See* SERPs
search engines
    conversion rates for PPC campaign on,
        52
    organic and paid traffic from, 51
    traffic source for websites, 47
search functionality, 115
Sears, countering FUDs in down
    economy, 148
Secure Sockets Layer (SSL) certificates,
    151
security and privacy concerns, 144
    caused by long forms and sign-ups,
        149
    giving customers a sense of security,
        151

protection of privacy, 208
security concerns in early days of
    ecommerce, 8
security services for ecommerce websites,
    111
segmentation of visitors, 215
self-actualization, 130
selling process, 1
    adjusting through personas, 83
    integrating marketing data, challenges
        of, 59
    as numbers game, 18
SEO (search engine optimization), 4
    blogs as strategy for, 178
    continuity problems from poorly
        constructed campaigns, 104
    spending on, 9
SERPs (search engine results pages), 4
    analyzing for information search
        buying stage, 126
    continuity problems from using as
        landing page, 104
    results for search term laptops, 121
    for VoIP telephone comparison, 132
service expectations, 138
shipping costs, bundling with products,
    218
shipping options and pricing, 218
shopping carts, 218
    abandoned cart incentives, 172
    add-to-cart buttons, 216
    cart page and multiple checkout paths,
        220
    cart page layout, 219
    continue shopping button, 221
    cross-sells and upsells on cart page,
        187
    navigation after clicking add-to-cart
        button, 218
    problems in locating calls to action,
        153
    proceed to checkout button, 222
    side navigation on cart page, 220

testing design of, adding assurance
    center, 200–203
update and delete buttons on cart
    page, 219
side navigation on cart page, 220
Skis.com, informational video on
    products, 189
social interaction, on-site, 176
social media, 178–182
    blogs, 178
    companies' use of to mitigate
        complaints, 112
    Facebook, 181
    following on, using as social proof, 111
    forums, 179
    perils of, 113
    Twitter, 181
social media websites, 11
    as major traffic source, 50
    value of traffic from, 51
social proof, 109–112, 208
    misuse of, 111
    for RHDJapan.com, 109
    techniques used on websites, 109
    testimonials, 206
social tools to increase engagement, 177
specialization, 135
spokespeople on video, 190, 206
SSL (Secure Sockets Layer) certificates,
    151
statistical significance of data, 56
Sterne, Jim, 141
stimulating customer needs, 122
    case study, 124
store clearance incentives, 163
store promotional incentives, 162
StumbleUpon, website traffic from, 50
subscription cancellation ratio, 27
subscription length, average, 27
supporting images, 206
supporting services, creative, 136
surveys, client, 70
SwissOutpost.com, freebie incentive, 169

SWOT (strengths, weaknesses, opportunities, and threats) analysis, 69

T

tagline, testing, 204
Target.com
    landing page for search term Dora Dolls, 101
    PPC ad for Dora Dolls, 98
temperaments
    history of four temperaments, 73
    using in persona development, 75–79
test hypotheses, 200
    case study, increasing account sign-ups at YouTube, 226
testimonials, 206
testing, 193–228
    A/B tests, 195
    basic website elements, 204–208
    brute force, 232
    cart page and checkout process, 218–223
    case against multivariate testing, 223
    creating successful test, 199–202
    determining type of test to conduct, 198
    follow-up experiments, 233
    general layout, 208–210
    increasing account sign-ups at YouTube (case study), 225–228
    multivariate tests, 196
    product pages, 215–218
    test results and confidence level, 198
    types of testing on websites, 194
    usability, 224
time spent on a page or site, 43–46
    average time on site, measuring engagement, 176
    based on traffic sources, 49
    resources for further information, 58
    time on page calculation, 44

time on site calculation, 45
visitors from social media sites, 50
Toyota, advertising campaign following recalls, 112
Toys R Us, PPC ad for Dora Dolls search, 98
traffic on websites. *See also* quality of traffic; visitors to websites
    advertisiing media used to drive traffic, 51
    breakdown of search traffic, 49
    conversion rate breakdown based on traffic sources, 48
    social media sites as source of, 50
    sources of, 47
    time spent on site based on traffic sources, 49
    value of direct traffic, 48–50
transaction abandonment, 145
    addressing, using personas, 147
    caused by discount codes, 156
    rate of, 25
transaction rating email, 139
trust, establishing with customers, 85–118
    case study, increasing conversion rate by 400%, 117
    circle of trust, 146
    congruency, 105–110
    continuity, 96–104
    design, 114–117
    external reputation, 112
    memberships/affiliations with professional organizations, 111
    perils of social media, 113
    social proof, 109–112
    steps in process, 86
    value propositions, 87–96
TV buying guide from CNET, 129
Twitter, 113, 181
    measuring engagement on, 182

U

uncertainties (of customers), 144, 152–157. *See also* FUDs
    bounce-around effect, 152

inability to locate call-to-action buttons, 153–155

    providing help with widgets and tools, 156

uniqueness of value proposition, 95

Unique Selling Proposition (USP), 90

upsells, 184–188

    cross-sells versus, 185

    placement of, 186

    placing on product pages, 187

    placing on shopping cart page, 187

    testing placement on product pages, 216

usability

    customers' uncertainties raised by site failures in, 144

    in website design, 115

usability studies, 73

usability testing, 224

V

value proposition, 87–96

    analyzing web page support for, 95, 105

    communicating on websites (examples), 87–93

    defining, 93

    images connecting with, 205

    incentives versus, 163

    and primary conversion goal, congruency in page support for, 107

    supporting main objective of selling products, 108

    tagline communication of, 204

video games, personas in, 64

videos

    informational, customer engagement through, 189

    product videos on B2C sites, 137

    spokespeople on, 190, 206

virtual help, 190

virual closets, 190

visitors to websites

    acquiring, costs of, 17, 30

    converting to buyers, 2, 9

    monthly visitors for content websites, 26

    quality of traffic, 47–58

        controlling with keywords, 53–56

        effects of ad copy on, 56

        from social networking sites, 50

        sources of traffic, 47

        value of direct visitors, 48–50

    segmenting and testing design for, 215

    time spent on page or site, 43–46, 58

    voice in design process. *See* testing

W

Wal-Mart

    fake blog, "Wal-Marting Across America", 113

    sales optimization, 2

    trying to be something it's not, 114

    value proposition, 93

warranties, 146, 208

web browsers, issues with, 151

web page for this book, xiii

websites

    categories of business websites, 10

    continuity problems within, 102

    ecommerce platform limitations affecting conversion optimization, 232

    evaluating from perspective of personas, 79–81

    navigation, 115

    options for increasing profitability of, 36

    testing basic elements, 204–208

    testing general layout, 208

    time spent on a page or site, 43–46

    tool-specific metrics, 177

    traffic sources, 47

well-known customers, using as social proof, 110

whitespace in site design, 116

widgets and tools, 156

wizards (guided selling tools), 128

Massage-Tools.com wizard, 128
wording on call-to-action buttons, 209
word-of-mouth marketing, 163

X

Xerox, use of need identification on its
      website, 131

Y

Yahoo! search engine, 47. *See also* search
      engines; SERPs
   conversion rates for PPC campaign on,
      52
   organic and paid traffic from, 52
   results for search term laptops, 121
YouTube, 189
   case study, increasing account sign-
      ups, 225–228

Z

Zappos.com, 90–93
   incentives, matching value
      proposition, 163
   Insights forum, 179
   maintaining congruency on product
      pages, 107
zip code analysis, 70

About the Authors

Khalid Saleh is cofounder of Invesp, a conversion optimization company. Saleh is an in-demand speaker who has presented at industry events such as Emetrics, SMX, Conversion Conference, DMA, PubCon, and ACCM, among others. Quoted in publications including *Internet Retailer*, California Executive, and *Chicago Sun-Times*, Saleh has over 12 years of experience in conversion optimization, ecommerce architecture, design, and implementation. Saleh's work has helped generate an average 65% improvement in conversion rates for Invesp's customers. He is also the chief architect behind Pii, the first conversion intelligence software.

Ayat Shukairy is cofounder of Invesp, a conversion optimization company. Shukairy's work focuses deeply on conversion optimization, usability, and online persuasion. She is a frequent speaker at industry events such as Search Engine Strategies and Web 2.0. She is regularly quoted in publications including *Internet Retailer*, RetailWire, and Medill. Ayat is Invesp's lead conversion architect, helping her customers generate an average 65% improvement in conversion rates and online revenue

Colophon

The cover fonts are Akzidenz Grotesk and Orator. The text font is Adobe's Meridien; the heading font is Akzidenz Grotesk; and the code font is LucasFont's TheSansMonoCondensed.

Get even more for your money.

Join the O'Reilly Community, and register the O'Reilly books you own. It's free, and you'll get:

- $4.99 ebook upgrade offer
- 40% upgrade offer on O'Reilly print books
- Membership discounts on books and events
- Free lifetime updates to ebooks and videos
- Multiple ebook formats, DRM FREE
- Participation in the O'Reilly community
- Newsletters
- Account management
- 100% Satisfaction Guarantee

Signing up is easy:

1. **Go to: oreilly.com/go/register**
2. **Create an O'Reilly login.**
3. **Provide your address.**
4. **Register your books.**

Note: English-language books only

To order books online:
oreilly.com/store

For questions about products or an order:
orders@oreilly.com

To sign up to get topic-specific email announcements and/or news about upcoming books, conferences, special offers, and new technologies:
elists@oreilly.com

For technical questions about book content:
booktech@oreilly.com

To submit new book proposals to our editors:
proposals@oreilly.com

O'Reilly books are available in multiple DRM-free ebook formats. For more information:
oreilly.com/ebooks

O'REILLY®

Spreading the knowledge of innovators   oreilly.com

Have it your way.

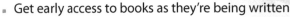